Transport Investment

and Economic Development

Gary Fromm, *Editor*

The Brookings Institution

TRANSPORT RESEARCH PROGRAM

Washington, D. C.

THE BROOKINGS INSTITUTION is an independent organization devoted to nonpartisan research, education, and publication in
economics, government, foreign policy, and the social sciences generally. Its principal purposes are to aid in the development of sound public
policies and to promote public understanding of issues of national importance.

The Institution was founded December 8, 1927, to merge the activities of
the Institute for Government Research, founded in 1916, the Institute of
Economics, founded in 1922, and the Robert Brookings Graduate School of
Economics and Government, founded in 1924.

The general administration of the Institution is the responsibility of a self-
perpetuating Board of Trustees. The Trustees are likewise charged with maintaining the independence of the staff and fostering the most favorable conditions for creative research and education. The immediate direction of the
policies, program, and staff of the Institution is vested in the President, assisted by the division directors and an advisory council, chosen from the
professional staff of the Institution.

In publishing a study, the Institution presents it as a competent treatment
of a subject worthy of public consideration. The interpretations and conclusions in such publications are those of the author or authors and do not purport to represent the views of the other staff members, officers, or trustees of
the Brookings Institution.

541

and Ext...

Transport Investment
and Economic Development

Foreword

THE BROOKINGS INSTITUTION is conducting a major research program on the role of transportation in the economic and social development of the emerging nations of Africa, Asia, and Latin America. One aspect of this program is a series of graduate seminars at Harvard University, designed to bring together students, faculty, visiting scholars, and public officials for research and training in transport investment planning. The essays in this book, based on the first series of Harvard seminars, comprise the second publication of the Brookings Transport Research Program, which is being financed by a grant from the Agency for International Development.

The Harvard program, which is directed by John R. Meyer, has focused on devising analytical methods for improving the quality of transport planning decisions. More explicitly, the program has three primary tasks: (1) deriving in a more rigorous fashion the implications of modern economic theory, engineering, and operations research for transport planning; (2) formulating more complete models to simulate or otherwise adduce the relationships between transport investments and the broader national goals of economic development; and (3) applying these techniques to the problem of discerning which transport technologies, new and old, might best serve the economic goals of underdeveloped countries under varying geographical, industrial, and population circumstances.

The initial transport seminar was established at Harvard during the 1963 spring semester. This seminar, with weekly sessions, was conducted by Gary Fromm and Richard B. Heflebower and had as its purposes the awakening of student interest in the topic and an introduction to the complexities of the subject. A number of guest speakers were invited to participate in the experiment, and their willingness to contribute time and effort has made possible the present volume.

The Brookings Institution expresses its appreciation to Dean Don K. Price of the Harvard Graduate School of Public Administration and to John T. Dunlop, Chairman of the Department of Economics, for their support and assistance in making the seminar a reality.

The reading committee included John R. Meyer; Merton J. Peck, Yale University; and George W. Wilson, Indiana University. Jane Lecht edited the manuscript and prepared the index. The Transport Research Program, under the direction of Wilfred Owen, is conducted in the Economic Studies Division, headed by Joseph A. Pechman.

The comments and suggestions of the following are gratefully acknowledged by the authors: Leon Moses contributed helpful criticisms of Chapter III, "Characteristics of Transport Modes." John H. Kaufmann generously contributed materials for the preparation of Chapter V, "Design of the Transport Sector," and Charles H. Berry and Robert T. Brown provided useful comments. In the preparation of Chapter VI, "Economic Development and Regional Growth," helpful suggestions were contributed by S. Chakravarty, R. S. Eckaus, John R. Meyer, and Gary Fromm. An earlier version of the paper was presented at a conference of the National Bureau of Economic Research in April 1963. Bilsel Alisbah rendered assistance and Robert T. Brown provided valuable comments on an earlier draft of Chapter XI. Carlos Massad, Carlos Hurtado, Manuel Metz, and Rada Yumba made significant contributions to the preparation of Chapter XII, "The 'Railroad Decision' in Chile."

Opinions expressed by the authors do not purport to represent the views of the Agency for International Development, or the trustees, officers, or other staff members of the Brookings Institution.

Robert D. Calkins
President

January 1965
The Brookings Institution
1775 Massachusetts Avenue N.W.
Washington, D. C.

Contents

List of Tables

I

Introduction: An Approach
to Investment Decisions

GARY FROMM*

THAT ECONOMIC DEVELOPMENT requires adequate, effective transportation services is axiomatic. That there exists, for given countries at specified stages of development, a theoretically optimum amount of transport capacity is generally accepted. Nonetheless, agreement on the determination of these capacities and their implied rate of investment is far from unanimous. This probably is due as much to the failure of economists to study the role of transportation in contemporary economic development as it is to basic disparities in views. It is apparent from Katherine Warden's selected bibliography following the text of this book that few, if any, comprehensive analyses of normative transportation-development theory have been conducted to date. This volume is intended as an introductory contribution to the subject.

Prior to a discussion of transport investment, however, it is well to establish the development context within which such expenditures are undertaken.

The Development Context

The less developed nations exhibit a vast diversity of geographic, demographic, political, economic, and social environments. Nonetheless, within each set of these characteristics, common elements which have similar effects on development and transport programs can be grouped. First, these countries, with few exceptions, can be classed into four geographic-demographic categories: (1) tropical lands with

* The Brookings Institution.

1

high population densities; (2) tropical lands with low population densities; (3) temperate zone mountainous lands possessing an altiplano or coastal plain of high population density with low densities elsewhere; and (4) desert lands with low overall population densities but concentrations along rivers or coastal areas. Development and transport problems are generally more intense in tropical areas and where population densities are low. Inordinately high densities, of course (as in India), pose other difficulties.

Second, in the political field, there are countries where development is limited by technical factors, the resources available, and the imaginations, inclinations, and skills of planners and the government; there are other nations where strong vested-interest groups exercise sufficient power to retard development significantly from otherwise attainable levels. Not only may such groups block essential programs, but they may also divert resources into investments that contribute little to development.

Third, in the economic-social area, a large number of characteristics are pertinent to investment decisions, although only a few can be cited. Most importantly, there are the dominant factors of low per capita income and highly unequal income distribution. Also, the agricultural sector usually suffers from low total productivity, enjoying only pockets of highly developed plantation or commercial farming of cash export crops. Farming methods are likely to be primitive, and the output of many farmers is adequate only for their families' subsistence. Furthermore, there is little incentive for producing a surplus. Because of lack of knowledge of marketing possibilities and the unavailability of rapid, dependable transport to domestic markets, much of any surplus that could be produced would be spoiled before it could be exported or consumed in urban centers. Often, the existing transportation network to the hinterland was built to export minerals and cash crops and not to serve internal transport needs.

A related characteristic is the extensive unemployment or underemployment of labor in rural areas. Notwithstanding the use of inefficient agricultural techniques, the low quantity of foodstuff production requires only a fraction of the available labor force, especially where population is high. Because of this lack of local employment opportunities and low rural living standards, as well as the attractions of city life and an unawareness of true conditions in urban areas, large numbers of people migrate to the larger urban centers. This urbanization is, at the least, unfortunate for the welfare of both the individual and the nation. Not only is the demand for unskilled labor at early stages of industrialization extremely limited, but living conditions in crowded cities frequently are less satisfactory than the migrants' villages. Yet, the unemployed migrants must be fed and housed, however inadequately, causing a drain on the economy that would have been avoided had they remained in rural areas. If rural employment opportunities are not created, improved transport between urban and rural areas may, unfortunately, increase excessive migration. Louis Lefeber's essay (Chapter VI) develops this point in greater detail.

The industrial and commercial sectors also suffer from a dualism that is similar to that in the agricultural sector; some industries operate at (or near) internationally competitive levels of productivity, while others are extremely backward. As in agriculture, too, many goods are not manufactured domestically (or only in limited amounts) and must be imported to satisfy consumption and production requirements. With great import needs and with foreign exchange earnings restricted largely to those arising from raw material or commodity exports, balance-of-payments deficits are common and pose a constraint to domestic expansion.

In all sectors of the economy, including government, productivity and development could be advanced by additional basic and vocational education. Since private initiative in this field is sure to prove woefully inadequate, government must bear the prime educational responsibility. It must also carry the burden of much of the new infrastructure investment (especially basic transport facilities), since the private sector is generally incapable of doing so except under politically untenable or economically undesirable conditions (cf. p. 94n below).[1]

Financing these investments and other public expenditures is one of the prime difficulties faced by government. Confronted by an initially low proportion of the national product which can be devoted to governmental purposes, long histories of tax evasion and avoidance,

[1] Expansion in the industrial and commercial sectors can largely be left to private initiative within some broad bounds and incentives established by the government. (However, there are exceptions when large capital investments, high risks, and new technologies are involved, resulting in a requirement for direct government intervention.) In the agricultural sector, too, private entrepreneurs should be able, with the assistance of agricultural extension services and government guaranteed or provided loans or credits, to raise productivity significantly.

archaic tax structures, and ineffective (if not corrupt) tax administration, most governments in less developed nations are hard pressed to meet the financial burdens of accelerating growth.[2] Certainly, some help is obtained from foreign aid and loans, but these normally satisfy only a fraction of the needs and sometimes entail onerous political or economic repayment obligations. Tax reform clearly should have high priority among development administrative measures. (Other legal reforms, especially those relating to contract law, are also imperative in many nations.) The importance of reimbursement by users for publicly produced goods and services (other than welfare services, such as primary education or public health) is also greatly heightened (cf. Chapter X by James R. Nelson and Chapter XI by A. Robert Sadove and Gary Fromm).

Finally, as to transport itself, a wide spectrum of technologies generally may be found, ranging from primitive footpaths and dirt roads with human or animal portage to modern superhighways, railways, and high speed aircraft. Moreover, the same diversity often prevails in the geographic distribution and integration of transport facilities and services; some (partially due to historical happenstance) are scattered haphazardly, while others are bound together in efficient subsystems.

Development Objectives and the Role of Transportation

The preceding brief generalizations of the development context are not universally applicable, especially in all of the details, to all less developed nations. Nevertheless, they are useful in formulating the objectives of many economic development programs and lending perspective to them. These might broadly be defined as: (1) growth in aggregate national income, accompanied by an equitable distribution between and within population, business, and regional groups; (2) increases in the kinds and amounts of final goods and services available to consumers, industry, and government; (3) development of a national industrial structure capable of earning foreign exchange and of supplying domestic markets; and (4) establishment and maintenance

[2] Harry T. Oshima, "Shares of Government in Gross National Product for Various Countries," *American Economic Review*, June 1957, pp. 381-90; also, Harley H. Hinrichs, "The Changing Level of Government Revenue Share During Economic Development," mimeographed, University of Maryland, 1964.

of a high level of employment. Most of these goals, of course, are subject to intertemporal trade-offs—the attainment of one can be sacrificed for increased achievement of another.

For these objectives to be realized, it is normally necessary (among other requisites, many of them noneconomic) that the agricultural sector be expanded and improved; that there be growth of the industrial sector and development of rural and urban markets; that a skilled labor force be trained; that urban centers with all their diversified productive, social, and cultural services be developed; and that an economical and reliable transportation system be furnished that is efficient from a resource allocation standpoint.

The Role of Transportation

Transportation plays a many-faceted role in the pursuit of development objectives. Its function as a factor input requirement is obvious—it enables goods and passengers to be transferred between and within production and consumption centers. Since much of this movement is between urban and rural areas, transport supplies an essential ingredient in extending the money economy to the agricultural sector and raising its productivity. In the process, if rural incomes can be increased, it may help to retard pathological urbanization.

Somewhat less apparent is the role of transport in shifting production possibility functions by altering relative factor costs. Improved transport lowers travel time, resulting in savings of labor man-hours spent in transit, and it permits reductions in inventory, capital, interest, and obsolescence costs. Of course, shipment costs fall, too, making otherwise unfeasible production possible. Thus, transport creates internal economies for many sectors, thereby fostering external economies for all sectors.

Increasing the speed and scope of the transport network also has beneficial effects on factor mobility, allowing human and material resources to be transferred more readily to places where they can be employed most productively. Consequently, transport helps to attain preferred regional distributions of population, industry, and incomes.

Finally, transport is also a private and public consumption good. In its private role it enables individuals to travel for private reasons. As a public good, it serves to increase national defense capabilities, social cohesion, and political stability. As Hans Heymann has noted in his review of the objectives of transportation in economic development (Chapter II), the latter noneconomic and redistributive effects largely are incommensurable, qualitative, and related to social utility. They alter economic priorities and, therefore, pose difficult problems in formulating and evaluating transport investment programs. Since economists have not been elected by popular mandate to reveal social preferences, they can only indicate the economic consequences of different proposals, leaving the final selection to politicians.[3]

Still, the economists' task is important, for they are responsible for devising alternative, *efficient* development programs from an almost infinite set of possibilities. Moreover, because the costs of suboptimizing one sector (such as transport) while assuming *ceteris paribus* conditions for the others can be extremely great, such designs should take place within the confines of a comprehensive planning framework. Unfortunately, such planning is extremely complex.

Deriving a Comprehensive Plan

The approach to comprehensive planning suggested below (which, admittedly, is somewhat idealistic), utilizes a six-stage iterative process, forcing transport and other planners to repeat a sequence of analyses until a set of satisfactory alternative plans for near- and long-term action is devised. The choice among these alternatives then becomes a matter of social judgment and is to be exercised, at least in democratic societies, by the elected representatives of the people with the assistance of development planners and other experts. However, a few preliminary remarks are in order before this methodology is outlined.

From the outset it should be recognized that an economic development plan should be only one aspect of a government's program to improve national well-being. Much more is involved in this program than formulating and implementing a plan for public sector investments on the basis of anticipated and stimulated private sector activi-

[3] On occasion, this has led to allocations that are clearly nonoptimal from an economic standpoint. It is interesting, however, that even in the highly planned Soviet society, economic opportunity costs frequently overrode the stated political objectives of transportation policy when the political goals involved large economic sacrifices. (See Holland Hunter's discussion of this phenomenon in Chapter VII.)

ties. More is required than government expenditures for infrastructure (housing, water, power, transportation, etc.) or for commodity-producing capacity. In general, the government must create conditions that are favorable to development; it must awaken an awareness of development potentialities and advantages; and it must foster an atmosphere that encourages efficient resource utilization and facilitates and stimulates private economic activities. Furthermore, although a mild degree of inflation may be beneficial, rapid inflation is to be avoided since it creates uncertainty, distortion of resource use, undue speculation, balance-of-payments difficulties, and other effects that deter growth. Consequently, a wide range of policy instruments—financial, monetary, import, tariff, direct and indirect taxation, transfer, educational, and so on—must be employed, together with expenditures, to attain a high growth rate and the realization of growth potential.[4]

Even given all these tools, the formulation of *ideal* policies and their application might prove to be insuperably difficult in many countries because of the dearth of information on which to base decisions. One of the first tasks in the developing nations is to gather basic national (and regional where appropriate) statistics on population, resources, production, prices, income, income distribution, savings, investment, etc. so that expected changes and structural interrelationships between these variables can be estimated. The failure to do this not only makes the design of development more uncertain, but also makes evaluation of the results of policy measures impossible. Merely determining that a given effect has been beneficial is insufficient proof that justifiable actions have been taken or that greater gains might not have been otherwise attained. The planner or administrator who has an "ostrich complex" and bases his conclusions on unnecessarily scanty knowledge may be doing his nation more harm than good.

This is particularly true in the first step of the planning process, the specification of goals. Goals should be stated in terms of minimum and desired levels and growth rates to be achieved at 5-year intervals from the present to a horizon 30 to 40 years hence. This long time span is required in part to permit proper accounting for the lives of major infrastructure investments; more importantly, it is necessary so that long-run shifts in goals and in the regional distribution of population

[4] The above prescription parallels that of Jan Tinbergen, *The Design of Development* (Johns Hopkins Press, 1958), pp. 3-8.

and economic activities may be correctly weighed in establishing near-term development programs.[5] The particular goals to be specified will vary from country to country. In general, they will encompass a time spectrum for achieving the objectives in regard to Gross National Product, per capita income and its distribution, the composition (and minimum values for certain components) of final demand and production, the distribution of income and production by regions, and certain additional items of special significance in a given nation.

The minimum character of these desires must be stressed. The aim in planning is to maximize national welfare, which is presumed to be equivalent to (or at least positively correlated with) maximizing the achievement of objectives.[6] The function of the goals is to act as minimum constraints.[7] Regardless of the degree to which some aims are exceeded, all must at least be satisfied. This, in essence, creates implicit prices for weighting the goals when some variables are forced to meet the constraints. For this reason, the goals should accurately reflect social preferences and be set at, or below, attainable levels. Unrealistically high goals, although they may serve a politically useful propagandistic purpose, hinder rather than aid effective planning. If reasonable goals are to be established, considerable information on the characteristics and capabilities of the economy is required.[8]

A set of goals without a means for their implementation, of course, is quite useless. Thus, the second stage of the planning procedure is to integrate these objectives into a long-range, dynamic development

[5] When even longer-run factors than those included at the planning horizon (e.g., watershed requirements) might be expected to alter discounted opportunity costs significantly, these, of course should also be considered.

[6] Goals aimed at minimizing undesirable effects may be expressed as maximizing problems by the use of negative prices, e.g., industrial waste may be given a negative price equal to its disposal cost.

[7] Because welfare may decline if certain goals are surpassed by a wide margin, maximum constraints may sometimes also be specified, i.e., the desideratum should lie within a relevant range. Some goals, too, may be subject only to a maximum constraint.

[8] These characteristics and capabilities enter the planning process as additional constraints. Aside from technical production coefficients, savings and financial factors may be especially important. (See Chapter XI by Sadove and Fromm.)

Since at early stages of development a large percentage of new production facilities and material inputs are likely to be imported, much attention should also be given to the foreign sector, i.e., to potential foreign exchange earnings, the import content of output, the balance of payments, long-term loans and credits, foreign aid, etc.

plan. While there may be some divergence in the details, the concepts to be applied in formulating this plan essentially are identical to those employed by Lefeber in Chapter VI. They need not be modified or extended here; the end result is the same: a broad program of utilization and allocation of resources and production among industries and between regions over time (to the horizon), to yield an optimal set of goods and services for final demand use.[9]

Clearly, both the production and output sets of this program must satisfy the goal constraints and should also provide for a maximization of economic product. Beyond this, however, the dynamic long-range plan should also serve three other purposes: (1) to act as a focus for the establishment of other long-term development guidelines and policies; (2) to provide the basic long-run framework on which the near-term plans are to be hung; and (3) to ensure that the latter plans are consistent with long-term development objectives.

The near-term plans represent the next step in the planning process and are the bridge between short-term actions (e.g., investment in projects) and the long-range program. Although the long-term development plan is the general determinant for near-term prescriptions, its high degree of aggregation is insufficient to guide current period policies. For near-term planning, more detail is required—the number of industry sectors and the corresponding final demand categories must be expanded to several hundred; greater regional detail may also be needed. Second, while the long-range plan should broadly optimize resource use in the long run, it is not sufficiently detailed or precise to do so in the short run. Transitory elements are largely ignored and certain effects within macro-sectors cannot be treated. Therefore, a further degree of optimization is required. Finally, to maximize output and reduce inflationary pressures, there must be consistency between resource use and availability in the short run.

Although the need for near-term planning to fulfill these requirements is evident, the exact form it should take is not intuitively obvious. Ideally, dynamic activity analysis should also be utilized for the formulation of near-term plans; practically, this may prove difficult,

[9] Because the uncertainty and the data requirements are so great in planning over a 40-year period, the long-term program must be fairly aggregative, containing probably no more than 50 sectors and 6 regions.

One point does require emphasis: it is vitally important that account be taken of the impact of continuing technological change on production relationships.

and an approximate technique may suffice as an alternative. Instead of attempting optimization of the objective function (i.e., the satisfaction of goals and the maximization of output) in a single-stage process, planning may prove more feasible if it proceeds sequentially. This might be done by a series of 1- or 2-year linear programs to cover a span of 5 or 6 years. The procedure then would be to impose the initial conditions and output specifications of the long-range plan as constraints on the first program, enter any additional necessary information, and solve for the efficient solution.[10] This process can then be repeated for the next short period with the initial conditions modified by the previous solution. Where there is a conflict between the specifications of the long- and short-term plans, the latter should dominate.[11]

There are further technical problems which must be surmounted in preparing the series of linear programs. For example, activity analysis as usually formulated permits no cross-hauling between regions. However, given geographic variations and the dispersion of resources, production, and markets *within* regions, it may clearly be desirable for regions to be both importers and exporters of particular commodities, especially in areas near their borders. To some extent this can be accommodated in the program by including subregions in the regional set and arbitrarily differentiating certain otherwise homogeneous goods.[12] Another source of difficulty is the potential instability of programming solutions; small changes in prices or resource availabilities trigger large, rapid regional and compositional shifts in output. Such occurrences can be averted by the introduction of lags and inertial response constraints.

Even with its drawbacks, this programming methodology has several

[10] Except for the interaction with the long-range plan, the analysis at this stage is essentially similar to that of Mitchell Harwitz in Chapter VIII. To obtain the requisite intermediate-year values of the long-range plan for use at this stage, some type of interpolation is needed; this probably will take an exponential form.

[11] After successive iterations of the entire planning procedure, no such discrepancies will exist, since the short-term solutions are utilized to realign the long-range plan within the established set of goals.

[12] It might also be noted that all regional planning need not necessarily take place within the confines of a central planning group. Hierarchical decision making, in which basic allocations (to industries and regions) are made at the national level, while the detailed planning is performed at the regional level, is feasible and desirable when the regional geographic areas are large and the disparity in their characteristics is great. It is essential, however, that there be feedback between the regional and national plans in order to ensure consistency and optimization of overall objectives.

critical advantages over the static or dynamic Leontief input-output technique (which is a simplified, special case of linear programming) normally employed for near-term planning. While both techniques fulfill the resource consistency requirements-check mentioned earlier, input-output analysis does not optimize resource allocation because it does not admit joint products, or alternative production processes with variable mixes of labor and capital inputs, or a multiplicity of resource types, or differential resource constraints. With its very restrictive assumptions, the Leontief system is "locked" to an efficient static point or dynamic path, even when other efficient programs may be feasible and more socially desirable.[13] Clearly, the more general technique, which provides both consistency and choice, is preferred for planning purposes.

At this juncture, having programmed the near-term plans which determine industry capacities and outputs by region, it is necessary to fill in the details for those sectors that are to be the subject of government intervention. That is, the plan for each industry is cast in generalized output and capacity terms which, to be operationally useful, must be translated into discrete products, particular types of capacities, and precise locations. For transport, this requires that the potential types and volumes of traffic be moved from point to point, and the adequacy of the facilities (basic and terminal) and operating equipment to carry these loads, be ascertained. Projects may then be formulated to eliminate any capacity deficiencies. In these specifications, account should be taken of the economic characteristics of different transport modes (described by Richard Heflebower in Chapter III); current and future technological possibilities (see Wilfred Owen, Chapter IV); and a host of design considerations (see Gary Fromm, Chapter V). Also, of course, this planning should be done on the basis of a system—the entire transport sector should be designed, not just particular facilities.

The cost-benefit evaluation of these prospective investments and the determination as to whether they should actually be undertaken constitutes the fourth stage in the planning process. Since the subject has had considerable attention elsewhere and is discussed by Hans Adler in Chapter IX, it need not be explored further here.[14]

---

[13] For an excellent critique of linear programming as contrasted to input-output analysis, see R. Dorfman, P. A. Samuelson, and R. M. Solow, *Linear Programming and Economic Analysis* (McGraw-Hill, 1958).

[14] An example of the application of these techniques may be found in Robert T. Brown's analysis of the Chilean railroad decisions, Chapter XII.

The fifth stage of the planning process deals with elements that cannot be formally introduced into these analyses.[15] These are indirect economic effects not yet taken into account, and social and political factors that might limit the decisiveness with which the previous analysis can be utilized in specifying projects and designing the long- and near-term national plans. These elements must be identified, measured to the extent feasible, and listed as addenda to the planning documents. As a result of combining these elements with the plan data, the design of particular sectors will be modified. Regional allocations will also have to be made, equating the demands for "fair shares" of the development resources and product with the objective of maximizing national income within a given time horizon. Fair shares here comprise not only the quantity of goods and services, but also their quality. Thus, for example, the political as well as the economic demands for transport must be considered. Maintaining bumpy, rutted roads in one region while paving highways in all the others may be economically desirable, but politically unrealistic. These are decisions not to be dictated by the planners, however, but by the elected representatives of the people.

Furthermore, before such a choice is presented to the executive and the legislature, the planning process must be completed. This is the function of the sixth and final planning stage. Two tasks must be accomplished: first, the various results of the previous stages and the various sector plans must be made consistent; second, a set of alternative development programs must be prepared. Both of these functions may be realized by iterating through the prior planning stages, making marginal adjustments to assure consistency and alterations in the mix and specification of goals and other allocations to yield the spectrum of different optimal plans and plan subsets among which the politicians will choose.[16]

The number of iterations required to achieve a reasonable set of

[15] This is particularly true for sectors, such as health and education, whose outputs are not, for the most part, direct inputs to other sectors and which serve to modify the distribution of welfare among segments of the population. In these cases, the allocation of resources to their production is somewhat arbitrary and depends, to a considerable degree, on the specification of goals and the political process.

[16] Technically speaking, the aim in this process is to determine the efficiency frontier set and its mapping to the horizon within the relevant range of the social welfare function.

significant alternatives (each one of which is internally consistent) cannot, a priori, be specified in advance. Their magnitude will depend on the detail and care with which the initial iteration has been undertaken, the complexity of the economy in terms of the variability of production possibilities, resource availabilities and geographic dispersion, and the importance of social and political considerations in relation to economic factors. In any event, the amount of effort involved is likely to be substantial.

This, in and of itself, might create resistance to adopting a planning procedure as extensive as that just outlined. Furthermore, it is often true that nothing is so strongly opposed as that which is least understood. To be sure, the proposed planning approach is complex, its utilization would entail considerable efforts in data collection and analysis, and its implementation would require the extremely scarce talents of highly competent economists and engineers. The approach is also imperfect because there will be data gaps and inaccuracies, statistical problems of aggregation, a host of simplifying assumptions, and a myriad of other difficulties. Yet alternative approaches (which, of necessity, use the identical data) are even more dismal—not in their methodologies, which are simple, but in their results.

Planning, as it is practiced in most underdeveloped countries today, consists almost wholly of attempting to take desirable actions in the short run. At times long- or intermediate-range goals are set forth; there may even be a "five-year plan," derived on an input-output basis. Nevertheless, optimization of intermediate- or long-term objectives is rarely practiced, and primary emphasis is placed on individual projects to meet immediate needs. As numerous examples have now shown, such suboptimization can result in tremendous losses of development opportunity. Project analysis is truly one of the cornerstones of effective planning, but, when employed alone, it frequently leads to unsatisfactory consequences. It should therefore be supplemented by additional information and other techniques that provide long-run guidelines. This is the function that is claimed for the six-stage procedure. Notwithstanding the costs and imperfections of the procedure, it should contribute to more intelligent decisions and greater national welfare than present planning methods, not by supplanting but by complementing project analysis.

Three groups of potential critics must be answered: (1) those elected representatives and heads of government who claim that their prerogatives of establishing national economic policies are being usurped by the planners; (2) those businessmen who believe that planning destroys free enterprise by restricting their actions and diminishing their profits; and (3) those economists who believe that a maximum rate of increase of Gross National Product is stimulated by inducing shortages or excesses via the route of unbalanced growth. These reservations to planning will be treated in turn.

The politicians' fears are wholly unfounded, since they alone, in most countries, are given the power to legislate and approve (or disapprove) programs and to appropriate funds. The planners exist to fulfill a staff function, serving under their direction to assist them in making better decisions.

The alarm of the business interests is also, for the most part, unnecessary. The purpose of planning is to achieve the greatest growth of real per capita product consistent with other social welfare objectives. With few exceptions, private initiative, productive activity, and efficiency are encouraged and assisted, because the planners' goals require increased production and higher absolute profits in all sectors. Toward this end, infrastructure in the form of transport, power, housing, sewage, etc. is often provided; several countries also have granted tax concessions for new plants. It is true, however, that planning includes a careful review of the economy and therefore tends to focus attention on certain aberrations and inequities that otherwise would be undetected and uncorrected. Thus, exorbitant speculative returns from landholding or the exploitation of minerals and other natural resources, especially if foreign-owned, may be limited or prevented.

At times, too, a country's development plans and policies may prove restrictive to certain industries, particularly in pricing or capacity-expansion decisions. In some instances, actions that would not voluntarily be undertaken by firms are compelled. Nevertheless, it should be recalled that the development plan takes its form partially from the anticipated actions of the private sector. Its aim is not central dictation of decisions or control of activity in each microcosm, but rather the achievement of a set of guidelines within which, hopefully, income and output will be maximized and economic losses—such as undesired excess capacity—will be minimized. As these development efforts bear fruit, internal markets will broaden and effective demand within the country will increase, raising sales and profits. Firms that enhance development should truly have little to fear and much to gain from planning; but firms that hope to reap unjustified, undue windfall or monopoly returns at the expense of social welfare may experience some difficulties.

These views seem even less extreme when it is recalled that nearly all industrialized countries employ some planning (and limit abusive practices) to guide their economic policies. Interestingly, none of these countries has intentionally utilized the shortage-excess unbalanced growth technique advocated by some economists.[17] The concept involved in this process is the use of disequilibrium as a driving force (e.g., by providing an excess or maintaining a shortage of transport capacity), depending on private profit and public political pressures (and also demonstration effects) stemming from external economies and complementarities to induce additional investment and production. Whether in fact such disequilibria do generate sufficiently strong incentives to bring about a greater increase in savings, capital expenditures, and output under this type of unbalanced growth, as contrasted to other forms of balanced or unbalanced growth, is unknown. In any event, the validity of the programming methodology previously described is not affected, since the sequence of induced effects can be taken into account.[18] Nonetheless, this does require that the proponents of induced unbalanced growth quantify their technique: without parameters, any consequences of lagged gaps between desired and actual production are largely problematical.

Transport Investment Planning

Planning transport investment is a difficult task, whether it is an integral part of comprehensive analyses of the type just outlined or it is in the more traditional milieu of suboptimizing an individual sector. The essays that follow describe some of the elements and problems involved in achieving an ideal allocation of development resources to transport.

Hans Heymann's essay focuses on the objectives of transportation in

[17] For example, A. O. Hirschman, *The Strategy of Economic Development* (Yale University Press, 1958).

[18] Programming of the dynamic form presupposes no particular degree of balance or imbalance. Nevertheless, given the changing goals, inertial or time lag constraints, and initial disequilibrium conditions of "real world" situations, the planning solutions are likely to be of the unbalanced type.

economic development and particularly cites the difficulties of choice among different investments posed by noneconomic goals and effects. The economic characteristics of alternative transport modes—economies of scale, capital intensity, flexibility, and so forth—which so markedly influence the choice among transport investments are examined by Richard B. Heflebower in Chapter III. In the next chapter, Wilfred Owen indicates the impact of technological change on methods of transport and describes some of the future possibilities for lowering movement costs and increasing mobility.

Chapter V discusses the design of the transport sector for an economic development plan and reveals some of the unique problems confronted in preparing an investment program. Attaining maximal economic development and balanced regional growth is the topic of Louis Lefeber's essay; he outlines a comprehensive, dynamic planning model and discusses its implications for wage, pricing, regional, and transportation policies. Holland Hunter's review of transportation in Soviet development which follows is testimony to the unfeasibility of subverting efficient transport development in favor of fostering political goals. He concludes that the application of regional linear programming techniques of the type proposed by Mitchell Harwitz in Chapter VIII should enable currently developing countries, and the U.S.S.R., to plan and manage the development process with less cruelty and waste of resources than in the past.

Programming solutions alone, however, cannot be the guide to the desirability of individual investments. Hans Adler's chapter, therefore, is devoted to a description of the method of cost-benefit evaluation as a tool in establishing priorities for transport projects. The pricing policy for the resulting transport services is a matter of some concern, since not only does it affect the allocation of gains between different users, but it also may involve subsidies drawn from a government's general revenue sources. In Chapter X, James R. Nelson explores the implications of different pricing schemes and proposes a multi-part charging scheme for obtaining full cost recovery. Pricing and financing of transport are, of course, intimately related. Inadequate consideration of financing requirements can have grave consequences for the availability of public investment funds and the creation of inflationary pressures, a subject which is discussed by A. Robert Sadove and this writer in Chapter XI. Finally, to illustrate the principles involved in project evaluation, pricing, and financing of transport expenditures, Robert T.

Brown's examination of the "railroad decision" in Chile is presented as a case study. Mrs. Warden's selected bibliography follows.

These brief, preliminary excursions into various aspects of transport investment and economic development provide far from definitive answers to the many questions and problems of allocating ideal amounts of resources to transport. Yet, it is hoped that the reader will gain an appreciation of the broad, and some of the narrow, issues and be stimulated to add to knowledge in the field.

II

The Objectives of Transportation

HANS HEYMANN, JR.*

Aɴʏ ɴᴀᴛɪᴏɴ, ʜɪɢʜʟʏ ᴅᴇᴠᴇʟᴏᴘᴇᴅ or underdeveloped, attempting to construct a national transportation system or to formulate a national transportation policy must come to grips with a most difficult first question: what are the national purposes that the transportation system is intended to serve? This at least *should* be the first question. Unfortunately, it is hardly ever asked at all. But in trying to make transportation decisions that fundamentally affect a nation's life, it is not enough to ask "how much?" and "where?" but also "what for?" Toward what larger ends should the transportation system be designed? The moment one asks that question one becomes aware of the painful fact that a large, complex society invariably embraces a multiplicity of conflicting objectives.

Incompatible Objectives

Transportation—the movement of goods and people—is hardly ever desired for its own sake; it is merely a means to serve other objectives. Some of these objectives are economic: to exploit natural resources, to raise agricultural productivity, to increase industrial output, to enhance per capita consumption, and so forth. Side by side with these are noneconomic objectives: to promote political cohesion, to strengthen the country's defenses, to bring about certain socially desirable locational patterns, etc. Clearly, the economic and noneco-

* The RAND Corporation, Santa Monica, California. Any views expressed in this paper are those of the author. They should not be interpreted as reflecting the views of The RAND Corporation or the official opinion or policy of any of its governmental or private research sponsors.

18

nomic objectives do not always pull in the same direction. Transportation decisions made to promote the national defense are likely to be in conflict with, and might even contradict, decisions designed to promote economic efficiency. The fact that transportation objectives are competing, incommensurate, and often incompatible with one another raises a serious dilemma for the economist trying to develop an optimal system.

Objectives of U.S. Transportation Policy

Does the United States have a transportation policy which reconciles conflicting objectives? Two examples from recent U.S. experience help answer the question. One is the President's transportation message to Congress of April 5, 1962, which attempts to spell out the objectives of U.S. transportation policy in some detail:

> The basic objectives of our nation's transportation system must be to assure the availability of the fast, safe and economical transport services needed in a growing and changing economy to move people and goods without waste or discrimination in response to private and public demand *at the lowest cost consistent with health, convenience, national security and other broad public objectives.* Investment or capacity should be neither substantially above nor substantially below these requirements—for chronic excess capacity involves misuse of resources and lack of adequate capacity jeopardizes progress. The resources devoted to provision of transportation service should be used in the most effective and efficient manner possible and this in turn means that users of transport facilities should be provided with incentives to use whatever form of transportation provides them with the service they desire at the *lowest total cost both public and private.* [Italics mine]

The emphasis in this statement of objectives is on economic efficiency in the broad sense of the term, with a polite bow in the direction of other "higher level" objectives, without admitting that the latter may conflict with efficiency. In fairness, however, it should be pointed out that the very purpose of the message was to underline the efficiency considerations in order to bring greater rationality to our muddled transportation policies.

A more dramatic example is provided by the formulation of objectives in the recent White House statement on International Air Transport Policy, issued on April 24, 1963:

> To develop and maintain an expanding, *economically and technologically efficient* international air transport system best adapted to the growing needs of the Free World, and to assure the international air carriers of the United States *a fair and equal opportunity to compete* in world aviation markets so as to maintain and further develop an economically viable service network wherever a substantial need for air transportation develops. [Italics mine]

This statement makes no concessions at all in the direction of noneconomic objectives, such as the strengthening of national security, the furtherance of certain foreign policy aims, enhancement of national prestige, and a host of other high-level national purposes that could be served by international air transport and that would almost certainly come into conflict with the norm of efficiency.

How do we explain this shying away from the existence of incompatible objectives in transportation policy? There are at least two explanations. There is first of all a belief that where transportation is concerned a hierarchy of objectives can be established—that it is possible to rank the national purposes according to the degree and quality of the impact that transportation can have on these purposes. In a highly developed economy like the United States, with a predominantly privately owned and operated transport system, it is probably true that the economic criteria are most relevant, that some noneconomic goals are automatically met by following them, and that other noneconomic objectives can somehow be accommodated as exceptions or special departures from the optimal system. By putting economic considerations first, we think we can avoid the dilemma that arises from the fact that there is no single optimum transportation system that would satisfy all of the diverse purposes simultaneously.

But there is also a second reason, inherent in the economist's special interest in efficient resource allocation and in the limitations of his special skill. The theoretically minded transport economist, eagerly in pursuit of an optimum, is attracted by the clarity and precision of his equilibrium theory which gives him a formula for allocating resources so as to achieve an optimum transport system. According to the rules, he does this by equating the ratio of marginal value product to marginal cost for each transport mode and, indeed, for every producing unit in the economy. The fact that the market mechanism in the real world does not lead automatically to the perfect competitive solution can always be taken care of, it is hoped, by regulatory intervention. Not that this is easy, but it is at least something that the economist can grapple with. The moment noneconomic objectives which are inconsistent with these solutions are introduced, however, the contradictions become unmanageable and the economist's prescriptions based on market values break down.

The Role of Economic Analysis

Economics deals primarily with the logic of the allocative process—it tells us *how* to choose but not *what* to choose. It provides no magic formula for choosing the right objective or complex of objectives. The economist is at his best in finding the most efficient or the least-cost method of achieving a simple and well-defined objective.

For example, he would do very well in answering a question such as: what is the least-money cost combination of transportation investments that will increase coal deliveries from the northeast Indian coal mines to the Port of Calcutta by 10 percent per annum? This is a simple means-end problem, in which the objective, the means, and the criterion are clearly stated. The objective is to achieve a specified increase in delivered output; the means, investment in transportation; and the criterion, least-cost. While there may be many different ways of measuring "least-cost," the selection of a minimum money-cost method of producing a given output is at least a familiar problem.

Limitations of Economic Analysis

The task, however, becomes much more difficult when the economist is confronted with a complex set of objectives many of which may not be quantifiable and where the utility trade-offs among them cannot be clearly specified. For example, the economist might have difficulty in tackling a question such as: how should India's $100 million transportation budget be allocated among the various transport modes so as to maximize India's national growth? Clearly, "national growth" is not a single output, but a combination of goals, most of which are not measurable. It is a general goal that includes a long list of independent subgoals, including increases in real per capita consumption, social cohesion, political stability, "the good life," and much else. If these intangibles could be quantified and placed on a pseudo-market basis, an "efficient" solution could still be found. But unfortunately they cannot be so quantified. Often economists make the simplifying assumption that "national growth" is adequately measured by the rate of growth of Gross National Product or some similar quantifiable factor and proceed to maximize that. But this is little more than an evasion of the issue, which is that the choice-of-objectives problem is not very congenial to the economist's tool kit. The fundamental problem is choosing the appropriate mixture of goals and, since most of these goals involve individual or community values, it is best to acknowledge that these are matters about which subjective decisions have to be made.

The transport economist must recognize that the choice among alternative national transport systems fundamentally affects and in part determines the nation's development path and its strategy for growth. This is not an economic efficiency problem but a high-level policy decision to which no single criterion is appropriate. Decisions aimed at "maximizing national growth" are bound to be somewhat intuitive and based on the faith that certain objectives are of a greater order of importance than others.

Usefulness of Economic Analysis

Recognizing that economics holds no magic for choosing a strategy for "national growth" is not the same thing as saying that economic analysis has no role in this choice. On the contrary, it has a very special and useful role. It can fulfill the important function of providing the decision maker with the terms of exchange, or trade-offs, among different objectives, so that he can better choose among the possibilities open to him on the basis of his own utility pattern or of the community's system of preferences. By providing such trade-offs, the economist can clarify, though not resolve, the community's question of how much of one goal it should be willing to trade to obtain more of another. While systematic analysis cannot select a single best transport system, it can present the relevant data on the costs and benefits of different transport systems that will achieve different combinations of objectives. These costs and benefits are useful factors in the decision, but do not in themselves supply the answer. The rational decision-maker surely would be ill advised to make his strategic choice on the basis purely of a least-cost consideration.

The transportation planner, seeking to maximize his nation's growth, would hardly be rational if he chose an inland waterway system over a highway system purely on the grounds that the former could perform the required transportation functions at lower cost. This would make little more sense than if a doctor, seeking to correct the effects of ill-health and stunted growth in an undernourished child, prescribed a particular vitamin instead of a balanced diet because the vitamin costs less. In both cases one must determine the meaning of "growth" and "health" and recognize all of the ingredients that constitute "growth" and "health." And the problem is one of understanding the organic relationship between the means and the end—between transport and growth, between food and health—and, finally, of selecting one combination of ends, one pattern of results, over another.

The economist, confronted with choice-of-objectives questions, is exposed to at least three temptations: (1) The temptation to lose sight of the distinction between choosing a strategy and obtaining efficiency. The risk here is that when development strategy is under consideration he will proceed in search of a "scientific" answer and act as if there were no large and irreducible element of subjective judgment involved in his choice of ends. (2) The tendency to make decisions that are justified mainly because they are supported by numbers. It is well to remember that estimates of trade-offs or of exchange ratios, can be made only on the side of costs; they cannot be made on the side of objectives. Utility maps exist only in the textbooks. Lack of quantitative guidance is a permanent condition with which the transport economist must learn to live. (3) The temptation to ignore the intangibles and the complexities of the real world, to exclude important insights, and to oversimplify complicated reality. The objectives of a society will always be vague and incommensurable, the course of development uncertain, and the hope of providing a precise model unlikely to be realized.

In short, economic analysis can be very important in large national transportation decisions; but its role does not lie mainly in the application of high-powered mathematical techniques that might be appropriate to economic efficiency questions. Its contribution should be in the form of formulating a problem logically, and of providing relevant

information on the productivity and cost of various systems so that it
will be easier to make subjective decisions.

Role of Economic Analysis in Developing Countries

The points in the preceding section are particularly important for
decisions in the less developed countries where the logical ordering of
problems, the systematic examination of alternatives, are among the
more important functions that the economist can perform. He can use
his skill most effectively by illuminating choices open to the community; by formulating and portraying alternative future paths that
could be followed and by clarifying both the cost and the value implications of choosing one or another of these paths. Most developing
countries are in need of help in this area. For, as Max F. Millikan
points out,[1] one notable fact about the developing countries is that
their systems of preference are still relatively unformed and in a state
of rapid flux. There is a kind of circularity here, since economic development demands a radical change in the motives, attitudes, and
values of the community. When the economist illuminates choices, he
can affect the evolution of these values, not by imposing his own
preferences upon the society but by broadening the society's understanding of these choices. By and large, people in transitional societies
have a limited conception of the options open to them for future patterns of life, both as individuals and as communities. What individuals want is related to what their experience tells them is possible. The economist's efforts can broaden, or narrow, the perception
of alternatives open to them.

This point is of particular importance to the transportation planner.
For transportation decisions have an enormous potential impact on the
quality and character of community life and on the locational pattern
of economic activity. It would be a serious error for the transportation
planner to accept the community's current objectives and values as
given and to try to build an optimal transportation system to match
them. It would be an error because the goals will almost certainly be
fundamentally changed by the social transformation that goes with

[1] Millikan, "Criteria for Decision-Making in Economic Planning," *Science,
Technology, and Development*, Vol. VIII, U. S. papers prepared for the U.N.
Conference on the Application of Science and Technology for the Benefit of the
Less Developed Areas (U. S. Government Printing Office, 1963), pp. 28 ff.

growth and by the very transportation path that will be followed. Instead, the transportation planner should attempt to present to the community a range of feasible and reasonably efficient alternatives. He should show for each alternative the consequences (to the extent they can be foreseen) for their future welfare and their way of life if the community were to pursue that alternative consistently.

This will not be easy, but it need not be a highly rigorous undertaking initially. The economist can make good use of his skill in applying cost and efficiency criteria to the discovery of optimal systems. In this way the locational decisions inherent in transportation development can be made in greater awareness of their purely economic consequences and, at the same time, in a fashion which will stimulate the clarification of goals.

Past Performance in the Developed World

If the economist hopes to contribute to the clarification of a society's goals, it may be well to ask whether, in the field of transportation planning, the economist has in fact shown a perception of changing social values in the more highly developed societies. Unfortunately, even the economic history of the United States suggests that the economist's performance has been less than inspired. Transportation decisions in the United States have been marked more by irrationality, waste, and insensitivity to social values than by a sophisticated consideration of alternatives.

Urban Transportation

In the Washington metropolitan area there are today no less than seventeen agencies concerned with urban transportation. Each of these agencies has some say on the direction that transportation development should take in this important urban area. Of the numerous plans that have been publicly submitted, however, none offers a systematic presentation of alternatives for public discussion. None appears to recognize explicitly the enormous uncertainty and abysmal ignorance about changing community values and consumer preferences. The plans typically serve up ingenious and elaborate schemes for *public* transportation systems on the ground that these are more efficient than private transportation. However, the planners cannot really be sure that the urban twentieth century American really *wants* public transportation. Most urban transport planning seems to be little more than a mechanical process of projecting into the indefinite future various indices of traffic growth, locational changes, and population growth. The authorities seem to assume that the forces which have shaped urban transport development in the past will simply continue unchanged into the indefinite future. Surely, in order to anticipate the future development of urban society, they should be taking a much harder look at the changing locational patterns of industry and at the changing preferences of consumers. Then they might find that, precisely because of the excellent access and mobility provided by our existing transportation system and because of changes in industries' factor proportions, enterprises are becoming more dispersed. They are locating themselves closer to their now highly diffused markets rather than to their sources of supply. The planners might also find that personal services occupy a growing share in the product mix of the economy. All this means that employment patterns are likely to become much more highly dispersed and journey-to-work patterns correspondingly more complex and intricate.[2]

A close look at people's desires suggests that with rising real per capita incomes most Americans want *higher quality* in their transportation systems. They are willing to pay a substantial premium for privacy, flexibility, and timesaving. (On the other hand they might think twice about this if each individual had to bear his share of the full social costs overtly!) This raises the interesting question of how much cheaper a public transportation system would have to be to induce people to give up privacy and flexibility. Similarly, increasing homeownership and growing preferences for recreational and cultural activities will almost certainly alter the location and time pattern of transportation demands. Whether or not these changes will be large enough to stop the relentlessly rising cost of combating congestion is not easy to predict, but these are the kinds of changes that will deeply affect the success of future transportation systems. So far, however, transportation planners in the most highly developed countries have paid relatively little attention to these matters. This does not augur well for our ability to guide and enlighten the less developed coun-

[2] Charles J. Zwick, *The Demand for Transportation Services in a Growing Economy* (The RAND Corporation, P-2682, December 1962).

tries where social and economic changes of the most fundamental sort greatly complicate the task of transportation planning.

Performance in a Planned Society

It might be argued that the deficiencies in transportation planning in the United States are the problems of a market-oriented society that has not developed the habits and techniques of broad national planning. Surely, in a centrally planned economy, transportation and locational choices can be made much more deliberately and consistently. There may well be some validity in this view, but in at least one country, the Soviet Union, experience does not bear out the hypothesis that transportation planners in centralized economies display a much higher order of sophistication and insight.

The Soviet case provides an excellent example of the frustration of policy engendered by the pursuit of contradictory objectives. Soviet objectives, both economic and political, are stated explicitly. Observers are thus able to examine the extent to which they have been met.[3]

In regard to the location of economic activity, the Soviets embraced three major political objectives:

1. The first objective was to redress the "unevenness" of economic development that had been inherited from the prerevolutionary capitalist era, in which the center (European Russia) had waxed fat, while the provinces had been exploited. Their first injunction therefore was to locate economic activity "more evenly."

2. The second related objective was to raise the proportion of output coming from the formerly neglected and culturally backward regions of the country.

3. And the third, associated with the doctrinal principle of autarky, was to rupture the Russian economy's links with the world economy and to enhance the country's safety from invasion.

All three objectives point to a strong drive to shift the economic center of gravity away from European Russia to the eastern and underdeveloped parts of the country. Was such a shift actually accomplished?

The record of Soviet development shows that the eastward movement, in fact, proceeded extremely slowly and that the old centers of European Russia continued to receive, as they do to this day, more

[3] Holland Hunter, *Soviet Transportation Policy* (Harvard University Press, 1957), pp. 21-38, Chapter 5.

attention and investment resources than the outlying regions. The explanation is that, side by side with the three political objectives that have been described, the Soviet leadership embraced two economic objectives that pulled them unwittingly in the opposite direction. One was the determination to secure the benefits of economies of scale in production, which meant that very large production units had to be located in densely populated regions if transport costs were to be kept within reason. The other was the well-known objective of maximum tempo of development, the policy of forced industrialization. The Soviet planners soon discovered that much larger increments of output could be obtained by expanding the capacity of the established centers than by developing new centers from scratch. The established centers yielded more rapid growth in production at lower cost than investments in new plants in underdeveloped regions. The Soviet discovery merely confirms the fact, well known in the West, that speed of development and dispersion of economic activity are inversely correlated.

Soviet location and transportation decisions were further distorted by the persistent determination of the planners to minimize the demand for transportation. The Soviets have had, from the outset, strong doctrinal and rational preferences for keeping investment in transportation to a minimum, so as to plow all possible resources into more directly productive or form-changing activity. However, the locational policies that were actually adopted, far from reducing the demand for transportation, began, as early as the 1930's, to generate very large traffic flows. To this day, the effort to hold down the demand for transportation is a stubborn preoccupation of the Soviet planning community.

The rigid insistence that transportation investment shall be held down has imposed and continues to impose significant locational inefficiencies and other socially costly choices on the Soviet economy. For example, Soviet pricing policy has persistently sought to force cargoes off the overburdened railroads and onto inefficient waterways. The location of industrial plants and the location of workers' housing near industrial plants are often motivated by the desire to economize on transportation rather than by broader economic and social considerations. The practice of subsidizing certain shipments to redirect haulage from distant rich-ore areas to nearby poor-ore areas is another economic irrationality imposed by transport stringencies. In short, the Soviet experience can hardly be held up as a model for those seeking an answer to the problem of responding rationally and consistently to the existence of conflicting objectives, and certainly not for those hopeful of efficiently limiting the demand for transportation. Transport demand was ultimately held down, but at an economic and social cost that hardly recommends Soviet policy for emulation.

Relative Importance of Transportation

The discussion thus far has dealt largely with the subject of *overall* transport objectives and goals. It has pointed up their multiple and conflicting nature, the need to distinguish choice-of-objectives problems from efficiency problems, the importance of broadening a society's perception of alternative goals and values, and the rather unimpressive record of economists and planners in dealing with these issues. I turn now to the more specific problem of transport objectives in *economic development,* having in mind the earlier point that investments in transportation are made not for their own sake but as a means to larger ends. How good is transportation as a means to the broader goal of economic development?

There seems to be a widespread faith in the United States that there is some magic in transportation, that it is of fundamental importance in a growing society, and that it acts as a development catalyst. The assumption is often made that an enlarged availability of transportation is an essential precondition for economic development in most low-income societies. Since it is so difficult to evaluate objectively how much investment in transport infrastructure is indicated in any given situation, there is a tendency to be profligate and wasteful in this field. Unfortunately, in practice, the question of "how much transportation?" cannot be answered on the basis of any objective principle. It is no easier to cut a rational transportation slice out of the national pie than it is to cut a defense slice or a public education slice. The overall choice of the quantity of resources to allocate to transportation can be made only as a reflection of the affirmative decisions concerning numerous individual transport projects. The choice is not a single decision based on a rule of thumb or in answer to the global question of how important transportation is in toto. The decision on total resource allocation to transportation must emerge as a result of evaluating individually, and in combination, the various transportation uses to which resources can be put in the quest for economic growth.

However, a close look at the overall resource claim of the transportation sector in the developing countries reveals that it is very large. In most of these countries, transportation regularly consumes anywhere from one-third to two-thirds of all available public investment funds. The International Bank for Reconstruction and Development (IBRD) has allocated about 40 percent of all of its loans to the transportation sector—certainly a resounding vote of confidence in the propitiatory qualities of transportation. Perhaps, as Albert Hirschman points out, one reason why Western development planners have been particularly attracted to the transportation sector is that it is a "safe" field of investment. Development planning is risky, and there is a real attraction to investing in ventures such as transport that cannot be proven wrong before they are started and that are not easy to prove to have been obvious failures.[4]

But in a more serious vein, another explanation for this heavy stress on transportation is the view that it represents a kind of diversified investment in the general growth of an economy and the associated belief that it not only permits but calls forth directly productive activity through its dynamic impact. But is such a belief really warranted? Can transportation *create* new tradition-breaking activities? Undoubtedly transportation affects the course of economic development very strongly, but whether it is able to *call forth* other economic activities is doubtful at best.

Transportation and U.S. Development

Perhaps some of this faith in the dynamic qualities of transportation stems from a misreading of the history of transportation development in the United States—that it was the canals and railroads that "opened up the West." One need not detract from the drama of the Erie Canal and the relentless march of the railways across the continent; but one might question the thesis that transportation *brought about* the economic development of the West. The great migration in the United States was set in motion by the golden opportunities, the powerful attractions of the West: the vision of denser forests, richer mines, wider fields, and busier towns that pulled the trapper, the lumberman, the

---

[4] Albert O. Hirschman, *The Strategy of Economic Development* (Yale University Press, 1958), p. 84.

miner, the farmer, and the cattleman irresistibly westward. The migrants were also helped along by the element of push, the dissatisfactions and dislocations in the areas from which they migrated. The men who provided land transportation by building the railways merely responded to the economic opportunity, admittedly enhanced by the government's land grant policies. Their aim was not to develop the hinterland but to make a quick fortune for themselves. In the process they contributed importantly to the *rate* of change, to the *pace* of the migration. They also determined the paths along which it flowed, and in this way helped to shape the regional distribution of economic activity. Thus the new transport links exerted strong locational attractions along the length of their routes. But they did not create the underlying motivations. The real thrust of the nation's westward development clearly was rooted in powerful economic and social forces that were quite independent of, and exogenous to, the transportation industry.

Developmental Impact in Underdeveloped Countries

The case should not be overstated. Obviously some transport investment which provides access to an area is indispensable before other economic activities can unfold there. Also, as was pointed out, a transport link, once established and used productively, will have important locational attractions. But there is no evidence that endowing a country with highway or rail transportation will ensure that new industrial or agricultural activity will result. Nor is there any real indication that it is the inadequacy of transportation that constitutes the key bottleneck in the growth of underdeveloped countries. Apparently the expansion of transport capacity is permissive: it allows a dynamic developing situation to work its way, and it can reinforce motivations that already exist. The degree to which transportation creates or compels new activity will surely depend upon the existence of other conditions within the economy: the quality of its administrative structure and social order, the character and drive of its educational system, the nature of legal and property relationships, and all the other dimensions of a nation's "propensity to grow." Where these qualities are deficient, no amount of transport investment will be likely to create an economy-wide dynamism.

The thought that our past transport development policies may have been based too largely on faith has begun to spread among Western economists. Recent economic surveys in a number of countries suggest that transportation may have received an excessive share of total investments, and some concern is now expressed over the high cost of providing mobility in the capital-poor countries. Efforts are being made to discover new ways of limiting investment in transportation and of lowering transport costs. These efforts are aimed most prominently at two areas—reducing the demand for transportation and utilizing more advanced technology. Some of the interesting possibilities in these two areas have been explored by Martin Meyerson and Wilfred Owen.[5] But if one of the objectives of transportation in economic development is that of economic efficiency, it may be well to insert a note of caution: a too enthusiastic attempt to limit the demand for transportation and an overly energetic pursuit of new technology could easily lead to unhappy results.

Reducing the demand for transportation may mean better land-use planning, efforts to reduce peak loads, and attempts to introduce efficient substitutions, such as the transmission of electric power for the transportation of coal. Such measures could result in important economies, provided an overall efficiency calculus in fact justified them. But if it means shifting the burden of transport costs to other economic activities or to consumers by imposing locational or other inefficiencies upon them, it would simply be a case of transferring costs from one sector to another, and no net gain would accrue.

Similarly, in the field of new technology, if the concern is to find more efficient transport vehicles or power sources adapted to the special environments of the developing countries, then important benefits may be gained. But if the pursuit of technology is motivated merely by worship of novelty, by a passion for discovering ever more glamorous propulsion systems, exotic fuels, and esoteric-effects machines, the economic benefits to the developing countries could turn out to be negative. In transportation, as in all other fields bearing on economic development, one quickly discovers that there are no short cuts and there is no magic.

[5] Martin Meyerson, "Strategy Planning for Transportation and Economic Development," and Wilfred Owen, "Transport Technology and Economic Development," in *Transportation,* Vol. V, U.S. papers prepared for the U.N. Conference on the Application of Science and Technology for the Benefit of the Less Developed Areas (U.S. Government Printing Office, 1963), pp. 5-13, 14-22.

Conclusions

Transportation in any society serves a variety of conflicting and incommensurable objectives. The selection of a national transportation system implies a choice among these goals. Such a choice cannot be approached as a straightforward economic efficiency problem; it constitutes a high-level policy decision. The economist can best contribute to this policy decision by offering up his transportation plans as a range of feasible transportation alternatives together with a prognosis of some of their foreseeable social implications. In this way he may help the community to broaden its own perception of its goals and values.

On the other hand, the past performance of economists and planners in this sphere, both in the market-oriented West and in the centrally planned East, has been less than inspired. Finally, the validity of a widely held faith that transportation stimulates new productive activity is questioned. Where a nation is deficient in the factors conducive to growth, no amount of transport investment will create the economic dynamism that is so ardently desired.

III

Characteristics of Transport Modes

RICHARD B. HEFLEBOWER*

In this latter part of the twentieth century, ways of moving people or commodities over space are almost as varied as are the reasons for movement. The methods range in technology from head-carrying or pack animal to (in the near future) supersonic jet aircraft. In degree of specialization, they vary from the pipeline or high-tension electric power line to the railroad that can carry anything anywhere track is laid. The five major traffic modes to be considered here—rail, water, road or highway, air, and pipeline—differ widely. They differ one to another and within each mode in speed, capacity, adaptability, and investment cost.

A transport investment decision involves, therefore, the choice among transport modes made in light of the economic-technological characteristics of each mode and its adaptability to the types and volume of expected traffic. Also required is a study of the handicaps, or aids, that nature offers that affect the cost of construction and operation of particular transport modes. Because decisions must give weight to alternative uses of the limited capital and foreign exchange available, the fact that modes differ significantly in investment per mile of route acquires unusual significance.

Applying the standard of optimal uses of resources becomes especially complicated when the desirability of investment in one transport mode rather than another is being evaluated. All nonspecialized modes have some capacity and traffic-handling characteristics to serve many production processes in a given economy. But a specific estimate of the efficiency added to a particular production process by the agency that hauls the materials used in, or the products of, that process is difficult to make, because it is vitiated by the high proportion of

* Northwestern University.

34

joint and common costs. The fact that transport can be a direct consumer service also adds to evaluation difficulties; railroads, for example, use the same fixed facilities and some of the same operating equipment for both passenger service and freight service. To simplify the analysis here, passenger transport will be disregarded and for commodity hauling the simple index of "ton-miles" (number of tons hauled per mile of route) will be adopted.

Nonspecialized forms of transport can also yield indirect economic and socio-political benefits. These gains (detailed in other essays in this volume) result usually because excess capacity is virtually inherent in the basic facilities of most transport modes. Availability of transport may, for instance, stir a population's entrepreneurial capacities to develop operations complementary to transport or made possible by it. The movement of people and goods tends to weld localities into larger economic and more viable political units. But the extent and character of such indirect benefits are often tenuous.

This fact, combined with the ambiguity, noted before, of transport's specific contribution to the efficiency of particular production processes, underscores the uncertainty of social returns from transport investment. The uncertainty is even more apparent when part of the investment is "sunk" in facilities that are physically fixed to the land—river improvement, road construction, and so on—that are not recoverable except by successful use in the particular activity.[1]

Putting all these considerations together, an uncertainty deduction should be made from the expected rate of return on the transport investment before comparison is made with potential returns from other uses of capital. As will be discussed later, the significance of uncertainty about the rate of use of transport capacity can be mitigated to some extent if it is feasible to build lower-capacity (which usually also means lower quality) facilities at first, and to add capacity later if needed. But any way one looks at the investment decision, the uncertainty of future traffic makes less attractive, all other things being equal, the types of transport that offer high potential economies of scale, for they usually require correspondingly high investment per mile.

[1] For a concise discussion of direct and social benefits, and an application of these concepts in the study of highway investment in a specific country, see *A Long Range Transportation Plan for Argentina* (Transport Planning Group, Ministry of Public Works and Services, Buenos Aires, 1962), Appendix II, pp. 3-8.

In the pages that follow, the major topics to be considered are: the transport plant; the length of investment planning periods; the general character of transport cost functions; cost behavior of various forms of transport with particular reference to economies of scale; the adaptability of various types of carriers to different kinds of traffic situations; some influences affecting multi-mode transport systems; and, finally, external benefits to be expected from certain transport modes.

Characteristics of the Transport Plant

The theoretical concepts that are commonly used when analyzing investment and cost functions of the manufacturing industries can also be applied to the transport industries, but they need adaptation. A manufacturing plant changes the form of materials and does it usually on one site; the essence of transport is to move materials from one site to another. In manufacturing, the long-life facilities are the buildings that protect equipment and personnel from the elements. Except for terminal facilities, the long-life facilities of transport are the means (other than in air transport) by which operating equipment moves over space, and these facilities often represent the major investment.

Such concepts as "plant" and "economies of plant scale" can be more readily adapted if a distinction is made between physical assets of the "basic facilities" and those usually denoted as "operating equipment." Basic facilities are the pathways over which movement between points of origin and destination occurs plus the immovable terminal facilities: for railroads—right-of-ways, trackage, and stations and yards; for inland waterways—channels, locks, and docks; for road transport—one-way dirt tracks to superhighways; for airlines—airports and air traffic control facilities. Operating equipment includes the vehicles or vessels that move on, or otherwise use, the basic facilities. (This distinction is not meaningful for pipelines or electric transmission lines.) In general, basic facilities are longer lived and less flexible in use than operating equipment.

Indeed, a large part of the investment in basic facilities is "sunk," or recoverable only from revenues (or from social benefits not reflected in revenues) in excess of shorter-period variable costs. Except for terminal buildings, rarely can basic facilities be diverted to other uses or sold at values (above removal costs) comparable to the net investment in them. Investment in operating equipment is more certain to be re-covered for it can be shifted from one location to another, or can be sold for use in distant places.

Also related to the above distinction is that it is often feasible for basic facilities to have one ownership and operating equipment an-other. Public investment often provides the former, while the latter is privately owned. Sometimes transport operating equipment is owned by the shipper of goods and is denoted "private carriage," as distinct from "for hire" carriage. Private carriage means that the shipper's business—whether crude material production, manufacturing, or trad-ing operation—is vertically integrated with the operating equipment part of the transport industry. Although, under such ownership ar-rangements, it is not difficult to conceptualize the costs and benefits of a transport mode, it is hard to measure total *social* costs.

Basic facilities have two dimensions of capacity for transport service of a given quality: capacity per mile of route and the length of route provided. The former dimension is much affected by the speed at which movement can occur; for example, more vehicles of a given weight can pass over a route in a day if movement is at 50 miles per hour than at 30. Speed also affects the quality of the service from the viewpoint of the shipper. At this point, speed will be considered an element of capacity but quality of service as such and length of route will be as-sumed to be constant.

But ton-mile cost behavior is also intimately bound up with length of haul as well as with capacity per mile, largely through differences in cost of terminal operations of different transport modes. The facili-ties used and costs are those of getting the shipments under way and of handling them when they reach their destination. For example, vehicles, or vessels, must be loaded and unloaded, and shipments must be billed; in railroading, cars must be switched and trains formed and broken. These facilities and equipment and costs are distinguished for analytical purposes from those involved in "line haul" movement be-tween areas of origin and destination of shipments.

The Long and Intermediate Periods

The life of the basic facilities is as long as the transport mode is used over a given route. The foundation of the basic facilities, the right-of-way, is permanent; rivers remain; the land that forms the pathway of the highway or railroad exists.[2] Additions to this right-of-way in the form of roadbed and surface, or railroad track, or the channel and locks of a river, tend to be permanent. Capacity changes are ordinarily a "one-way street"; they can be increased but are not often decreased (except by lack of maintenance) as long as the transport mode is used at all on a given route. Abandonment occurs only when there is a change in traffic routing or another form of transport becomes so advantageous that short-term variable costs cannot be covered.[3]

On the other hand, the effective use life of operating equipment is measured in years, or at most a few decades. Furthermore, capacity can be added, shifted, or reduced in small increments by purchase, relocation, or sale, respectively.

For these reasons, it is convenient when examining cost functions in the transport industries to identify *three* "length-of-time periods" or "runs." The "long run" when all costs become variable is of little relevance once the investment in basic facilities is made, but it is the fundamental consideration before the commitment of capital. Because the amount of operating equipment used in connection with basic facilities of given capacity can be changed in a much shorter period of time and in either direction, much attention is given below to the "intermediate run." There is, of course, a "short run" during which the quantity of basic facilities and of operating equipment is fixed, but such a period is of only incidental interest here. The concern is with investment decisions, and the relevant cost functions are of the intermediate- and long-run planning sorts.

Interrelations Among Cost Functions for Different Periods

The general character of the relation between volume of traffic and costs per ton-mile is illustrated in Figure III-1. At this point each specific route is considered separately and its cost-quantity relationships examined. This is a necessary step before considering a transport system made up of interconnected routes of quite different traffic densities, often served by different transport modes. What is shown first are

[2] The United States Bureau of Internal Revenue has ruled that a railroad tunnel is a permanent, nondepreciable asset. The track through the tunnel is depreciable, however.

[3] One can find exceptions to the fixity of investment in basic facilities. Obviously a double track can be reduced to a single track. Railroad right-of-ways and highways are straightened. But these are minor and infrequent occurrences compared to the usual fixity of basic facility investment.

the effects on costs on a specific route of different combinations of basic facility capacity and amounts of operating equipment.

For each capacity of basic facilities, greater or lesser economies of scale are obtained according to whether more or less operating equipment is required by the traffic volume. In turn, these volume and cost relationships are portrayed for each of three sets of basic facilities each of which has markedly different capacity with the corresponding amount of operating equipment.

The curves on the chart are hypothetical. Although they are not based on operating data or on the estimates of engineers, they have been drawn with railroad transport in mind. In that industry, for a

FIGURE III–1. *Transport Costs for Different Periods and Capacities*[a]

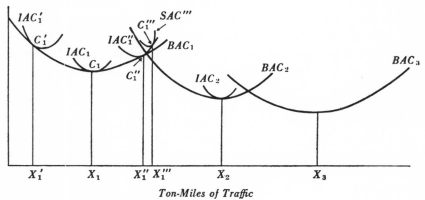

Costs per
Ton-Mile

Ton-Miles of Traffic

[a] *Assuming fixed length of haul.*

given capacity of basic facilities, there is an optimal number of cars and locomotives whose use will result in lowest cost per ton-mile. In turn, each amount of operating equipment during the period of its commitment to a particular railroad can be underutilized, utilized to capacity, or overutilized. Corresponding to these differing amounts of operating equipment, there are optimal quantities of short-period inputs required to use the equipment most efficiently. If less or more short-period inputs were used, costs per ton-mile would be sharply higher. To illustrate these points about each of the three periods—the long, the intermediate, and the short—the corresponding curves are drawn on Figure III-1.

Each of the three curves labeled *BAC* shows the behavior of total cost per ton-mile for different volumes as it is affected by the capacity of the basic facilities. For a railroad, for example, capacity of the line-haul basic facilities is determined by the quality of the grading, the number of "sleepers" or "ties," the ballast, the weight of the rails, strength of bridges, and whether a single track line is equipped with electronic controls or whether the line is double track. Each BAC curve reflects the potential cost per ton mile of basic facilities of particular capacity when used with varying amounts of equipment and short period inputs to haul different volumes of traffic. More importantly for an investment decision, such curves indicate the analysis necessary to decide upon the capacity of basic facilities to install. Parenthetically, it should be observed that no one of these curves is a true long-run average cost curve (or LAC curve) in the strict sense because this major and more lasting feature of plant capacity is held constant by assumption. (If an LAC curve were drawn, it would be a scalloped "envelope" of the BAC curves.)

The IAC curves tangent to a particular BAC curve show the cost per ton-mile for the intermediate period, based on the differing amounts of operating equipment adapted to various traffic volumes. Thus, given the basic facilities that govern that part of the cost reflected in BAC_1, if volume is X_1, by use of the optimal amount of intermediate-term and short-period inputs, cost per ton-mile would be C_1X_1 per ton-mile, where IAC_1 is tangent to BAC_1. Were volume X_1' in the intermediate-run, the optimum amount of operating equipment on this railroad would result in a per ton-mile cost of $C_1'X_1'$.[4] On the other hand, were the volume X_1'', the appropriate volume of equipment would result in a cost of $C_1''X_1''$.

To complete the steps, in a short-run period when volume is X_1''', but the operating equipment committed to the railroad is that which gives rise to the cost reflected in IAC_1'', the sharply U-shaped SAC''' curve indicates the cost effects of using equipment above its capacity on basic facilities also used above their capacities.[5] Cost per ton-mile

[4] The fact that this equilibrium is at the point at which IAC_1' is tangent to BAC_1 stems from assuming continuous variations in the amount of operating equipment. If equipment could only be added in discrete, discontinuous amounts and the figure were drawn with technical accuracy, the BAC curves would be scalloped.

[5] Unless one modifies the usual method of stating costs empirically, a curve like IAC_1'' for volume X_1'' understates the cost of transport service to the shipper because the quality of that service will be distinctly lower when the basic facilities are used far above capacity. Note consideration given to quality of transport service below, pp. 47 and 66.

would be above $C_1''X''$ and be at $C_1'''X'''$. A situation of this sort has existed on some Indian railroads recently and on the Russian railroads in one prewar period of rapid industrialization.[6]

BAC_2 reflects the lower potential costs traceable to higher capacity basic facilities. For this capacity, the optimal volume would be X_2, the corresponding intermediate-period cost curve would be IAC_2, and the cost per ton-mile would be C_2X_2. Furthermore, for any volume above the point at which BAC_1 and BAC_2 intersect, costs along the latter curve are lower because of the higher capacity basic facilities.

Finally BAC_3, which reflects the maximum potential economies of scale, is introduced. Rarely, if ever, in developing countries is rail traffic heavy enough to warrant investment in basic facilities of this capacity. Few rail lines in the world have enough traffic to fully utilize this much capacity.

So far, the expected traffic volume has been taken as a datum; actually the prospective volume is uncertain in amount and in date of development. The sunk character of the investment in excess capacity (for a particular route) of basic facilities underscores the social cost of an optimistic error in predicting volume. On the other hand, the sharp diseconomy of attempting to use a set of basic facilities above its capacity—above volume X_1'' for basic facilities that give rise to costs along BAC_1—emphasizes the social cost of a pessimistic error. What considerations enter into a choice then?

Uncertain Future Volume and Capacity Decisions

The greater the uncertainty about future traffic volume,[7] and the more distant its probable development, the more advantageous is a conservative or pessimistic estimate. If the most probable traffic is X_1''', for example, the more uncertain that estimate is, the more attractive would be basic facility capacity whose influence on costs is reflected by BAC_1. Bias toward BAC_1 is enhanced also to the extent that either of these volume rates is expected to develop some years in the future. If the higher capacity that explains the lower level of BAC_2 were built, the capacity idle at rates of use above X_1'' would represent resources that make no contribution to net national product.

[6] Holland Hunter, *Soviet Transportation Policy* (Harvard University Press, 1957), pp. 50-88.

[7] This is aside from such uncertainties as the future prices of inputs and future changes in transport technology.

Second, the advantage of building initially according to planning curve BAC_1 is enhanced further in proportion to the ease of rebuilding the basic facilities *toward* the quality and capacity that would make possible costs indicated by the curve BAC_2. Ordinarily one would expect that the total investment to build to the BAC_2 capacity level in two steps would exceed the capital that would have been required to build the higher BAC_2 capacity initially. How great the percentage difference would be is an empirical question, and probably is not the same for all types of transport. For example, the author suggests that the percentage difference would be higher for a railroad than for converting a low-grade highway to a high-grade one. But the point to underscore is that a higher capital requirement for two-step building of capacity of basic facilities is not necessarily uneconomic. As noted in the paragraph above, had the higher capacity been built originally but greatly underutilized, the additional resources committed to construction of the differential capacity would have been unused until traffic increased substantially. Such a situation is shown (Figure III-1) by the segment of BAC_2 that is above BAC_1; the higher level of costs per ton-mile shown in BAC_2 for traffic volumes less than X_1'' reflects primarily the heavy capital charges for capacity used below the optimal rate.

Some Evidence on Cost Functions

The amount and quality of information about longer-run costs differs among types of transport. Some of the available figures are based on operating experience of existing transport facilities, and others are cost estimates for facilities and equipment to be built de novo. The former costs reflect past investment decisions, whether they were optimal for that date or not, and also the technology and relative factor prices of earlier years. Of particular importance in transportation is the further fact that very costly features of basic facilities are often unique to the terrain and weather of a locale. Perhaps equally important is the availability decades ago of the capital needed (capital rationing or not).

The differences in costs of various railways or highways may be dominated by these influences, not by volume of traffic. One might expect that some of these difficulties are avoided by those making cost estimates. But estimates of cost are also made for a particular locale and are subject to substantial error in predicting both construction costs and traffic rates even for that locale.[8] Where costs related to very long-life sunk investment are a low percentage of total costs, and hence most costs are of the intermediate-run or shorter-run sorts, actual cost experience becomes a correspondingly better basis for a planning cost curve.[9] With some exceptions, projected transport operations can be instructive only in the sense of indicating ordinal differences among cost levels and the extent of potential scale economies of transport modes.

A Generalized Transport Cost Function

The cost per ton-mile for a particular transport mode is the sum of terminal costs and line haul costs. For a given set of factor prices each of these components of cost per ton-mile is, potentially, a function of the volume of traffic and the length of haul. Terminal costs $[C_t]$ are a sum to be spread over the length of the haul, and in order to compute terminal costs per ton-mile, the function becomes $C_t = f(Q)/L$, in which Q is number of tons and L is length of haul. But in line haul there is no a priori basis for assuming a linear relation between costs and either quantity of traffic or length of haul. Hence, C_h (or line haul cost per ton-mile) is equal to $f(Q, L)$. The total cost function per ton-mile becomes, therefore, $C = f(Q)/L + f(Q, L)$.

Railroad Cost Functions

There is a paucity of data indicating the character of actual cost functions for railroads. While operating figures from developed countries are abundant, analyses of these that show cost functions have not

[8] See Chapters IX and XI by Hans Adler and by Robert Sadove and Gary Fromm.
[9] The discussion here centers on economies of plant scale, which in some forms of transport is equivalent to firm scale. Generally, where plant scale economies are high, which usually means that investment in, and costs related to, basic facilities dominate costs, there is little point in going on to economies of firm size. Having parts of a continuous railroad or pipeline in a developing country under separate ownership makes little sense. Nor is there much occasion, if any, in developing areas to construct competing rail or pipe lines. But it is feasible to have competing trucking, air, or water transport lines that use the same basic facilities. In such cases, costs by size of firm may be quite important, as will be seen.

FIGURE III–2. *Estimated Operating Costs for Rebuilt Argentine Railroads by Freight Traffic Densities*

(Costs in pesos; tons in thousands; length of haul 200 km.)

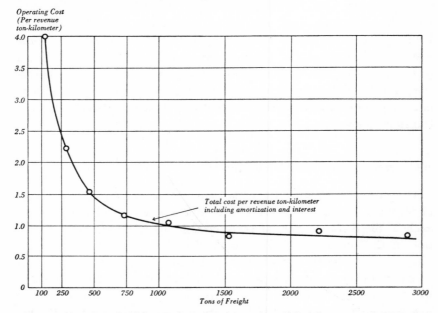

Source: Ministry of Public Works and Services (Republic of Argentina), Transport Planning Group, *A Long Range Transportation Plan for Argentina* (Buenos Aires, 1962), App. III, graph 2a.

been found by the author.[10] But the results of such studies would be of limited general value since the cost experience of railroads is affected uniquely by terrain, length of haul, and different ratios of terminal to line haul expense. For example, the heavy traffic, coupled with costly duplication among lines and excess capacity (for line haul

[10] For an extensive and valuable discussion of the character of railroad costs and the statistical derivation of cost functions for particular categories of expenses for U.S. railroads for 1952-55, see John R. Meyer, Merton J. Peck, John Stenason, and Charles Zwick, *The Economics of Competition in the Transportation Industries* (Harvard University Press, 1960), pp. 33-63 and 321-47. But these authors did not develop a composite (of all expense categories) cost function for railroads. They did estimate a total dollar cost and the regression coefficients for each of numerous phases of terminal and line haul operations, but even for a given phase of operations it is not possible to derive a cost per ton-mile. For average volume, a typical long-run marginal cost of 3.27 mills per gross ton-mile of bulk commodities hauled is reported. This amounts to about 8.2 mills per revenue ton-mile on the assumption that the weight of freight hauled represents two-fifths of the total weight of the cars hauled both loaded and empty. (*Ibid.*, pp. 62-63.)

but less so for terminal operation), make the operating data of United States railroads largely inapplicable to transport investment planning in developing countries.

Estimates of how average costs per metric ton-kilometer for Argentine railroads could be expected to differ for a range of traffic densities are presented in Figure III-2. These are not actual costs for railroads of different lengths and densities of traffic, but estimates made by a series of adjustments of data for Argentine railroads for 1958-59.[11] To minimize the effect of length of haul and to give effect to certain expected improvements in facilities and equipment, all estimates were developed to show how average costs per ton-kilometer for a line 200 kilometers long would differ for various traffic densities. Estimated costs (for broad-gauge lines) range from about 4.0 pesos per ton-kilometer for 0.134 million revenue ton-kilometers of traffic per year to less than 0.7 pesos if volume were over 5.5 million ton-kilometers. The costs drop dramatically in the range from the lowest volume to about 0.7 million ton-kilometers of annual volume and then fall gradually for higher traffic densities.

One should be cautious about drawing precise conclusions, by using these estimates, about expected cost differences for varying densities of traffic. This is not so much because the estimates refer to Argentine conditions, but because the same quality and capacity of basic facilities were assumed for moving widely differing volumes of traffic per kilometer. But, as pointed out above, for lines built de novo or radically rebuilt, the optimal investment and capacity of these facilities would differ substantially for light traffic densities compared to heavy. Consequently, estimated costs per ton-kilometer in Figure III-2 must be higher for low-density traffic relative to high-density than they would be if the line were built de novo to handle the respective traffic volumes.

A second major variable in a complex cost function for railroads is length of haul. An indication of its importance can be obtained from the estimates by John R. Meyer and his colleagues based on United States data, presented here in Table III-1. In the Meyer study (see footnote 10), length of haul affects transport costs entirely through spreading terminal costs over more or fewer line haul miles. In the early 1950's terminal cost per ton was estimated to average $3.28 in the United

[11] See *A Long Range Transportation Plan for Argentina,* "Main Report," *op. cit.,* pp. 23-27, for a full exposition of the methods used in making these cost estimates and for the estimates themselves.

States if the shipment is picked up by truck at the shipper's place of business and delivered to the consignee's establishment by truck.[12] This outlay becomes a rapidly decreasing amount per ton-mile as the length of haul increases, as is shown in Column 2 of Table III-1. (No data are available on costs where both establishments are on rail sidings.) But nearly half of the estimated terminal expense, or $1.58, was for loading the goods into a boxcar and unloading at destination, for billing and other office costs, and for switching. These likewise become rapidly decreasing costs per ton-mile as hauls become longer. (See Column 3 in the table.) Add to these costs the constant 0.32 cents per ton-mile of line haul expense, and the result is a rapid drop in long-run marginal costs incurred by the railroad as length of haul increases (Column 4). For 200-mile hauls, costs per ton-mile are estimated at less than a third of

TABLE III-1. *Long-Run Marginal Costs, Rail Boxcar and Truck, by Distance, 1952-1955*

(Distance, miles; cents per ton mile)

Distance	Pick-up and Delivery	Terminal Costs	Line Haul Costs	Total Rail Costs	Service Differ-ential	Total Rail Costs Including Differ-ential	Truck Costs
(1)	(2)	(3)	(4)	(5)	(6)	(7)	(8)
50	3.40	3.16	0.32	6.88a	3.12	9.94a	8.80
100	1.70	1.58	.32	3.60	1.72	5.32	6.00
200	0.85	0.79	.32	1.96	0.98	2.94	4.80
400	.43	.40	.32	1.15	.63	1.78	3.85
600	.28	.26	.32	0.86	.53	1.16	3.27
800	.21	.19	.32	.72	.43	1.05	3.24

Source: Adapted from John R. Meyer and others, *op. cit.*, p. 190.
a Apparently there is an error of 0.06 cents in this row of the table.

those for a 50-mile distance; for 800-mile hauls, the costs are only a third of those for 200 miles.[13]

[12] The sum of columns 2 and 3, second row, multiplied by 100.

[13] For a statistical analysis of the effect of amount of pick-up and delivery service, of traffic density, and length of haul on rail and on highway transport costs, see Jeanne Pierre Baumgartner and Pascual Santiago R. Palazzo, "Estudio de la Estructura Económica Típica del Transporte de Carga por Carretera y Ferrocarril," *Caminos Revista Tecnica,* February 1962, pp. 32-36.

But these data understate the *costs to the shipper* of rail service on short hauls because the quality of service is markedly inferior to that of truck transport. Meyer and his colleagues estimate the money value of loss to shippers from the longer time required for the shipment by rail and the reduced ease of making small shipments. These "losses," converted to a ton-mile basis for hauls of different lengths, appear in Column 6 of Table III-1. When this differential is added to the railroad's own expenses, the total, which is roughly equivalent to shippers' rail transport costs, is higher for 50-mile hauls than are truck transport costs. But for increasingly longer hauls, even when cost of shipping is computed this way, rail costs drop off very rapidly, while those of trucks decline only gradually. For distances of 600 miles or more, rail costs to shippers are about one-third those of truck.

Petroleum and Gas Pipelines

Transportation by pipeline provides the highest degree of potential economies of plant scale of any form of transport.[14] The major input is capital invested in the right-of-way, pipe and its laying, and pumping stations. Practically all of this investment is sunk: the cost of digging up the pipe, cutting it into transportable lengths, and hauling it to a new site would ordinarily exceed its value for re-use. The major source of scale economies is in the increased capacity of a pipe as a function of its diameter, without there being a comparable increase in the cost stemming from investment in the pipe and expenses of its laying or of operating the line. In contrast to railroads, length of line does not affect the per-barrel-mile costs of pipeline transport materially because terminal expenses are a nominal percentage of total costs. The capacity of a pipeline is also a function of the pressure exerted by pumps. Consequently, there is something of a parallel between the pipe diameter (as the indefinitely fixed input) and the railroad right-of-way and track; and another parallel between installing fewer or more pumping stations (that result in less or more capacity of a line of given diameter) and the intermediate-run character of a railroad's use of fewer or more locomotives and cars. But there is one important difference: railroad equipment is saleable,

[14] For a fuller discussion of pipeline costs, see Leslie Cookenboo, Jr., *Crude Oil Pipe Lines and Competition in the Oil Industry* (Harvard University Press, 1955), pp. 8-32.

but the resale value of a pipeline pumping plant would be scarcely more than the cost of moving it.[15]

Nevertheless, Figure III-3, which reports well-authenticated estimates of total cost per barrel-mile for crude-oil pipelines, has a kinship with Figure III-1.[16] The *level* of the curve for each diameter reflects the effect of diameter of pipe for given pressure on costs per barrel-mile; hence the curve for each diameter of pipe is roughly equivalent to a *BAC* curve of Figure III-2.[17] The *contour* of each curve shows how the cost per barrel-mile is made higher, or lower, by installing fewer, or more, pumping stations and capacity, and hence each curve reflects the points of tangency of a set of *IAC* curves.

Using the curves in Figure III-3, one can select the optimal planning curve for any expected volume of crude oil. If only 50,000 barrels a day are expected, the 14-inch line would be lower cost than a 12-inch line, even though the 14-inch line would not require the pumping capacity which would result in the lowest cost per barrel for its diameter. If 70,000 barrels were expected, there would not be much difference in cost per barrel between a 14-inch line operated at its optimal pressure and a 16-inch line operated below its optimal pressure. The relevant cost per barrel of the latter is shown in the segment of its cost curve that lies to the left of its low point. One can go on to study the optimal combinations of pipe diameter and of pressure for various expected volumes.

If there is uncertainty as to whether the volume will be 70,000 barrels, there would be an advantage in building the 16-inch line but

[15] In *ibid.*, p. 12, Cookenboo refers to adding pumping stations as giving rise to "intermediate-run cost curves which include cost of varying amounts of capital equipment [that] *are not reversible.*" (Emphasis added.) Because of this fact, the character of the curves, for lines of different diameters in Figure III-3, differ somewhat from those in Figure III-1.

[16] While these estimates were made for conditions in the United States, they are closely applicable to other areas. Terrain does not often affect pipe-laying costs to a marked degree, and the price of pipe and the methods and costs of laying and operating the line are such that scale advantages are not affected materially by geographic rate differentials. Note, however, that I added the broken line with the subscript *14 + 14* to illustrate the effect of having two pipes of 14-inch diameter rather than one of 20 inches and about equal capacity.

[17] Given the diameter of the pipe and the installed pumping stations, practically all short-term costs are fixed as long as the line is operated at all. Were it possible to add the "envelope" of the curves in Figure III-3 without making the chart unreadable, such a curve would be the true long-run cost curve. The *BAC* curves would not be tangent at their respective least-cost points to such a *LAC* curve because of discontinuities in sizes of pipes.

FIGURE III–3. *Costs per Barrel, Crude Oil Trunk Pipelines, 1952*

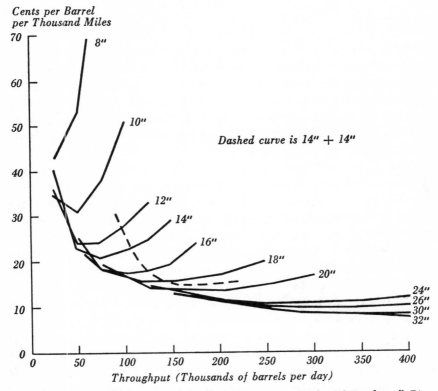

Source: Leslie Cookenboo, Jr., "Costs of Operating Crude Oil Pipelines," *Rice Institute Pamphlet* (April 1954), pp. 106-07, Table 19.

initially installing only a few widely spaced pumping stations. The line would not be markedly inefficient for hauling 50,000 barrels and could at any time be made distinctly more efficient (than a 14-inch line) for 70,000 barrels by adding pumping stations. And by adding pipeline pressure beyond that for which cost per barrel is least, the 16-inch could haul 100,000 barrels without being grossly less efficient than an 18-inch line.

Laying a second pipe is another way to expand the capacity of an established line. The level of costs achieved by two 14-inch lines, as suggested in Figure III-3 by the broken curve *14" + 14"*, would be higher than for the same capacity provided by a 20-inch line. However, adding the second 14-inch pipe would result in lower long-run *marginal* cost per barrel-mile than could be obtained by abandoning the original 14-inch and laying a new 20-inch.

Road Transport

Cost information that combines the cost of the road or highway with the users' expenses poses unusual analytical difficulties. Further difficulties stem from the fact that the road is publicly owned while the vehicles are often privately owned. Even where both are publicly owned, decisions about investment in, and use of, vehicles are apt to be distinct from decisions about routings and capacities of the basic road facilities.

A complete cost analysis should include: (1) the relation between the costs (interest on capital plus maintenance) of roads of various widths and quality of road base and surface; (2) the relation, for *each* road quality (i.e. capacity), between costs per vehicle- or ton-mile, and (a) the number of vehicles using it, (b) the weight of the vehicles, (c) the speed at which the vehicles are operated; (3) the relation between vehicle operating costs per ton-mile, and (a) the weight of vehicles, (b) the speed at which they are driven, (c) the length of hauls (load factor disregarded), (d) the effect of road surface on vehicle maintenance and depreciation; and (4) the relation of various combinations of the preceding variables to the costs of carrying on the shippers' own operations, as affected by the speed and certainty of time of deliveries and by damage to shipments. The least information is available about (4), the most about (3); some is available about (1) and (2). The best that can be done is to present some of the various possible combinations of (1) and (2), modified by some indication of the significance of (3).

Assuming that the use made of each type of road is optimum in terms of the number, weight, and speed of vehicles adapted to the quality of the road base and surface, the road costs per vehicle-mile appear not to differ widely among roads of different quality. Road quality (in terms of surface and width) ranges from a one-lane dirt road, through a two-lane gravel road, one with a light bituminous surface, then a heavy bituminous surface, to a heavy concrete surface road (possibly four-lane). A corresponding quality of roadbed is assumed for each type of surface. Capacity of roads and highways in terms of the optimal weight and speed and number of vehicles to be operated on them, differ in the same order as do the qualities of road just listed.

FIGURE III—4. *Returns to Scale, Venezuelan Highways, by Quality, Early 1960's*

(Cost in centimes of bolivars)

Annual Maintenance and Construction Cost (Per vehicle-kilometer)

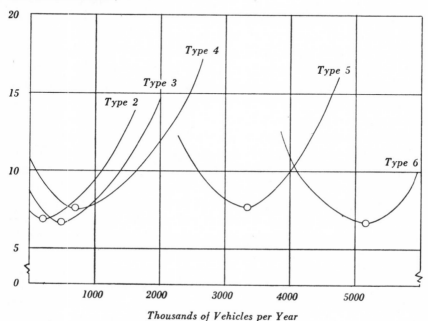

Thousands of Vehicles per Year

Source: Adapted from Charles J. Stokes, "Analysis of the Decision to Build the Tejerias-Valencia Autopista," (Brooking Institution, 1964), Table VIII (multilithed).

Figure III-4 presents the relationship between costs for such a range of road qualities and the number of vehicles (all assumed to be of the same weight) estimated for Venezuela in the early 1960's. Note that the low points of the cost curves for the respective road qualities do not differ much in level; it should be emphasized, however, that this reflects the assumption that each quality of road carries the optimal traffic for its roadbed and surface. But for any rate of use of a given quality that is lower or higher than optimal—measured by number of vehicles per year—road costs per vehicle are higher; the cost curve for each quality of road is almost V-shaped. At lower than optimal use rates, the annual charges stemming from construction costs and the effects of weather become progressively higher per vehicle-mile. At higher than optimal use rates, the declining cost per vehicle of such fixed charges is more than offset by the upsurge of maintenance costs; this is true particularly for roads that lack a heavy base and a concrete surface. Heavy vehicles are particularly damaging to low-quality roads but, as will be seen later, where larger vehicles can be used, truck operating costs per ton-mile are reduced sharply.

A number of studies have been made in the United States that show the effect of weight as well as of number of vehicles on the long-run marginal costs of highways (see Figure III-5). The assumption is made that a highway of minimal quality needed for traffic of automobiles and light trucks up to 6,000 pounds would exist over any particular route. For such light vehicle traffic on a "low-type" pavement, operated for about 1.3 million "axle-miles"[18] per year, the estimated road construction (interest on investment) and maintenance cost would be about 4.5 cents per axle-mile. But if there were *in addition* about 0.1 million axle-miles of 6,000–10,000 pound vehicles, the estimated long-run additional or marginal cost would be sharply higher, or about 34 cents per axle-mile. This is an excellent way to isolate the effect on highway costs of weight of vehicles and their relative numbers, but is not necessarily applicable where one cannot assume a substantial volume of light vehicle traffic as a datum.

For medium-type pavement, the cost per axle-mile of light vehicle use was estimated to be only two-thirds of that for the low-type pavement, even though the traffic is twice as heavy. When 6,000–10,000 pound vehicles operate on the medium-type pavement, the estimated marginal costs of this added and heavier vehicle traffic is less pronounced than on low-type pavement, but still substantial; 10 cents per axle-mile for 6,000–10,000 pound vehicles and 14 cents for still heavier trucks, as shown by the broken line in Figure III-5. For heavy-type pavement, estimated marginal costs do not rise at all until it is used by 10,000–14,000 pound vehicles; under modest use by the even heavier 14,000–18,000 pound vehicles, marginal costs actually fall.

Considering now the cost of operating trucks of a given size on roads of different qualities, it is obvious, first, that dirt and gravel roads force lower speeds on drivers than paved highways do. Thus, driver pay per vehicle-kilometer is reported to be 60 percent lower on paved roads than on dirt or gravel. Depreciation charges are also much

---

[18] Number of vehicles per year, multiplied by the number of axles per vehicle, multiplied by the number of miles each vehicle is operated.

FIGURE III—5. *Long-Run Marginal Costs of Highway Construction and Maintenance by Qualities of Highway, Number and Weight of Vehicles*

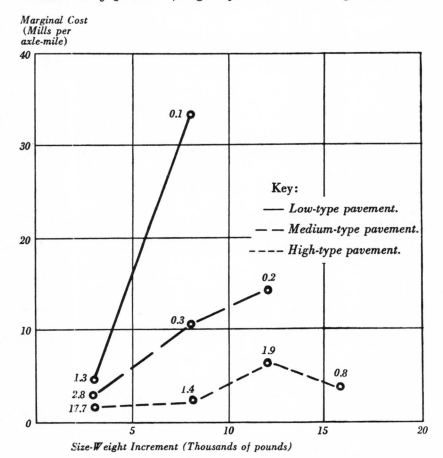

Size-Weight Increment (Thousands of pounds)

Note: *Numbers by points in curves are millions of axle-miles of vehicles of specified weight brackets. On horizontal axis, points are marked at mid-points of weight brackets.*

Source: Adapted from summary by John R. Meyer and others, *The Economics of Competition in the Transportation Industries* (Harvard University Press, 1959), p. 80, of data published in W. B. Ross, *Financing Highway Improvements in Louisiana* (Louisiana State University, 1955).

TABLE III-2. *Estimated Truck Line-Haul Operating Costs in Venezuela, 1961*[a]

(Truck capacity in metric tons; cost in bolivars)

Truck Capacity	Cost per Vehicle-kilometer			Two-way Load as Percentage of Capacity	Cost per Ton of Load at Specified Load Factors		
	Paved Road	Gravel Road	Dirt Road		Paved Road	Gravel Road	Dirt Road
7.8	0.69	1.31	1.49	70.0	.126	.240	.273
11.4	0.75	1.44	1.66	55.0	.120	.230	.265
15.9	0.90	1.74	2.06	50.0	.114	.219	.259
21.0	1.02	2.03	2.42	42.5	.115	.227	.271
23.5	1.11	2.18	2.58	40.0	.119	.232	.274

Source: Richard M. Soberman, "The Cost of Road Transportation in Venezuela," Report made for Corporación Venezolana de Guayana, División de Estudios, Planificación e Investigación (April 17, 1963), pp. 58, 60. mimeo.

[a] No terminal costs (including pick-up and delivery) are included. See Table III-1 above and page 55 below for effect of length of haul—chiefly as influenced by terminal cost—on per ton-mile costs.

higher when vehicles are not operated on a smooth, hard surface.[19] Data in Table III-2 show that the benefit of paved roads to users is striking even on a vehicle-kilometer basis. To some extent the benefit is correlated positively with size of truck.[20] Comparison of the left and right halves of the table indicates that, where size is adjusted by assumed load factors, the percentage of cost saving for larger versus smaller trucks drops sharply. Estimates made for Argentina are similar. Operating costs per vehicle-mile for automobiles are one-fourth higher on gravel roads than on paved surfaces, and for dirt roads three-fifths higher. Truck and bus costs are one-half higher on gravel than on pavement, and almost double on dirt roads.[21]

For any size vehicle, cost per ton-mile or per vehicle-mile is affected by the length of haul. (This is evident in the last column of Table III-1.) A study of truck operations in the United States reports out-of-pocket terminal costs of 30 cents per hundred-weight for a 100-mile haul, but that is less than a third of the 92-cent total out-of-pocket cost for a 400-mile haul. Where numerous small shipments have to be picked up, loaded, and delivered to a consignee at destination, cost per

[19] Actually, different speeds were reflected in the costs in Figure III-4 and ranged from 40 KPH (kilometers per hour) for type 2 roads to 100 KPH for types 5 and 6. (See reference cited for Table III-2.)

[20] Analysts assume that autobus operating costs and the effect of these vehicles on roads of different types are equivalent to those of trucks of the same weight.

[21] Richard M. Soberman, "The Cost of Road Transportation in Venezuela," *op. cit.*, p. 45.

FIGURE III–6. *Line Haul Trucking Costs and Average Speeds, General Freight in California*

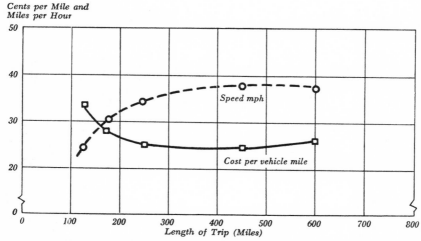

Source: *Line Haul Trucking Costs in Relation to Vehicle Gross Weights*, National Research Council, Highway Research Board Bulletin 301 (Washington, D. C., 1961), p. 33.

hundred-weight is far higher, but for a 30,000 pound shipment falls to 12 cents.[22]

There is also a higher line haul cost per mile on short hauls because of lower average speed. Figure III-6 shows that average speed is sharply lower for hauls under 200 miles, presumably because of traffic congestion in areas of origin and destination; it is not surprising, therefore, that cost per vehicle-mile is also sharply higher for these shorter hauls. Had data been gathered for 50-mile hauls, the effect on costs of average speed and on cost per vehicle-mile would have been even more pronounced.

The final step for estimating total line haul cost is to combine highway costs with vehicle operating costs to arrive at a composite relation between line haul costs, volume of traffic, and weight and speed of vehicles for each type of road. Estimates of this sort for Venezuela, as presented in Figure III-7, are planning-type curves for the line haul part of truck transport. Some attention is given to speed of operation by weight of vehicle and by type of road, as well as to numbers of vehicles. The curves are useful illustrations of the general ordering of

[22] Data adapted from U.S. Interstate Commerce Commission, "Cost of Transporting Freight by Class I and Class II, Motor Common Carriers of General Commodities," Middle West Territory (May 1960), Tables 2, 4, and 12.

FIGURE III–7. *Costs of Road Transportation in Venezuela, Selected Variables,* [a] *1961*

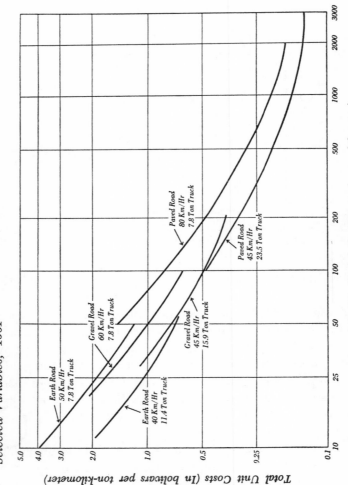

Annual Freight Hauled (In 1000 ton-km per kilometer)

Total Unit Costs (In bolívars per ton-kilometer)

Source: Reproduced from Richard M. Soberman, "The Cost of Road Transportation in Venezuela," Report made for Corporación Venezolana de Guayana, División de Estudios, Planificación e Investigación (April 27, 1963), p. 66. Mimeo.

[a] At 10 percent interest.

highway and vehicle operating costs per unit of weight by various traffic densities for different types of roads.[23]

Beyond economies of size of plant of the individual truck, the fact that truck transport firms may operate few or many vehicles means that economies of firm size should be considered. Studies of the costs of common carrier truck companies by size in the United States indicate that firm scale economies are nominal. A minimum of office staff and terminal facilities and personnel is required, but such items make up a very small percentage of total cost. Very small companies probably use their trucks and drivers with less efficiency, since such companies lack the "massing of reserves" advantage that comes from owning a substantial number of vehicles. Except for such cases, and after eliminating the effect of length of haul on costs, there is no clear evidence that costs per ton-mile are related significantly to size of firm.[24]

Finally, reference is made again to the comparison of the long-run marginal cost of railroads and of highway transport presented in Table III-1. The data for the latter, in the opinion of Meyer and his colleagues, include payments for fuel taxes, licenses, and other charges that approximate the long-run marginal cost of constructing and maintaining highways of the quality required for heavy truck traffic.[25] On the basis of transport costs per ton-mile, railroads are at a disadvantage on very short hauls and have a very marked advantage on long hauls. But from the shippers' viewpoint, truck service is so superior on short hauls that they are willing to pay more per ton-mile.

Air Transport

Total costs of air transport per passenger-mile include those of such basic facilities as airports and air traffic control, as well as those of plane operation. The basic facilities are normally provided by public agencies. To widely varying degrees, but seldom fully, the capital and other costs of these facilities are covered by user charges. Combining these costs with those of airplane operation is not easy, even when the

[23] Comparison of these estimates with later construction costs showed that costs of the higher quality roads had been underestimated by a wide margin.

[24] For a critique of studies by others and the conclusion cited here, see Meyer and others, *op. cit.*, pp. 95-99.

[25] *Ibid.*, pp. 81-85. But this is an estimate only of the *added* cost of building and maintaining better highways, with all costs of low quality roads assigned to light vehicles. However, in developing countries most roads are built from scratch and all costs enter.

airlines are publicly owned, because planes more often than not use the basic facilities of more than one jurisdiction.

Airport capacity limits the size, type, and number of planes that can use it. It can range from a short runway with a turf surface for very light planes through a series of increases in capacity (in terms of strength of foundation and surface) to the long, heavily built runways required for giant jet transports. Very light traffic areas rarely need to have heavy and long runways, but if any flights occur in a particular area, investment in airport facilities is necessary.

Because of the newness of the industry and the variety of operating conditions in the United States, data for American air operations have more relevance to other areas than do railroad cost figures, for example. Operating costs of United States airlines include practically nothing toward the costs of the federally provided air traffic control and guidance system. Landing fees and rentals of terminal facilities at a sample of municipal airports amounted to 85 percent of current airport expenses in 1958, but provided nothing for depreciation or interest.[26] Some heavy-traffic airports do better, and a few report a profit.

Airline costs per passenger-mile (or per ton-mile, a measure used at times) are a function of size of planes—the "plant"—traffic density or quantity, and length of flight, called "stage length." Many comparisons of costs with these variables are vitiated by the fact that speed of plane is correlated with size of plane, but speed is also a measure of quality of service. The "product" thus is not the same, a nuance not taken account of in reported cost. Continuous change in plane design, speed, size, and type of motive power also inhibits precise comparisons. Finally, data that seem to indicate an advantage in increasing the size of firms actually are dominated by relative size of planes, lengths of hauls, and traffic densities between terminal points.

In the United States small airline companies are engaged almost exclusively in the short-stage, or local business between small cities or between them and a major metropolitan center; consequently small, slow planes are used. Even though local carriers rarely face competition from another line, they have a low load factor. Lines serving small population centers experience less of the averaging effect of large numbers. But the major adverse influence on the costs of these companies is the short-haul character of their traffic.

The effect of length of haul on costs stems primarily from the ratio

[26] Richard E. Caves, *Air Transport and Its Regulators* (Harvard University Press, 1962), p. 415.

of terminal expense to flight costs. Once a plane has reached its flying altitude, the cost per mile is constant. The idleness of the plane and the crew while at the terminal adds considerably to costs, but this addition is presumably included in the reported category of flying operations cost. For short-haul carriers, aircraft and traffic servicing costs per ton-mile in 1958 were three times those of the largest carriers, a fact that goes far in explaining why the total costs per ton-mile of small lines were 1.9 times those of large carriers.

There is also some evidence of diseconomies in very small firm size. General and administrative expenses of small carriers, exclusive of passenger service, sales, and promotion expenses, were 2.9 times those of large companies.[27] But among the trunkline companies that vary greatly in size (but all of which are larger than any local service carrier), there was no clear evidence of the effect of size on cost.

Water Transport

General statements about inland and coastal water transportation are difficult to make because the length, capacity, and routings of bodies of water or river channels differ so much among locales. That rivers sometimes are available for part of the year only, due to freezing or low water, substantially affects the cost of using them. However, basic facility costs are usually low, unless channels or harbors have to be dredged or protected against flood waters or storms.

Water movement is slow. Turnaround time for loading and unloading is lengthy, except for bulk commodities such as oil or ore, and the route is often far less direct than that of a railroad. A freight train can make the trip from New Orleans to Chicago in 60 hours or less, whereas a barge on the Mississippi River system takes 500 hours. The quality of water transport service is correspondingly low, but the significance of that fact varies according to what materials are being shipped.

Inland water transportation is usually the cheapest method of long-distance movement of nonperishable bulk commodities, but because of the long turnaround time and the high cost of loading and unloading, cost advantages are lost rapidly for short hauls. For all hauls from 1936 through 1938 over Gulf Coast rivers and canals, terminal costs accounted for about half of all barge operations costs. On the Mississippi River system, where hauls are longer, terminal costs represented

[27] The data are taken from Caves, *ibid.*, p. 58.

about 40 percent of total costs. Before World War II, total cost per ton-mile of petroleum carriers on Gulf Coast rivers and canals ranged downward from about 6.0 cents for hauls of 70 to 100 miles, to 2.0 cents for hauls ten times as long. Coal carrier costs on the Mississippi River system ranged downward from the neighborhood of 3.0 mills per ton-mile for hauls of 50 to 100 miles to about 2.0 mills for 200 to 250 mile distances.[28] Great Lakes freighter line costs are estimated at 1.2 mills per revenue ton-mile with no return loads and 0.6 mill with full return loads of bulk commodities, compared to about 4.0 mills line haul costs for railroads with full return loads. But freighters have no clear advantage in package freight largely because of expensive pick-up and delivery costs from docks to places of origin and destination.[29] But for long hauls over comparable routes and volumes, operating costs of tankers and often even barges are below those of giant pipe-lines.

Low operating costs of water transportation are misleading to the extent that investment in basic facilities must be made, and the costs related thereto are not added to vessel operating costs. River channel clearing and lock, harbor, and dock building are usually financed from public funds.[30] Charges, if any, to users are nominal and reimburse only a small fraction of the costs incurred by the financing jurisdiction. A study made decades ago indicated that investment in river and canal improvements (after the railroads were well established) quite often provided far less social benefit than the public outlay.[31] To this should be added the social loss that occurs where

[28] The data are adapted from National Resources Planning Board, *Transportation and National Policy* (U.S. Government Printing Office, 1942), pp. 438, 439. Since the overwhelming portion of barge movement is now by contract carriers or by fleets owned by shippers, few operating data for recent years have been published.

[29] Meyer and others, *op. cit.*, pp. 147-148, 155-156.

[30] An estimate of the public (and also of total social) cost of waterway improvements is often complicated by the fact that such improvements are part of what is deemed to be a multi-purpose project—e.g. flood control—as well as transportation. At best, the allocation of the cost among "purposes" is a guess and, in the United States' experience, the division of the total outlay among purposes often has been influenced by a desire to make the least politically acceptable purpose appear economically advantageous.

[31] H. G. Moulton, *Waterways vs. Railways* (Houghton Mifflin, 1912), pp. 370-438. For a discussion of more recent waterway improvements and the principle of "user taxation" and of its difficulty of application, see Meyer and others, *op. cit.*, pp. 122-26.

railroads already exist or are to be built as the advantageous major transportation mode: with diversion of rail traffic to waterways, the railroads' costs become higher per ton-mile than they would otherwise have been. If shippers do gain from using water transport, it is not necessarily because the *total social cost* of water transport is lower than that of rail or equivalent routes, but because the rates which railroads charge (or are forced to charge) for hauling bulk commodities over such routes exceed what intermediate-run marginal costs would be if railroads were to handle the traffic now moved on the publicly supported basic facilities of water transport. Hence, reference to the low costs of barge traffic may mean only that the cost of operating the barges is low. On the other hand, where the advantages of building a railroad are doubtful or the basic facility cost of water transportation is low, this form of transport can easily have the lowest (social) cost per ton-mile.

Adaptability to Characteristics of the Traffic

Making a choice among transport modes involves not only their respective planning cost functions, compared to traffic volume, but also their adaptability to various combinations and routings of traffic. Combinations include length of haul, extent of two-way traffic, and type of commodity, particularly as to perishability and adaptability to bulk handling. Routings depend on two major items: degree of the mode's adaptability to a wide variety of points of origin and destination, and whether or not the mode can pick up and deliver at shippers' and consignees' places of business and thereby avoid a local transfer haul. Further, for particular areas, adaptability of the mode to particular conditions of terrain, soil properties, and weather must be appraised.

Potential Variety of Routings

Every transport mode is limited in routing to what the basic facilities provide, but what nature supplies and/or the capital-output ratio that stems from basic facility construction make some modes more flexible in this regard than others. Water transport is, of course, usually limited to routes that nature has provided, especially since canals are rarely a part of modern transport planning except as very short connections between major waterways. Consequently, some other mode must ordinarily supplement water transport. Thus it is the composite of the water transport and of the supplementary land-spanning facilities that must be appraised.

Pipelines have very high capital-output ratios and very high potential economies of scale. Lines will be built, therefore, only where a heavy volume of one commodity—gas, crude oil, or light refined fuel products—is expected.

Railroads are less restricted in route than either water transport or pipelines. Compared to water transport, railroads can make their own map, although they incur heavy expense when some of nature's obstacles must be overcome by tunnels or by circuitous routes where the gradient is above two feet per mile. The capital-output ratio of railroads is lower than that of pipelines, but because rails are able to handle almost any commodity that is movable, they can usually expect more traffic per mile of route.

Airlines are limited in routing only if airports have not been built at desired points of origin and destination. If adequate terminal facilities are provided, length of route can be that of a straight line.

Road transport is the mode least restricted in routing, in part because highway traffic is usually able to operate on very steep gradients, and in larger part because roads of widely varying quality, capacity, and investment outlay can be built according to expected traffic density.

Pick-up and Delivery

There are wide differences in the extent to which transport modes are adapted to picking up and delivering goods without a local transshipment at each end of the haul. Highway transport has the clear advantage here, for local streets and roads can be used in picking up goods from the shippers and in delivering them to the consignee. Railroads must rely on local transshipment by truck for less-than-carload lots, and even for carload lots where there is no railway siding at the shipper's or consignee's place of business. However, when carload shipments are consistently of substantial volume, provision is usually made for direct loading at a siding on the shipper's premises. Air transport inherently involves local transshipment, but whatever this costs, it is inconsequential when goods of high unit value are involved.

Traffic Adaptability

The traffic-handling capacity of transport modes varies from that of the pipeline which hauls only one type of product continuously in one direction, to that of a mode which hauls almost any commodity, in almost any size of shipment, both ways over the same route and in a variety of supplementary directions. Adaptability also has to do with the size of equipment unit that can be operated autonomously. Highway transport, for example, can not only pick up and deliver small items, but can also move a truckload of goods whenever a shipment of that size is available without waiting for any subsidiary, and usually costly, transshipment help. But truck cost savings with size of shipment stop at the truckload weight.

Rail transport gains over truck progressively with size of shipment, a full carload as compared with a truckload, and a trainload as compared with a carload. Recently, special trainload rates in the United States have been approved on a showing of cost savings. Integrated trains that are not "broken" and that move back and forth between coal fields and power plants show large cost savings. Highway transport, however, is uniquely adapted to a wide variety of lengths of haul. Because each operated vehicle is self-powered, it can enter and leave the highway, and intermingle with long-haul traffic, without being coupled to any other vehicle or itself being loaded on a rail car or a boat.

Railroads and highway transport rank first among transport modes in the variety of commodities that can be handled effectively. Where special types of equipment, such as tank or hopper cars, will be an advantage, these can be fitted into the railroad's car inventory. Truck lines can do much the same, as can barges and ships in a few cases. But the more specialized equipment becomes, the lower the percentage of time it will be in use for any given volume of traffic. And a major disadvantage of all specialized transport equipment is that its use is ordinarily only one way. For low traffic density, the cost of general-purpose equipment (e.g., the box car or the van-type truck) that can be fully utilized is apt to be lower than that of partially used specialized equipment. Air transport is, at least at present, essentially a type of specialized equipment, in that its adaptability to types of traffic is limited by the size of planes and by the high cost per ton-mile.

Modes of Transport as Parts of a System

So far the analysis has been directed to the cost, capacity, and traffic handling characteristics of each transport mode for a given route. Yet each route is part of a transport system. This introduces further complexity and necessitates the use of additional criteria for the evaluation of transport investment decisions. Nevertheless, only those aspects of the topic that follow logically from the preceding sections can be considered here.

Different routes often have different types of traffic, involve movement over different terrains, and promise different traffic densities. As a consequence, different modes appear to be optimal for various parts of a system, but the choice does not rest solely on the efficiency of each segment of the transport system considered separately. Furthermore, a system is not normally planned de novo, for in most cases some facilities already exist. Their type, the cost of their use, or the basis for their abandonment, must all be appraised. Then, too, as per capita income increases significantly, the character of traffic and of shippers' criteria of the efficiency of transport usually changes.

The transport system for an area can be thought of as having one or more "backbones" or main routes, from which "ribs" or feeder routes run off in various directions. The backbone ordinarily has higher capacity and a longer average length of route and of hauls than do the ribs. Usually, but not necessarily, the backbone will be of one transport mode (particularly if traffic is fairly heavy), while the ribs may be of one or more other modes, in part at least to minimize diseconomies of small volume. Such differences in types of mode or of their capacities, if arranged so that each mode is best for the traffic and terrain of the section it serves, point to another aspect of the skeletal analogy: in an integrated transport system, each bone should be of such size, length, and direction that all parts of the economy with traffic enough for a small bone can be tied by transport to all other parts.

Since most areas have some transport facility, investment planners must usually consider first whether the old capacity should be enlarged and its routes extended. Where usable facilities exist—even cleared right-of-ways for a very low-quality rail line or road—only capital charges (depreciation and interest) and maintenance expenses for *added* investment in basic and intermediate-period facilities are usually relevant. (The fact that debt service remains on funds used for the previous investment is irrelevant in the current transport investment decision.) However, replacing the established mode with another may be optimal, either because of technological advance in other modes or because actual volume has proved to be so small that relevant marginal costs of the established mode would exceed the long-run marginal costs of the substitute mode.

Both of these principles are emphasized in a study of the Argentine transport problem. The conclusion is reached that the long-run marginal costs per ton-kilometer of rehabilitating the basic facilities and operating equipment of a number of light-traffic rail lines would exceed the long-run marginal cost of maintaining existing parallel highways and of operating trucks over them. In some cases it also appears that highway-truck costs would be lower if new highways were built.[32] If railroads were to be retained, the only capital costs that would be relevant are the long-run marginal costs of rehabilitation and new investment in basic rail facilities and equipment.

A second point that must be emphasized (whether some facilities already exist or not), is that the lowest cost per ton-mile (taking account of scale economies) should not be the sole guide in selecting the mode for the "ribs" or branch lines. Transshipment must be made from the branch to the backbone mode and vice versa. If both modes are the same, no problems arise because operating equipment is merely shifted from one line to the other. But if the modes differ, goods must be moved from one type of equipment to another, such as from trucks to railroad cars. This is an expensive, time-consuming task. Only when traffic has reached the level where goods are "containerized" ("piggy-back" or highway trailers hauled on railroad flat cars is a promising form) can inefficiencies in intermode transfers be made negligible. Consequently, rail branch lines that could not be justified on a

---

[32] The first of these principles is stated explicitly on pp. 19-27 of *A Long Range Transportation Plan for Argentina, op. cit.* (1961), App. III, and the second is implicit in pp. 33-34.

per ton-mile cost basis may be efficient as part of a rail transport system. Alternatively, a railroad may be inefficient as the backbone mode of a system because of numerous connections with light-volume highways or water transport.

A third consideration in planning a transport system is the effect of rising per capita income. As income approaches the level of developed countries, more highly manufactured goods will make up a larger proportion of the freight to be shipped. Because transport is a lesser part of the value per pound of these manufactured goods than it is for crude materials, the location of production becomes increasingly market-oriented (instead of resource-oriented) as development progresses. As this takes place, shippers will demand quicker deliveries and more reliable delivery schedules. The added variety of goods increases the potential inventories of manufacturers and sales distributors. However, these enterprises have been adroit at avoiding a rise in their inventories/sales ratio by putting their businesses as nearly as possible on a "flow" basis. This practice is feasible only to the degree that deliveries of materials to plants or goods to customers can be dated with some precision. When this coordination breaks down, it is cheaper to draw on a surplus somewhere and have it shipped rapidly, even by airplane, than to maintain larger inventories. This explains the use of trucks in the United States for shipments of several hundred miles when railroad rates are much lower. Rapid development of "piggyback" with scheduled delivery times has enabled railroads to recapture some of this business.

Although it is hazardous to generalize, taking the above and several additional factors into account, it does appear probable that in the earlier stages of development a road-highway system will be the most efficient means of satisfying a nation's transport needs. Even if built de novo, a gravel surface road adequate to handle the sparse traffic of an area in the early stage of development costs far less than a low-capacity railroad. And capacity of roads can be increased progressively as traffic needs develop; thus the uncertainty of return from investment in them is less than for railroads.

Finally, the unique ease of handling traffic of widely varied size of shipment and length of haul, and of movement off and on backbone and feeder routes, all point to the superiority of road-highway systems, especially where heavy long-distance traffic does not yet exist. Even for areas beyond the early stages of development, where rail routes now exist, it may be predicted that consumption-travel use of roads will be a result of increasing per capita income and will warrant more highways—often paralleling rail routes. In any case, roads of a quality only for light automobile traffic can handle a substantial amount of light truck traffic at almost zero marginal cost of highway.

External Benefits from Various Transport Modes

The improvement of transport makes various social contributions as well as reducing transport cost for identifiable production operations. An increase in mobility can, for instance, augment a citizen's sense of being a member of a larger group. General availability of transport can also re-order production and consumption behavior quite widely, although the ways are difficult to predict from a product-by-product or locality-by-locality analysis. One promising economic effect is the commercialization of self-sufficient activities. Along with this comes the growth of specialization in production by areas that are often stimulated by increased availability of goods for agriculturalists to buy.[33] Opening the doors to entrepreneurship puts more minds and imaginations to work on the task of integrating private, small-scale enterprise into the development of market economies.

To widely different degrees, transport modes stimulate such entrepreneurship and the necessary related experience of workers. Formal education assists in preparing persons for participation in the hired labor force, but so does work under direction. Most skills can be taught, but the more elementary skills are acquired by experience. Entrepreneurship, to cite Schumpeter, responds to conditions favorable for its exercise, and the improvement of road and highway transport appears to be one of these conditions.

The process of creating transport in itself offers unusual opportunities for indigenous entrepreneurship. Because of the very low entry barriers and small scale of firm requirements, private firms in road transport owned by local persons can easily spring up.[34] Low-quality road construction and maintenance can be carried on by labor-inten-

---

[33] Shown for a variety of areas in the essays in *Markets in Africa*, edited by Paul Bohannan and George Dalton (Northwestern University Press, 1962).

[34] For example, see E. K. Hawkins, *Road Transport in Nigeria* (Oxford University Press, 1958), pp. 40-50 and 89-94.

sive methods, where the alternative employment of labor yields a very low marginal product. Many workers then learn to work in teams, and some of them to supervise and coordinate the activities of one group with another. For railroad construction and maintenance much more skilled supervision is required.

Private ownership reduces the administrative load of the new governments, already burdened with more tasks of this sort than they have the staff or experience to handle well. It also puts domestic savings to work. Moreover, the small size of motor transport firms means that they probably cannot undertake their own repair or service work economically. Thus, motor vehicle service enterprises can be expected to develop.

External benefits can be expected from any expanding commercialized activity, but transport development has a unique feature. To the degree that transport capacity must precede its extensive use by the industries expected to respond to its availability, the incidental training of workers and supervisors during road construction and the spur to small-firm entrepreneurship in motor transport, add further to the conclusion that roads will often provide the most advantageous form of transport in developing areas.

IV

Transport and Technology

WILFRED OWEN*

COUNTRIES WITH LOW STANDARDS of living are char-
acteristically countries with inadequate methods of moving. The reason
for this relationship is obvious. Transportation is an essential ingredient of almost everything man does to supply himself with the neces-
sities of life.

Science and technology now provide the means of overcoming the
obstacles to movement which throughout most of history have restricted the effective use of the world's resources. Man has at his disposal a choice of technological methods not even conceived of a few
decades ago. It is no longer necessary to move slowly and laboriously
through each successive stage in the process of transport evolution as
it was for nations that developed in an earlier period. The newly developing countries can reap all at once the accumulated benefits of
the transport revolution, and of innovations outside the transport field
that affect both the problem and its solution.

Tremendous strides have already been made in the transport systems
of Africa, Asia, and South America. Transport has opened the way to
previously inaccessible land and resources and has made possible new
agriculture and mining, new industry, new markets, and the communication of new ideas. In the past decade, railway freight on these
continents has more than doubled. Thousands of miles of road have
been completed, and the number of trucks and buses has increased
one and a half times. Air transport, too, has provided connections
among most of the key cities of the world, overcoming for the first
time the isolation that has so long perpetuated poverty.

The transportation gap between the rich countries and the poor,

* The Brookings Institution.

however, remains. Asia, with 53 percent of the world's population, has 3 percent of the world's motor vehicles. Africa and Latin America, with more than one-third of the land area of the world, have only 7 percent of its surfaced roads. Yet two nations—the Soviet Union and the United States—account for 75 percent of the freight that moves on the world's railways.

The transport revolution has by-passed two-thirds of the world's people. To date, the efforts of the newly developing countries have failed to break the transport barrier. If a breakthrough is to be achieved, it will be the product of a more effective application of science and technology. What is needed is a total strategy for mobility aimed at introducing effective technological advances both within transport and in other aspects of the development program affecting transport.

A Total View

Since mobility is essential to almost everything that underdeveloped countries are striving to accomplish, it follows that transportation is a factor in the success or failure of the entire development effort. Food, shelter, health, education, and useful jobs are the ultimate goals, but transport may be the catalyst essential to the realization of these objectives. This implies an approach which not only looks at transportation as a whole, but which looks beyond transport itself to the processes of production and distribution that the transport system is called upon to serve.

The point can be illustrated by food. A goal common for most of the countries of the world is to provide enough for people to eat and to supply the kinds of food that will assure an adequate diet. The role that transportation can play in attaining this objective is to provide access to arable lands, to help communicate new agricultural techniques, to make possible the delivery of seeds and fertilizer, to assemble and move the increased product to consumers, and to provide the incentive to produce for the market.

But even when we look at transport in this broader framework, solutions that seem satisfactory from a transportation standpoint may still be unsatisfactory from a development standpoint. The goal of increasing the food supply may not be served best by expediting movement at all. An alternative may be to introduce new methods of storing or preserving what is grown. When storage is made possible in producing areas, peak traffic demands typical of agricultural economies can be flattened by spreading the transport burden over a longer period of time, and investments in transport capacity may be reduced accordingly. Freezing, drying, or irradiation of foods may be the technology that is needed, not transportation. This type of solution may have the added advantages of creating local employment, providing a source of local capital accumulation, making agricultural wastes available for fuel or local manufactures, and reducing the weight and bulk of commodities flowing into the transport system. An entirely new approach to the transportation problem may emerge when science and technology are focused on the objective of increasing the supply of food rather than increasing the supply of transportation.

But the importance of scientific innovation lies also in the fact that conventional methods of providing mobility have been costly in time and material resources. The developed countries dedicated a very large proportion of their energy and wealth over a period of many years to providing adequate transport systems. Today's developing countries are too eager for immediate results and too hard-pressed to meet a variety of urgent needs to permit unnecessary delay or waste.

Stages of Transport Development

The effort to break the transport barrier in the now industrialized nations was a slow evolutionary process dictated by the rate of innovation. Progress had to wait for invention, and it has taken a century and a half to get things moving the way they move today. Five stages can be distinguished in the advance toward higher standards of transport. These stages are overlapping and their time and duration are by no means definitive. However, they represent a general sequence of events in which advances in transportation and progress toward higher levels of living are clearly related.

First was the period of immobility and the traditional society. In this period it was extremely difficult and costly to develop trade and cultural relations on any large scale except where channels of communication were provided by the rivers and oceans. The pattern of living emerging from these conditions was predominantly one of localized agriculture and handicraft industries with a minimum of economic integration.

Most of the people of the world still live in this initial stage of primitive transport, and their efforts to break out of a subsistence environment and to achieve a better life are being thwarted by the same barriers to movement that plagued all generations before them. The transport symbols of the traditional society today are the bullock cart, the camel, the donkey, and the jugs and trays carried on human heads.

A second stage of transport development was the period of internal improvements and the growth of trade. Human and animal power were made much more effective by the development of turnpikes and canals which reduced the cost of transport by traditional methods of moving on land and water. This period of declining transport costs saw both an expansion of capacity and a lengthening of the radius of trade and travel.

A third stage in the evolutionary process toward greater mobility and higher standards of living was that of transport mechanization and industrialization. During this period steam power introduced both the steamship and the first railways. It was a stage marked by heavy investments in transportation and by the establishment of a wide assortment of manufacturing industries.

A fourth period in the evolution of transport has been the development of motorization and the new mobility. This has been an era marked by growing dependence on trucks, buses, and automobiles, and by extensive efforts to provide all-weather roads. This is the period when people and economic activity were freed from the limited mileage of fixed routes provided by railways and waterways.

A fifth stage is the air age and the conquest of distance, a period in which the world is being united by transport speeds that are obliterating political boundaries and adding a third dimension to the solution of transport problems. It is not a stage, however, that has yet made its impact in local and short-haul transport, which comprises a major part of the transport problem.

In the less developed areas all of these stages are being experienced simultaneously. Transport problems in Asia, Africa, and Latin America reflect both a continuation of the immobility that constrained societies of earlier times and a projection into the most advanced transport technologies. This mixture of the old and the new suggests that there are two very different types of transport problems to be dealt with in underdeveloped countries. The latest in technology serves the principal cities and major arteries of commerce. Here the problem may be little different from what is encountered in the economically advanced countries. In many rural areas, however, where immobility and bare subsistence go hand in hand, ancient and primitive methods still prevail, and further solutions may also require elementary measures. The choices open to the developing economy cover a wide range of possibilities, and these choices call for care to assure the use of facilities and services most appropriate to a nation's needs and resources.

How the World Moves

One indication of the direction in which developing countries can be expected to move in the planning of transport systems may be found in the fairly universal trends in freight and passenger movements throughout the world today. These trends, observable in both the developed and less developed countries, are gathering momentum regardless of different public policies that encourage or discourage them. Public policy has influenced their timing but not their direction.

Recent Trends

The most noticeable development of the past two decades has been the growth of motor transport and the construction of roads. In nearly all countries goods movement by truck and passenger movement by bus have become major new elements in the transport system. The use of road transport for local services, for short intercity hauls, and for small shipments suggests that under present technological conditions a substantial part of the transport problem in newly developing countries will be met through motor vehicles and highways.

For high-volume traffic, water transport and railways provide the principal means of movement. Most railways are carrying more than ever before, but they are losing short-haul business and much of the higher-valued manufactured goods that they used to carry. This traffic is rapidly gravitating toward the highways. The net result is that while freight traffic on the railways continues to grow in absolute terms, the railway share of total freight movement is on the decline. Other worldwide trends include the long-distance movement of passengers by air-plane and the use of pipelines for gas and oil. Both of these relatively new developments have added important new elements to traditional transport patterns.

For personal mobility the world depends predominantly on private means of movement as distinguished from public carriers that charge for their services. Many people walk wherever they go, and many others provide their own transport by camel, burro, bullock cart, coun-try boat, bicycle, motorcycle, motor scooter, or automobile.

For public carriers three transport patterns have emerged. One is characteristic of the economically advanced countries—the United States, Canada, and Western Europe; another pattern is found in less developed, densely populated countries, such as Japan, India, and Pakistan, as well as in the Soviet Union and other Communist coun-tries. Still a third trend is found in the underpopulated and underde-veloped areas of the world. In some respects these patterns reflect different stages in an evolutionary process; in others geography, pop-ulation, and income levels provide the basis for the particular approach to meeting transport needs.

Western Europe, the United States, Canada

Trends in the United States illustrate the transport matrix emerging in an affluent society. Freight traffic in 1960 was double what it was in 1940. Every mode of transport shared in this growth, but some shared more fully than others. Rail transport increased 53 percent and water transport 89 percent. But pipeline traffic registered a 400 percent in-crease, and truck transport expanded nearly 500 percent. As a result of these different rates of growth, the railways' share of total freight move-ment dropped from 62 percent in 1940 to 44 percent twenty years later. Pipelines and trucks, which accounted for 20 percent of total ton-miles moved in 1940, were handling 40 percent of the total in 1960. Water carriers showed a steady growth over the two decades, but in the end they had nearly the same share of traffic as in the beginning.

Technological changes in passenger travel resulted in even greater changes in public transport methods. From 1940 to 1960, the volume of travel in public carriers doubled, just as freight traffic had done. But the railways did not share in the expansion. The railway share of passenger business dropped from 64 percent to 28 percent. Bus

TABLE IV-1. *Intercity Freight Traffic in the United States,*
1940, 1950, 1960

Type of Transport	Billions of Ton-Miles			*Percentage Increase*
	1940	1950	1960	*1940-1960*
Railways[a]	379.2	596.9	579.1	*52.7*
Motor Trucks	62.0	172.9	299.4	*382.9*
Inland Waterways including Great Lakes	118.1	163.3	223.0	*88.8*
Pipelines	59.3	129.2	228.6	*285.5*
Domestic Airways	—[c]	0.3	0.8	—[d]
Total[b]	618.6	1,062.6	1,330.9	*115.2*
	Percentage Distribution			
Railways	*61*	*56*	*44*	
Motor Trucks	*10*	*16*	*23*	
Inland Waterways including Great Lakes	*19*	*15*	*17*	
Pipelines	*10*	*15*	*17*	
Domestic Airways	—[e]	—[f]	—[g]	
Total[b]	*100*	*100*	*100*	

Source: 1940 and 1950 data from "Intercity Ton-Miles 1939–1959," Bureau of Transport Economics and Statistics, Interstate Commerce Commission, Statement No. 6103 (Government Printing Office, 1961). 1960 data from Interstate Commerce Commission *Annual Report, 1960.*
[a] Revenue ton-miles including electric railways, express, and mail.
[b] Totals do not always add to 100 due to rounding.
[c] 14 million ton-miles.
[d] Percent increase, 5,614.3.
[e] 0.002 percent.
[f] 0.03 percent.
[g] 0.06 percent.

travel in 1960 was above the 1940 level but below 1950 and still declining. But the volume of air travel was 34 times higher in 1960 than it was two decades before.

Canadian experience has been comparable. Between 1940 and 1960, when the total volume of intercity freight movement increased 118 percent, railway traffic increased 73 percent and inland water traffic 64 percent. During the same period, however, truck transport increased 649 percent, and oil pipeline traffic increased from nothing to a level exceeding the ton-miles moving by truck.

In the passenger sector during the period 1948–1958, traffic by air increased 456 percent while travel by rail declined 40 percent and intercity bus travel fell 86 percent. Most passenger travel in Canada, as in the United States, is by private rather than public carrier.[1]

Many of these trends have been duplicated in Western Europe. However, some differences from North American experience have resulted from lower income levels, a higher density of population, shorter distances between major urban areas, and geographically

TABLE IV-2. *Interstate Passenger Traffic in the United States, 1940, 1950, 1960*

Type of Common Carrier	Billions of Passenger Miles			*Percentage Change*
	1940	1950	1960	*1940–1960*
Railways, Steam and Electric	24.8	32.5	21.6	−12.9
Intercity Bus	11.5	26.4	19.9	73.0
Inland Waterways	1.3	1.2	2.1	61.5
Domestic Air	1.0	10.1	34.0	—b
Total a	38.6	70.2	77.6	101.0
	Percentage Distribution			
Railways, Steam and Electric	*64*	*46*	*28*	
Intercity Bus	*30*	*38*	*26*	
Inland Waterways	*3*	*2*	*3*	
Domestic Air	*3*	*14*	*44*	
Total a	*100*	*100*	*100*	

Source: Interstate Commerce Commission, *Annual Report, 1940, Annual Report, 1950, Annual Report, 1960*
a Totals do not always add to 100 because of rounding.
b Percent increase 3,300.

smaller national units. European trends similar to those in North America include the general increase in passenger and freight traffic by all methods, the rapid growth of motor truck transport relative to rail, the stable position of water transport in the total picture, and the rapid shift of energy resources to pipelines. The outstanding differences are a continuing rise in rail passenger travel where population densities are high, and limited dependence on air travel where good rail service over intermediate distances eliminates the time advantage of air travel between city centers.

[1] W. B. Saunders, *The Problems of the Canadian Railways*, Vol. I, A General Appraisal, submitted to the Royal Commission on Railway Transportation in Canada (Washington, D.C., 1960), Table VIII-2.

These transport patterns are reflected in transport investment expenditures. In the United States, annual new highway construction is seven times greater than investments in railways; motor vehicle equipment outlays add further to the overriding importance of road transport in the total picture. In Western Europe half of the estimated $7.4 billion capital expenditures for transport in the period 1956–1960 was for motor vehicles and roads.[2]

U.S.S.R. and Japan

There are outstanding examples, however, of industrial countries with a markedly different pattern of transport development. Both the Soviet Union and Japan place major reliance on railways for passenger and freight traffic, and they began the shift to road, air, and pipeline transport much later than the West. The Soviet rail system has for some years carried up to 85 percent of all intercity freight, and in Japan a combination of rail and water transport, supported by local movement by cart and wheelbarrow, provided a largely railway-oriented system prior to World War II. Road construction in both countries was kept to a minimum during these earlier periods. It is only in the past decade that Japan has launched extensive roadbuilding and motor vehicle production programs, while the Soviet Union began to emphasize highway and air transport in its transport investment program even more recently.

Underdeveloped Countries

Like the Soviet Union and Japan, less developed countries with high population density and an extensive area are likewise rail-oriented. India, Pakistan, and China depend heavily on rail movements, supplemented by river transport. But in most of the developing countries with lower population densities, this pattern does not apply. In these countries reliance is primarily on road transport, with air transport or pipelines sometimes playing a significant role. In Colombia, for example, 57 percent of 1960 traffic was carried by truck, 19 per-

[2] $2.5 billion for vehicles and $1.3 billion for roads. Eighth Report of the Organization for European Economic Cooperation, *Europe Today and in 1960*, Vol. II, April 1957, p. 52.

TABLE IV-3. *Freight and Passenger Transport in the U.S.S.R.*

(In billions)

Type of Carrier	Total Ton-Km.		Percent Distribution		Total Passenger-Km.		Percent Distribution	
	1940	1962	1940	1962	1940	1962	1940	1962
Rail	415.0	1,646.3	85.1	77.7	98.0	189.3	92.2	63.7
River	36.1	109.8	7.4	5.2	3.8	4.6	3.6	1.6
Marine	23.8	173.1	4.9	8.2	0.9	1.3	0.9	0.4
Pipe	3.8	74.5	0.8	3.5				
Road	8.9	113.0	1.8	5.3	3.4	81.5	3.2	27.4
Air	0.02	0.89	0.01	0.04	0.2	20.3	0.2	6.8
Total	487.6	2,117.6	100.0	100.0	106.3	297.0	100.0	100.0

Source: Central Statistical Board, the Council of Ministers of the USSR, Moscow, 1963.

78

cent by inland rivers, 17 percent by rail, and 7 percent each by coastal vessels and pipelines.[3]

Transport trends in Colombia have been comparable in many respects to those of more developed countries. In the period 1951–1960, commodity movements other than crude oil increased 75 percent;

TABLE IV-4. *Distribution of Freight Traffic, Selected Asian Countries, 1957*

(Freight traffic in thousands of ton-km.)

Country	Total Ton-Km.			Percent Distribution		
	Rail	Road[a]	Water[b]	Rail	Road[a]	Water[b]
India	73,415	4,550	5,950	88	5	7
Japan	48,991	13,724	41,000	47	13	40
Pakistan	6,684	438	4,960	55	4	41
Thailand	1,025	780	500	44	34	22
Burma	621	388	1,400	26	16	58
Indonesia	1,044	1,568	3,491	17	26	57
Philippines	190	1,558	300	9	76	15
Vietnam (S.)	82	350	1,210	5	21	74
Cambodia	62	126	400	11	21	68

Source: *Economic Development and Planning in Asia and the Far East, VI. Transport Development,* U.N. Economic Bulletin for Asia and the Far East, Vol. XI, No. 3, December 1960, pp. 6–7.

[a] Road traffic is estimated by multiplying the following assumed annual performance by the numbers of registered vehicles by type:

Year	Type of Vehicle	Capacity	Rate of performance	Av. annual distance travelled	Annual performance
1957	Bus	30 pass.	0.80	40,000 km.	960,000 pass.-km.
	Pass. car	5 pass.	0.40	12,500 km.	24,000 pass.-km.
	Truck	2½ tons	0.50	20,000 km.	35,000 ton-km.

[b] Except in the case of Japan, Indonesia, and the Philippines, water transport refers to inland waterway traffic only, figures of which are worked out largely on the basis of the estimates of the number of vessels, inland country boats, the average load factor and informed opinion regarding the average length and number of journeys performed annually. For Japan, Indonesia, and the Philippines, figures refer to interinsular freight traffic. In the case of Indonesia and the Philippines, estimates are made by multiplying actual tonnage carried by an average haul of 500 km. for Indonesia and 200 km. for the Philippines.

transport by highway doubled; railway traffic increased 39 percent; and river traffic remained unchanged. There was some increase in coastwise shipping and in the use of product pipelines, but their contribution to the total remained small. A 23 percent increase in passenger traffic in Colombia during the same period was due entirely to

[3] Republic of Colombia, "Plan for Improvement in National Transportation," Parsons, Brinckerhoff, Quade, and Douglas (December 1961), pp. 8-9.

the expansion of bus and air services, with rail and water traffic actually declining 18 and 65 percent respectively.

Transport trends throughout the developing world are often the product of fairly obvious circumstances. Over much of the rural countryside where population density is low, the only feasible way of moving is by road—walking, cycling, headloading, hauling by animal, and possibly transporting by wagon, cart, or some type of motorized vehicle. Where rivers are navigable, both local and long-distance traffic may find these ready-made water routes indispensable. And on long hauls the airplane is often the obvious answer for moving people. In other circumstances, difficult choices and combinations of choices have to be made. Trends to date indicate how decisions have been made in the past. What we need to know is whether or to what extent these decisions have taken into account all the relevant considerations and how public policymakers might find additional guidance in the future.

The process of choosing among alternative transport media involves four principal sets of factors. One is comparative transport costs and capabilities. Another is the influence of transport costs on production costs. Third are the net effects on development of the several methods of transport: the different inputs and outputs of capital, managerial skill, labor, and other factors. These three are discussed by Richard B. Heflebower in Chapter III. A fourth set of factors are the potentials of transport innovation which may alter transport cost and quality in the foreseeable future. (A more extensive treatment of the choice of transport technology is contained in my recent Brookings book, *Strategy for Mobility*.)

The Outlook for Transport Technology

In a period of rapid advances in science and technology it has become increasingly important that developing countries take advantage of what is new or that they maintain flexibility in anticipation of coming changes.

The world is now on the threshold of extraordinary developments in transport as well as in areas that will have an important impact on transport. For the first time in 5,000 years the world is witnessing innovations that challenge the wheel as the symbol of mobility. Vertical takeoff aircraft, hydrofoil ships, ground-effect machines, and pipelines for solids as well as liquids and gases all operate without wheels. New forms of energy are also creating conditions for radical changes in transport, not only because they supply new motive power, but because they alter the nature of the transport problem itself by introducing substitutes for fossil fuels. Nuclear energy reduces the burden of fuel transport, and long-distance transmission of electric power substitutes wires for rails in the movement of coal. Telecommunications have now introduced effective substitutes for transport.

Pipelines

Among the relatively new transport media, the pipeline has a growing role to play in the whole transport investment picture. Continuing improvements in the quality of pipe and in the ease of installation and operation have resulted in a rapid expansion of this form of transport, with important implications for conventional methods of hauling coal.

The feasibility of pipelines for developing countries lies in their ability to traverse even the most difficult terrain, to be practically unaffected by weather, and to furnish transport of bulk commodities at low unit costs. Land costs are held to a minimum by burying the pipe to avoid interference with the use of the land. Another advantage of pipeline systems is the relatively routine nature of operations, which can be performed by the novice after a short period of on-the-job training. Periodic inspection and overhauls requiring greater skills can be accomplished by a small number of technical personnel moving over the system at regular intervals by air. The pipeline also has the advantage that its construction is not disassociated from the purpose it is to serve, so that investment is determined by known rather than imaginary needs. Finally, the pipeline must be in good working order if it is to function at all, with the result that the economic drain from poor maintenance and low operating efficiency typical of road and rail transport is not experienced.

Further potentials for pipeline transport are now evident from recent success in piping bituminous coal. The coal is ground to the consistency of coarse sand, mixed with an equal share of water, and pumped a hundred miles in thirty hours. What can be done with coal is also possible for a wide variety of other materials. Moving solids by pipe, and doing so more cheaply than by rail or water, presents a real possibility for heavy-traffic routes in newly developing countries. It is now clear that any substance that can be broken into small pieces and suspended in a liquid can be moved by pipe. Thus far the technical drawback has been the cost of preparing solids for the trip and then reclaiming them at the other end. Engineering advances are overcoming some of these problems.

Aviation

Despite its promise in a variety of other uses, aviation continues to make its major contribution in long-distance passenger travel. Its application to the short haul and to cargo movement may still prove to be a major potential for economic development. Special importance attaches to the progress being made in vertical take-off and in the new designs for cargo carriage. Most of the aircraft that developing countries have so far had at their disposal for air cargo are used piston planes that were displaced by jets. As a stopgap these aircraft offer the advantage of small initial capital outlay, but they also have the drawback of high operating costs.

But conventional aircraft purchased secondhand are not the type of vehicles that would be specifically designed for developing countries. What is needed is an air vehicle that moves at relatively slow speed in order to reduce the cost of ground and navigation facilities and to increase safety and reduce operating complexity. A satisfactory cargo plane should also offer ease of loading and unloading and the ability to take off and land at small airports and on rough runways.

The variety of conditions encountered throughout the world does not suggest that any one aircraft can meet the need for economy and performance in developing countries. But aircraft designed to provide local or feeder service in developing countries might have some characteristics in common. Most developing countries have limited surface carrier competition and are therefore able to move cargo by air over relatively short distances. If aircraft are designed for a four-hundred-mile range instead of a thousand miles, therefore, the ratio of payload to gross weight will be higher, with consequent reduction in ton-mile costs. For short distances, increases in speed do not achieve important time savings, so there is no need to incur the expense of higher speed.

Another possibility is aircraft capable of vertical takeoff and landing. Helicopter operating costs are still high, but the introduction of jet power has been an important breakthrough. The helicopter introduces important economies by eliminating costly ground facilities and by reducing the problem of pick-up and delivery by surface carriers. Recently designed helicopters could carry cargo short distances for about 16 cents per ton-mile. For hauls over fifty miles, however, some combination of direct lift and fixed wing would be necessary to achieve an economical transport vehicle that would take off vertically.[4]

Air transport can do much more than it has to date to serve the development program. Local air carriers can stretch the supply of scarce technicians by enabling them to visit more people and more places than would be conceivable by surface travel. Aircraft can carry doctors, medical supplies, and government and business officials quickly to where they need to be. The airplane can help discover and map a nation's resources, can spray, dust, and fertilize crops, and can fight insects and disease. It can survey sites for new construction projects and carry supplies to remote locations. The need for these and many other local services points to the important role that specially designed aircraft might play in the future development of the poorer nations.

Hydrofoils

A more experimental but potentially significant method of movement for developing countries is the ground reaction vehicle which operates just off the surface of the ground or water on a cushion created by downward jets of air. The air-cushion vehicle has particular applicability for travel over unstable ground or difficult waters where shoals or other obstacles impede navigation. Its applicability to newly developing areas is apparent. It would provide transport service over low-cost tracks of cleared land without a heavy investment in roadways and bridges, and it would be able to operate in the rainy season where existing roads are impassable. The hydrofoil ship may be another significant move toward improved transport by river and coastal transport.

[4] Philip R. Carlson, "Application of Air Cargo Transport to Feeder Operations in Less Developed Areas," in *Transportation*, Vol. V, United States papers prepared for the United Nations Conference on the Application of Science and Technology for the Benefit of the Less Developed Areas (U. S. Government Printing Office, 1963).

Road and Rail Transport

To date, however, about three-quarters of all transport investment in developing countries is for conventional rail or road transport. This emphasis will continue for some time to come, so that innovations that enhance the advantages of these forms of transport will be highly significant. Gas turbines, for example, can reduce the complexity of motor vehicle engines and introduce further economies in vehicle operation. The turbine engine contains fewer moving parts and can operate on a variety of liquid fuels. Turbine-powered trucks have a power plant that weighs less than a tenth the weight of a diesel engine with equivalent power. Further cost reduction may lie in the use of lightweight materials, the improvement of roadbuilding techniques, and in new sources of railway motive power and traffic control systems.

In addition to these developments, improved methods of packaging and cargo handling offer important advantages. Containerization makes it possible to transfer cargo quickly and cheaply from one method of transport to another. It is possible for containers to be moved on barges or railway flat cars over long distances and then transferred to trucks for the shorter haul at destination. Container traffic is protected from pilferage and damage from handling or bad weather during transshipment. The economy of this type of operation suggests that for suitable types of commodities, railways may retain traffic in the future that might otherwise have shifted to other modes.

The Impact of Nontransport Technology

Scientific innovations outside the transport field may significantly affect the nature of transport problems and the steps taken toward their solution. We have noted that the movement of mineral fuels accounts for as much as 25 to 40 percent of total railway operations. A nation's energy policies will be a major factor, therefore, in determining both the volume and the type of transport required.

The railways of India, for example, are heavily burdened with coal movements, and very heavy investment in rail equipment is required to meet the anticipated growth in coal usage during the next decade.

One-third of the coal is for use by the railways themselves, so that electrification or conversion to diesel power would substantially reduce the volume of coal to be transported. Further reductions might be accomplished through the development of natural gas or oil, the use of nuclear power, and the long-distance transmission of electric power.

Preservation of Raw Products

Other innovations that may alter the demand for transport include facilities for the storage, processing, and preservation of agricultural products. The predominant role of agriculture in underdeveloped countries means that the demand for transport is highly seasonal and that peak tonnages at harvest time create extraordinary pressures on transport facilities. It may be possible to reduce these peaks as new methods of food preservation are developed.

A number of new devices are available for preserving food and thus reducing the need for investing in refrigerated transport and high speed transit. They include radiation, dehydration, and antibiotics. Preserving perishable foodstuffs through dehydration has a special advantage in tropical climates where high temperatures make it difficult to preserve fresh foodstuffs by refrigeration. Various techniques for prompt dehydration can reduce the volume of goods to be moved as well as level the seasonal variations in production.[5]

Experimental work has been conducted in Kenya using antibiotics to prolong the freshness of meat and poultry. Although none of the drugs can replace cold storage, they extend the keeping quality of meat for almost two days after slaughter. This critical period is of great importance in tropical and subtropical countries where the farmer is interested in preserving what he markets until it is sold and where unforeseen delays often occur during distribution.[6] Food preservation through gamma irradiation is another significant innovation that makes it possible to stop reproduction of insects in stored cereal crops and to delay ripening of fruits. All these processes are of vital

[5] M. B. Rouge, "Dehydration of Foodstuffs in Countries of the Tropical Zone," United Nations Conference on the Application of Science and Technology for the Benefit of the Less Developed Areas (Geneva, 1963).

[6] Alfred Ginsberg, "Antibiotics in the Preservation of Fresh Meat and Poultry," United Nations Conference on the Application of Science and Technology for the Benefit of the Less Developed Areas (Geneva, 1963).

importance to the task of reducing losses and getting food to those who need it.

Communication

New methods of communication also provide new approaches to transport problems. In developing countries transport is still the principal means of spreading ideas, of achieving political unity, and of making it possible for people to communicate. The volume of passenger movement relative to freight movement on public carriers is generally high, and the volume of travel being performed on foot and by animal or country boat is also substantial. Despite the heavy total volume of movement, however, most people have neither the time nor money to travel. They pass most of their lives within a radius of a very few miles of where they were born. Transport does not begin to provide the communications that are necessary.

A century ago transport and communications were closely allied activities because communications were possible only through the transportation of messages. This is why the Post Office in the United States has always had a keen interest in all forms of transport, from the early development of roads for rural mail routes to the payment of subsidies to airlines. With the development of telegraph and telephone services, however, the link between transportation and communications was broken. The gap was widened by radio and television, and by the transistor.

In the United States, for example, it was once necessary to maintain thousands of one-room schools in order to provide education for a relatively immobile population. The consolidated school with adequate teaching staff and physical plant was made possible by an extensive roadbuilding program to permit the transporting of pupils by bus. It cost some $40 billion for the roads alone and took several decades to accomplish. Now electronics provides a means of reaching every village and community with speed and economy. Classroom television and radio have demonstrated the ability to multiply the effectiveness of scarce teaching personnel in Egypt, India, Iran, and several Latin American countries. These efforts have important implications for investment in transport and in education.

In Chile 100,000 children in more than 1,300 rural schools, both public and private, are receiving lessons by radio.[7] A similar radio system in Colombia provides a widespread network of instruction in public health, agriculture, and in reading and writing. In Egypt seminars and discussion groups are conducted by radio and television covering such fields as agriculture, health, national history, and analysis of current affairs.

Transistor television now introduces further improvements over transistor radio, and the communications function of the transport system can be supplied through the air to hasten the benefits of education, to disseminate ideas, and to stretch the scarce supply of teachers and technicians. But if the underdeveloped countries were to attempt a duplication of the educational television system in the United States, they would find both the cost and time far in excess of what would be feasible. Since each station serves only about 6,000 square miles, a ground-based TV system involves hundreds of broadcasting stations and interconnecting microwave communications.

Now it appears that the use of an earth satellite repeater system would be more economical than a ground system. Programs would be transmitted to the satellite and rebroadcast directly to community sets. The area over which the satellite signals could be seen would range from one to three million square miles. This would be equivalent to the size of India or Brazil, or might encompass a group of countries that could conduct television education programs jointly.[8]

For India a ground-based system such as the developed countries now use would require 224 telecasting stations connected by an 18,000 mile microwave system. Even if the satellite is assumed conservatively to have a life of only one year, this method of achieving a national television network would cost substantially less than the conventional ground system. Transistors make it possible to provide the necessary power for community sets without a central supply, and local assembly could substantially reduce the cost per set. But the main advantage of the satellite system is that it could achieve the objective quickly.

[7] Hernan Poblete Varas, "Communications and Audio-Visual Systems in Rural Education," United Nations Conference on the Application of Science and Technology for the Benefit of the Less Developed Areas (Geneva, 1963).

[8] N. I. Korman and A. Katz, "Television Broadcasting from Satellites," American Rocket Society, 17th Annual Meeting, Los Angeles, California (November 13-18, 1962).

88   TRANSPORT AND TECHNOLOGYTRANSPORT AND TECHNOLOGY

Conclusion

Modern technology has greatly improved the possibility that the obstacles to development imposed by poor transport can be overcome. In some cases the solution will be in doing conventional things better, and in others the answer will lie in approaching old problems in entirely new ways. There are thus two basic problems to be overcome. One is to take better advantage of what is already possible, and the second is to undertake the research and development efforts necessary to accelerate further innovation.

If the first problem is to be overcome, it will be necessary to provide the basis for selecting among alternative technologies, as well as the organizational and policy frameworks in which wise choices can be made. The principal drawbacks now are partly the absence of sufficient information on cost and performance records in developing countries. But a further obstacle to decision-making is that each segment of the transport system is separately provided and programmed. The result is that transport alternatives may never enter into consideration when investments are being planned. Finally, the larger view of the relation between transport and development goals too often conceals alternative approaches to solutions that may not involve transport at all.

The situation calls for overhauling transport administration and planning procedures to permit a total transport approach in the context of the economic development effort as a whole. At the same time there is urgent need for an imaginative program of research and development that will focus on new transport techniques and new techniques for meeting transport requirements in more effective ways through scientific innovations outside the transport field.

V

Design of the Transport Sector

GARY FROMM*

Promoting economic development without plan-
ning is like attempting to reach home port in a rudderless ship. If an
emerging nation is to increase the rate of realization of its human and
material potential, normally it must establish an optimal framework
for both private and public economic activities. Adam Smith and
Thomas Jefferson to the contrary, reliance on market and political
forces and legislative intuition will seldom guarantee rapid growth
and prosperity in immature economies. Before ideal economic policies
can be implemented, a development plan is required. This plan should
encompass minimum final demand goals, production capabilities, intermediate output requirements, and other constraints, on a dynamic
national, regional, and industrial sector basis. Economic growth per se,
of course, does not depend on planning. Nor is planning a panacea for
all economic ills; indeed, it can be overdone and impede attainable
growth. Yet, both the social and economic consequences of development can be improved greatly by intelligent planning.

A development plan is the sum and product of its parts—each sector
is dependent on every other sector, and all sectors as a whole depend
on each sector. Nevertheless, each sector is also influenced by unique
factors unrelated to the forces impinging on the others. Thus the transport sector must be devised concurrently with other development sectors which transport is designed to support and promote. However, it
must also be structured partly from particular economic, political,
and social facts and directions of the country's economy.

This implies that a pattern of resource allocation for the various
segments of the transport sector can in some way be predetermined;

* The Brookings Institution.

that the relationship among investments in roads, railroads, ports, or air facilities has some validity in itself; or that at a particular stage of development a pattern of investment in certain types of facilities is called for. In turn, this pattern emerges from the need for integration of the segments of the transport sector and the goals of the overall development plan. Unfortunately, except for technological characteristics, patterns of transport investment in one country offer little guidance for others. Widely differing land masses and formations; differing demographic, social, and economic organization and locations; differing stages of industrialization; previous investments and attention to maintenance; dependencies on foreign trade; as well as differing national goals preclude any universal rule for resource allocation to transport investment, and it should not be sought.[1] Furthermore, because a development plan is a combination of sectors, while a sector is a function of discrete projects, attention from the outset must be devoted to an evaluation of projects. The merit of any project hinges on a large number of complementary and conflicting factors. Each must be taken into account and appropriately balanced in assigning project priorities.[2]

Common Factors in Sector Planning

The primary factor common to all sectors in development planning is the determination of economic returns (and other social effects) of projects in terms of costs and benefits. In other words, the investment, maintenance, and operating costs of projects should be compared with the measurable benefits of the investments. (See the methods proposed

[1] Certainly much can be learned from an examination of the transport investment and growth experiences of the developed and developing nations. Nonetheless, Tinbergen's conclusion that public and private transport investment consistently and *properly* comprises 20 to 25 percent of total gross capital outlays appears unwarranted. (Jan Tinbergen, *The Design of Development*, Johns Hopkins Press, 1958, p. 31.) Not only does this range not have any normative significance *per se*, but furthermore, Tinbergen's own (*ibid.*, pp. 90-91) and statistics of the International Bank for Reconstruction and Development reveal many observations outside of these limits.

[2] This is not to deny that projects should be examined in the light of an integrated transport system, or to minimize the importance of administrative reforms or inter-sectoral tradeoffs (e.g., between transport and communications or transport and inventory investment). These are matters which will be treated later.

by Hans A. Adler in Chapter IX.) However, an obvious perplexity remains. Because the benefits of transport facilities are frequently more indirect than direct, they are extremely difficult to quantify. Especially in the case of roads, total benefits cannot readily be measured in terms of value of receipts, value added, or even quantity of product as is the case in industrial investment decisions.

Benefits and Pricing Policies

In addition, the demand to be satisfied and the benefits to be derived therefrom are often not fixed, nor are they independent entities, since the demand will depend in part on a pricing policy. The pricing policy established by the government, which may be indeterminate during the planning period, not only influences the total demand for the facility but can also have different indirect benefits for various industries and trades affected. This results in further difficulties in calculating benefits.[3]

The problems of analyzing a new port project in an isolated and underdeveloped part of an emerging country illustrate some of the issues. The direct internal benefits to be derived from the port construction and the lower port costs can be estimated in terms of port revenues resulting from current traffic as well as from traffic to be diverted from other transport media. Additional internal revenues from the port can also be estimated (but in far less definitive fashion) from traffic from new industries which will be made economically viable by reduced transport costs. The economic benefits of the port are not, however, limited to economies reflected in these internal port revenue flows. If, for example, the level of port charges to an export industry is below that which the industry previously was paying, there will be external port economies and benefits in the form of higher profits accruing to the export industry. An increase of port charges could, of course, transfer these external benefits into internal port benefits; they would then be reflected in higher port revenues. Similarly, the external benefits derived by shipping companies from improved port facilities (quicker turnaround time, etc.) may or may not be reflected in lower shipping rates and increased volumes. Thus, pricing policies

[3] This presumes that there are oligopoly elements present in the economy and the government does not, and could not if it desired to do so, enforce price relationships which would apply under purely competitive conditions (and therefore would be subject to endogenous determination).

(government and private) affect the distribution of benefits from the facility, but they also can and do affect, through elasticities of demand, the total traffic and benefits which will accrue from the investment.

This is not an evaluation problem that is unique to transport, nor can it be averted by merely assuming that pure competition, constant and decreasing returns to scale, and marginal cost pricing are ubiquitous in the economy. The real world is indeed imperfect. Economies of scale, private enterprise monopolistic elements, inadequate foresight, and other abberations will all cause deviations from the market prices that would prevail in an ideal setting. The use of shadow rather than market prices (cf. the chapter by Louis Lefeber) will alleviate some, but not all, of the difficulties of benefit measurement caused by market imperfections; their use will also aid in quantifying developmental external effects.

External Developmental Effects

Transport and other investments frequently serve a dual function, playing both a passive and a dynamic role in the development process. The transport sector is passive in meeting the current and immediately foreseeable demands of agriculture, industry, and trade. It is dynamic in altering relative price relationships between production factors (by reducing distribution costs through the provision of ports, highways, pipelines, etc.), thereby facilitating the exploitation of unutilized, or underutilized, resources. Improved transport may also help to increase the spread of the market economy, entrepreneurship, and private savings and investment in productive activity.

Determining the extent of this dynamic stimulation of production is difficult, however, if not impossible. It is even more hazardous to place a value on these external developmental effects than to ascribe them to particular projects or sectors. Not only may a major portion of such gains have come about without the new facilities, but, when shadow prices are employed and substitution possibilities are admitted, their net benefit may sometimes be small, if not negative. This is not to say the beneficial effects are imaginary; indeed, they are frequently tangible and large. However, in most cases, especially when the stimulation of development by transport appears tenuous and the effects are problematical, these benefits should be classed with other non-quantifiable economic factors—to be identified and measured to the degree feasible and included in the cost-benefit project evaluation as an addendum.[4] Where several projects have interdependent external benefit or cost effects, they should, of course, be evaluated as a group as well as independently. This will internalize some of the external effects.

Sector Plans and National Welfare

Another common factor in the formulation of sector plans is their impact on income distribution among groups and regions (including urban vs. rural) within the nation. The location and type of investment in productive and social overhead facilities, though planned to be efficient on economic grounds, may cause the relative, if not absolute, well-being of some segments of the population to decline. These changes may or may not be desirable from a social welfare standpoint. It might be presumed that the most efficient economic plans should be adopted and that inequities for particular groups or regions could readily be corrected by appropriate tax and transfer policies. However, this is not necessarily the case in an underdeveloped country hampered by strong vested-interest groups, a lack of requisite data and trained personnel, and poor tax administration. Some modification in "efficient" plans may be required to compensate for possible undesirable effects on the distribution of income.

Regional disparities in income affect not only welfare, but national unity. Even without income discrepancies, political stability suffers when economic ties, communications, and transportation are limited and segments of the population are not cohesive. Such instability can lead to turmoil or a rapid turnover in governments (sometimes by revolutionary means), and it can retard economic activity. Therefore, for both economic and political reasons, certain transport projects may be accorded high priority in the investment budget because they tend to strengthen national bonds by linking isolated regions to the rest of the country.

Other things being nearly equal, some investments may also be preferred because they add significantly to defense and national security. Nevertheless, justification of outlays for productive and transport facili-

---

[4] External effects on the cost side should, obviously, be considered, too. For example, the opportunity use of scarce foreign exchange deserves careful attention.

ties on logistic or other military grounds should generally be avoided unless they satisfy a definite defense requirement. To do otherwise is to sacrifice economic efficiency for the sake of chauvinism.

Finally, other social factors must be considered. Destruction of scenic vistas or historic landmarks; the bastardization of local culture and customs; the substitution of haste, noise, and pollution of air and stream for nature's serenity—are all part of the price that is frequently paid for accelerating the rate of growth and "raising" the standard of living. Depending on its population density and climatic, geographic, and agricultural characteristics, a nation may not be indifferent to the loss of natural assets and social values.

The problems discussed are common to all sectors in development planning. Design of the transport sector, however, involves several distinctive features of its own. These features are not so much unique in kind as they are idiosyncratic in degree. Although found in other sectors, too, they pose particular problems for the transport planner.

Distinctive Features of Transport Planning

Public surveillance certainly is one of the difficulties of transport. The transport sector and its planning decisions are probably more closely scrutinized by the public and by politicians than other sectors. In addition to commanding a lion's share of investment resources, basic facility transport projects are primarily public investments; the private sector generally cannot or will not make them, yet they vitally affect private investment decisions as well as the regional interests which the politicians represent.[5] Furthermore, these projects are usually visible

[5] The willingness of the private sector to undertake infrastructure investments in the absence of government intervention is dependent on firms' aversion to risk and the expected values and variances of the rates of return. Where, due to large capital requirements and uncertain demand, the risks are high, private corporations may only invest if monopoly control can be exercised, if prices higher than competitive rates can be charged, and if extra-normal profits can be earned. For infrastructure projects, these requisites, especially when foreign ownership is involved, may be politically unpalatable and economically undesirable, giving rise either to direct government investment or regulation to insure adequacy of service, "reasonable" prices, and minimum wasteful capacity. If the regulatory course of action is chosen, then guarantees on rates of return and assurances against nationalization may be needed to induce private infrastructure ventures.

and affect large groups that can readily form and express judgments on the facilities and their use.

Lumpiness of Transport Investment

Difficulties also emanate from the "lumpiness" of investment decisions, since the supply functions for transport capacity are not continuous. Once a railroad expansion investment is indicated, the whole expansion must be accomplished for the major benefits to accrue; a road must be built between two points before it has much utility; for an airport to handle major international traffic, it must be built to accommodate the largest jet aircraft.

Complementary or supplementary investment requirements also increase the "lumpiness" of many transport facility projects. A new deepwater port planned to cost $20 million might be justified only if a road .system connecting the port with the hinterland were simultaneously constructed at a cost of at least as much as the port itself. The transport sector, of course, has no monopoly on lumpiness—other sectors also are confronted by the necessity of providing excess capacity in order to have any capacity at all. In the smaller emerging nations, however, the high capital requirements created by the lumpiness of transport investments can be particularly burdensome.

Problems of Time and Space

Coupling lumpiness with two other interrelated problems, long time horizons and the need for regional specificity, causes additional difficulties. The physical or economic life of transport projects is probably no greater than that for investments in many other sectors. Equipment may be expected to be *economically* useful for 10 to 20 years, while basic facilities (rights-of-way, roadbed, track, ports, airports, etc.), if maintained, will not normally become economically obsolete due to population shifts or alterations in the regional characteristics of production for 20 to 40 or more years.[6]

[6] Future technological change may appreciably shorten this period by causing faster economic obsolescence in the various transport media. Heavier trucks and diesel engines make road and rail beds obsolete; larger deadweight tonnage ships make ports inadequate; and higher specification international air equipment and safety standards rapidly make the foresightedness of airport designs of yesterday

This long life would pose no problems were it not for the lumpiness of investment. That is, the satisfaction of current transport demands automatically creates excess capacity which can be utilized to meet future needs. Thus, facilities provided in the present affect future transport costs; inadequate consideration of future needs and improper specification of capacities today, can engender wasteful expenditure of resources tomorrow. It should be noted that these capacities are not items in the abstract; they must be specific facilities, in specific locations, designed to handle specific levels and types of trade and passenger movement between specific points for a minimum of 10 to 20 years.

The long-range planning of industry or agriculture is rarely delineated in a manner which the transport economist can use in this time perspective. Long-range industrial sector planning may well anticipate and specify a fairly detailed list of industries to be developed, but usually without indicating the nature of the consequent transport requirements. Often industrial sector plans, particularly in the realm of private enterprise, place emphasis on the use of credit facilities to stimulate private initiative, thus contributing to the vagueness in timing and location of new industrial growth.

Similarly, long-range agricultural planning has usually been limited to indicating production goals by foodstuff types and means of increasing production through seed, fertilizer, mechanization, water, and credit programs. These programs are not readily translated, even in the short run and especially in the longer run, into transport needs.

Confronted with the dilemma of planning geographically quite specifically and well beyond the time period for which industry and agriculture plan, and yet having to fulfill their largely implicit future needs, the transport economist must develop (preferably in concert with the planners of other sectors) explicit projections of the extent, timing and location of transport demands. Obviously, the current and foreseen demands of the various sectors should be extended as far as the data and thinking permit but, because the horizon for these figures

---

appear to be nearsighted. Nevertheless, while such advances may make obsolete the construction put in place at an earlier date, they do not normally make the rights-of-way obsolete.

The physical life of equipment and basic facilities can, of course, be much greater than the economic life. Even today, one may find freight cars of 1910 vintage still in use. Whether these can justifiably be employed from the standpoint of operating efficiency seems extremely dubious.

will generally be short, another level of abstraction is necessary. To complicate matters further, the transport planner is not, and cannot be, given special timing consideration for the submission of the transport sector plan document; it must be integrated and bound with the rest of the plan. It must be submitted simultaneously, with specifications and cost estimates for transport facilities for yet partially undetermined industrial, agricultural, mining, and other developments.

Reasonable ranges of anticipated production by the other sectors (and their timing and geographic dispersion) can be derived from nationally specified, realistic medium- and long-range goals; population location and projection studies; and analyses of probable arable land, water, and labor skill resource development. The cost and pricing of the components of this activity do affect its total volume. It is assumed that the planners are aware of the need to formulate their projections so that the sectors are consistent with each other and with feasible and desirable output capacities. (Note that this does not imply that growth must be balanced.) The task could be simplified by ignoring the regional distribution of future development and by planning on the basis of the current pattern of industrial activity. However, adoption of this procedure might be extremely costly (due to the large, sunk nature of investments in basic facilities) were the current and future regional patterns to diverge.

The geographical dimension of a country's development is also shaped by transport costs and available capacity. Therefore, transport should not passively acquiesce to the demands of other sectors, but should endeavor to achieve a preferred areal distribution of production. This is far too important a matter to be left solely to the transport sector; the planning group as a whole should bear the responsibility for basic locational decisions and the studies needed to support them. Unfortunately, if the planning group is delinquent, this burden falls solely on the transport planner. If he is to prepare reasonably reliable estimates and help guide development into its proper regional allocation, he must conduct the studies himself.

Allocation Problems

The determination of the *best* regional distribution of production can probably only be done by some form of iterative process. Starting with an initial specification, the analysis moves on to consider its impli-

cations in terms of transport and other requirements. Once these have
been ascertained, it is necessary to reexamine the original allocations
to effect improvements, and so on.

Given a regional trade pattern, relating projections of transport
requirements per physical unit of production and delivery to the expected volume of final demand yields estimates of future transport
needs for the movement of goods.[7] The movement of labor inputs
(i.e., people) to satisfy production needs may be calculated on a
similar basis. For the most part these will be urban travel demands for
round trips from home to work. Assuming that the labor force and
employment grow proportionately, these demands are correlated with
increases in urban populations. In agricultural regions, urban and near-
urban demands are created by trips made to and from farms (trips for
the purpose of hauling produce to market and inputs to the farm have
been included in the goods production and distribution requirements
discussed above). The last segment of business travel, intercity trips,
will depend upon geographic conditions and the pattern and extent
of interregional and international trade.

Finally, aside from some relatively limited governmental and military
needs, only consumer demand for transportation services remains. (Any
special military requirements should, however, be communicated to the
transport planner.) Generally, extensive investment to satisfy personal
travel desires cannot be justified at early stages of development when
the alternative uses of scarce foreign exchange and domestic capital
and labor skills have such great value. Nonetheless, these demands
can be met partly by hitchhiking on private business vehicles (mostly
trucks) and by the use of intratemporal excess and off-peak load capacity of roads and public rail and bus facilities. Yet, as development
progresses, rising incomes and a keen desire for personal mobility and
travel can create a demand for transportation services, especially by
automobile, far in excess of these capacities. In countries where most
cars are imported, the satisfaction of this demand is, of course, subject
to government control through import restrictions. In other nations
where the production and sale of cars is dictated mainly by market
forces, potential purchases of automobiles and their use must be esti-

[7] More research on transport requirements (transport cube and density factors
per unit of product for basic commodities) would certainly serve a useful purpose. In this area, the strictures cited previously on the use of data from the
developed nations does not apply.

mated by conventional supply and demand analysis, i.e. by relating consumption to income, price, and other variables, and production to the availability and cost of inputs. Then, by applying weights indicating the probable distribution of ownership and use pattern of cars by region, the expected additional highway requirements can be forecast.

At this juncture, general information about the future economy has been obtained and translated into initial estimates of the level and timing of transport demands. The next step is the attempt to block out the basic framework and timing of the transport infrastructure so it can play its proper roles in development without misdirection and waste of massive amounts of resources. Before this task of design is completed a myriad of further problems will be confronted, some of which will now be examined.

Some Specific Design Problems

First and foremost is the consideration of complete transport systems. Too frequently transport planners succumb to the temptation to satisfy transport needs on a point-to-point basis without reviewing the overall implications of the implied composite system. It is not necessarily true that the most efficient transport plan is one that attempts to provide the lowest unit costs between each origin and destination. Given economies of scale and backhaul costs, circuitous routing, traffic concentration on a particular mode, and the use of general—rather than specific—purpose vehicles (and other seemingly inefficient procedures) may be desirable from a total transport cost standpoint. In other words, planned "inefficiency" may sometimes be efficient.

Most inefficiency, of course, is to be avoided. Where traffic volume is potentially high, circuitous and "broken" routes may be costly artifacts of inept planning.[8] Much inefficiency also arises from the need to

[8] There appears to be a tendency in transport planning to err on either one side or the other in linking points within a given mode; either all points are served by minimum distance connections, or the intramodal system is fragmented or inappropriately incomplete. Intercountry linkages at contiguous national borders seem especially to suffer from the latter condition, a fact which tends to delay economic integration over broad regional areas. Thus, it is likely that trade within the European Economic Community and Latin American Free Trade Association has been retarded by poor physical transport connections and differing rate structures and regulatory practices.

employ, due to location and cost, several modes in transferring passengers and goods from specific origins to specific destinations. For example, manufactured exports might be transported from the factory by truck, rail, truck and ship before they leave national boundaries. Certainly, some combination of modes may be necessary, but the number involved and the intermodal transfers should be designed so that efficiency is enhanced, not retarded. The transport plan should provide for integrating modes by selecting optimal locations for junctions, by establishing feeder routes and linkages, and by encouraging low-cost methods (e.g., containerization, gravity unloading, etc.) and terminals for intermodal transfers. The aim at all times should be to make available that capacity, regardless of mode, which minimizes total distribution and travel costs. Savings or losses in this area frequently can be large.

Costs and Specifications

The design task is also made more difficult by the variability of costs with relatively small alterations in specification. The change of a road from a weight-bearing strength of a 10-ton axle load to 13 (which in terms of truck volume would not appear appreciable) can increase the construction costs about 40 percent; dredging a harbor to a 10-meter depth, instead of 9, to accommodate ships at most tides might well increase harbor costs 15 to 20 percent.[9] Issues pertaining to such specifications often become the critical points of policy decision. Yet their benefits frequently cannot be, or are not, clearly defined and quantitatively analyzed. Furthermore, the crucial factor in making a decision of this sort may well be a political one which cannot be anticipated with any great certainty. For example, bearing specifications for roads often depend upon whether the government has the desire and the

[9] In part these basic facility costs rise rapidly because of the inability to substitute labor for mechanical equipment for some major construction operations (e.g., dredging), and the high cost of skilled labor input for others. The lack of economic substitutability of construction methods establishes a fairly constant range for many transport projects' costs (including foreign exchange requirements) once the specifications are determined. Here, clearly, is an area where the engineer and the economist should cooperate—both in ascertaining feasible limits of substitutability, given the current technology and the quantity and cost of available resources, and in devising lower cost and more flexible construction methods.

power to enforce a weight limitation and at what level it could be made effective.

Another aspect of the cost and specification problem is the possibility of tradeoffs between various cost components: basic facility capital costs vs. vehicle operating costs; basic facility capital costs vs. basic facility maintenance costs; and basic facility maintenance costs vs. vehicle operating costs. Operating costs, as used here, include vehicle investment charges per traffic unit (i.e., per ton-mile or car-mile). There are also other tradeoffs against vehicle investment and inventory costs. As the quality of a basic facility is improved, consequently raising its cost, the operating costs of vehicles which employ it tend to fall. This is most evident in the case of highways and railroads, where an improved roadbed permits higher speeds and heavier loads and lower unit fuel, labor, and repair costs. Some evidence on this phenomenon may be found in Chapter III.

Maintenance vs. New Construction

Depending on geographic, climatic, and soil conditions, there can be rather large variations in maintenance costs with alterations in design. This is especially true where seasonal or daily extremes in temperature or rainfall are experienced. Far too little comparative analysis of original construction costs with maintenance costs of transport media (under varying physical conditions, specifications, and input cost of materials, machinery, and labor) is done today in transport investment reviews. It is too often assumed by the engineer as well as the economist that input factors in the developing countries have comparable relative costs to those existing in the advanced industrial nations, for maintenance as well as construction.

Maintenance, of course, is not undertaken for its own sake, but because of its impact on vehicle operating costs. Within a relevant range, as maintenance expenditures rise, vehicle operating costs fall. Thus, there may be an opportunity to lower total transport costs by substituting one type of cost for another. Incompleted past maintenance or reconstruction of an existing facility should often have a first claim on resources, *ceteris paribus*, prior to further extension of new facilities. The existence of a road requiring maintenance should not, obviously, automatically command a priority on resources for its maintenance without an analysis of comparative benefits to be derived from the same resources used for an alternative investment. Unfortunately, in the developing countries there is a strong bias for constructing new transport facilities rather than maintaining existing ones. The bias stems from such factors as: the relatively high cost of maintenance; the shortage of technical skills; the requirement for foresight in terms of planned acquisition of equipment, training of personnel and organization for the execution of maintenance; and the lack of realization of the real costs (direct and indirect) of not taking preventive or restorative maintenance measures. Furthermore, the developing country frequently finds it easier to obtain foreign loans for new construction than to obtain increased taxes for maintenance.

A proper combination of maintenance and staged construction can do much to reduce initial (or discounted) capital requirements, permitting prospective demand to be met without overinvestment in excess capacity. This is particularly pertinent to road design and construction. It has been said of the Near East that some type of "road" exists between all inhabited points, having been engineered by the lazy camel seeking the surest and shortest route. Following this original "engineering," the traffic has assisted in stabilizing the soil. There is enough truth in this statement to assert that road construction often may be simply an improvement to provide sufficient capacity and durability for the anticipated traffic.

By projecting the type and level of traffic on road segments and comparing the total costs and benefits of developing the roads to alternative higher levels of capacity and specification, decisions on staged construction can be made consistent with long-range future road development plans at a far smaller initial (at each stage) cost, thereby freeing funds for other purposes. The gain here is in the potential productive use of the cost savings which otherwise would have gone into providing higher quality or capacity facilities on given segments than are really needed at a particular time. The absolute, total capital outlays (in constant dollars) for facilities built under staged construction will almost always be greater than if they had been built at a single date. However, if the staging dates have been properly selected, and if the alternative uses of the initial construction cost savings are considered, the discounted present value of the staged construction outlays (including extra maintenance) will be less than the unstaged.

Where this technique has been introduced in planning and design-ing roads, it has enabled the development of as much as one-third again the kilometer length of roads to a level of *needed* utility with the same construction budget. While this approach certainly does increase planning costs, these costs, which appear relatively large in the planning stage, are more than justified in terms of the opportunity uses of the savings in construction costs.[10]

Importance of Administration

Although these gains are great, the administration of transport facilities is probably as critical an issue in transport development as the allocation of capital funds. Improved administration to utilize the current physical capacities with greater effectiveness prior to further investment in the facility, particularly for ports and railroads, may obviate the need for additional capital outlays and should be a sine qua non to any additional investment to expand capacity. This be-comes evident when the costs of the alternatives are calculated.

The effective capacity of a port is not only determined by the physi-cal equipment provided, but also by the coordination of a series of acts and movements of equipment, cargo and administrative paper. For example, a port in a developing country was recently handling approxi-mately 400 to 500 tons per year per linear meter of quay; the same facilities handling the same types and flows of commodities in a Western European port averaged about 650 tons per year per linear meter of quay. Since the cost of constructing an additional quay, back-up warehousing, and facilities is about $4.0 million per 100 meters of quay, an investment of this magnitude to meet rising demands for port facilities might be avoided by only a 10 to 15 percent improvement in the administration of the port.[11] Similarly in railroads, where capital requirements are high, minor improvements in efficiency can frequently effect substantial increases in capacity and avoid unnecessary invest-

[10] Yet staging is not an unmixed blessing—great care must be exercised in formulating these programs, since there is danger of costly errors. Maintenance costs may become prohibitive on low-standard roads, routes may be poorly chosen, future costs may rise excessively, etc. Nevertheless, the mistakes with staging are probably no greater, and possibly less, than in conventional designs.

[11] John H. Kaufmann, "Planning for Transport Investment in the Development of Iran," *American Economic Review*, Proceedings (May 1962), p. 402.

ment. Since the cost of improvement in administration usually is significantly less than the cost of new physical capacity, the savings in capital resources are great.

Deriving the Optimal Plan

As should be evident from the preceding discussion, planning is a complex task involving the use of a mass of information ranging from precise engineering estimates to unknown economic responses to vaguely delineated social objectives. How then can an optimal plan be derived when the incommensurables are so numerous, the uncertainties so great, and the alternatives so many? The outline which follows is only an approach, not an answer.

Ideally, planning for any sector should take place within the context of a comprehensive planning strategy which rigorously maximizes a set of goals to a horizon. However, even if the highly sophisticated iterative programming process cannot be undertaken, approximations of its stages are still a valuable ingredient in effective planning. First, a set of goals based on resource availabilities and national desires is definitely needed as guidelines for sector design. Second, consideration of how to achieve these goals in the long-run (and their geographic implications) can aid in their attainment. Third, even if only on an ad hoc basis, some form of near-term analysis which examines the substitutions and complementarities in investments between sectors and attempts to increase their returns is desirable. This stage should also endeavor to ensure overall consistency in resource use and availability. Fourth, a determination of the costs and benefits of each sector's projects is essential to a rational allocation of resources. Fifth, provision for taking account of other indirect economic effects and social and political factors that might influence investment decisions must also be made. Finally, there must be an opportunity to revise sector plans to remove inconsistencies; also, because maximization of national welfare entails more than maximizing economic product and involves regional, group, and temporal equity and preference considerations, a set of development alternatives susceptible to political choice must be prepared.[12]

[12] While these stages have been presented as discrete, sequential steps, they will

Overall responsibility for this procedure should rest with the planning group as a whole. Each sector, to varying degrees, must contribute to every step in the process and must bear the primary burden of evaluating its own projects.

Since at early and intermediate stages of development the division of transport demand between production requirements and final consumption is almost wholly weighted toward the former, the transport sector has little role to play in the specification of goals. It enters importantly, however, in the determination of constraints on their achievement. Transport must receive from the planning group an indication of the future regional distribution of growth and any anticipations of transport needs. In response, it must develop estimates of the transport demands implied by this development and provide an analysis of the long-run spatial and economic character of the required national transport network. This entails a complete description of the existing system and detailed proposals for its expansion over time. By iterating this process in cooperation with the planners of other sectors and the central planning authority, feasible development programs (comprising different intensities and geographic mixtures of transport, industrial, commercial and agricultural production) which satisfy alternative goals can be formulated.

Similarly, for near-term analyses, a statement of expected demands must be communicated to the transport planners and an indication of the adequacy of capacity should be forthcoming as a response.[13] Sector investment projects can then be devised to fulfill long-term needs and relieve short-term bottlenecks. Their evaluation and the inclusion of noneconomic factors in an addendum to the plan submitted for political approval needs no further comment here.

In some countries, even the rather informal analysis just outlined cannot be undertaken because of shortages of skilled personnel, lack of adequate statistics and a data collecting and reporting mechanism, failure to organize a comprehensive planning group, and other reasons. To the extent that he is able, here the transport planner must: gather

be taken in practice with varying degrees of simultaneity. The resulting plans, too, would be subject to continuing review and periodic revision and submission to the legislature and executive for selection and approval.

[13] In both the long- and near-term cases, the pricing of output enters critically in all cost (supply) and demand functions (cf. Chapter X for a discussion of pricing transport services).

and derive his own information on the current and future characteristics of the economy; assume what are apparently reasonable goals;
and proceed to approximate their achievement by suboptimizing his
own sector along the general lines proposed above. Hopefully, the
resulting specifications will not be overly inconsistent with those that
would be obtained under formal or informal global planning.

Conclusion

The investment decisions made today affect not only the standard
of living of the present generation, but those of the future as well.
Because the need to raise the rate of growth and the income per capita
in the less developed nations is great, and because the economic returns and social consequences of a purely laissez-faire approach can
be so significantly enhanced, government intervention to improve the
allocation and utilization of resources is advantageous. Such intervention need not, and probably should not, take the form of direct control
over all directly productive activities. But there is a clear necessity for
establishing guidelines and policies under which the private sphere
will operate more efficiently, and for providing basic facilities, including transportation, that are needed. The most effective way of doing
this is by means of an intensive comprehensive planning effort. Whatever the limitations of this method, its solutions are superior to those
resulting when decisions are merely optimized for each sector independently and feedback and interdependent long-range effects are
largely ignored. Economy-wide planning should not be implicit, but
explicit. Nevertheless, for some countries, this technique cannot become fully operational in the near future because of gaps in requisite
data and shortages of trained personnel.

In the absence of comprehensive planning, the transport planner
must labor under decided disadvantages in designing his sector of a
development plan. He must detail the investment in transport facilities
to meet the requirements of other sectors in the economy not yet
specifically defined, and he must also work with a time perspective
appreciably greater than the usual sector-plan period. This forces him
to frame (with due regard for potentially desirable regional production
shifts and other tradeoffs) transport infrastructure programs in the light
of basic natural resources, geographic, demographic, trade and other

economic factors as well as transport needs derived from currently planned or prospective development projects. These basic factors can then be interpreted in terms of anticipated population, agricultural and industrial centers and types of commodity and trade flows; and then, taking account of technological and cost characteristics of different modes, they can be translated into transport requirements. With requirements seen in this perspective, the use of the various alternative transport media can be interrelated so that a more integrated system of facilities can be developed.

Too often plans for the transport sector are primarily a collection of individual project proposals for roads, railroads, ports, and pipelines. Many, if not all, of the proposals may have favorable cost-benefit ratios, but together they do not represent an efficient system of facilities which minimize resources to meet the estimated total transport needs. Planning an integrated system of transport facilities points up the imperative time sequence of engineering planning and construction for facilities which are related not only to one another (e.g., feeder roads to rail heads, roads to new ports, etc.), but also to projected industrial and agricultural programs. The long lead time for transport projects, from initial proposals through feasibility testing to facility use, also heightens the attention which must be given to this aspect of transport sector planning.

Analyses of transport sector projects, while not having to grapple with such imponderables as the benefits from possible health or education projects, nonetheless face obstacles in estimating both indirect (and sometimes direct) costs and benefits. In progressing from project to program to subsector and then to sector determinations, the conventional marginal investment analyses become less definitive and less precise. It is not suggested here that an aggregative approach to the transport sector can replace project cost-benefit analyses. However, if these evaluations are conducted within a framework of a national transport pattern developed as indicated, it appears that improved transport investment decisions in the light of pertinent regional or national plan objectives can be made, and that fewer misallocations of resources to and within the transport sector will occur.

VI

Economic Development and Regional Growth

LOUIS LEFEBER*

ECONOMIC DEVELOPMENT implies that national income grows at a faster rate than population and that the benefits from growing national income lead to improvements in the standard of living of low-income groups. Hence, not only income growth but also income distribution is involved.

In overpopulated countries, the functional distribution of income is bound to yield high incomes to owners of scarce resources as well as low wage rates to employed labor.[1] The unemployed (or equivalent underemployed) earn nothing. They exist on subsistence farming and on official or private charity. The functional distribution could move in the direction of greater equality only if unemployment were first eliminated. From then on, further increases in the relative scarcity of labor would be accompanied by corresponding relative increases in wage rates. One could, of course, conceive of various schemes for redistribution in favor of the unemployed. But it is unrealistic to assume that a continuous improvement in income distribution could, in the long run, be attained if the functional distribution itself did not move in the right direction. Hence, the minimization of the time needed to attain full employment is to be considered a primary social goal. The implication is not, of course, that other social goals do not

* Massachusetts Institute of Technology.

[1] Even if labor were not homogeneous, this conclusion would, in the long run, hold for all labor groups. The short run scarcity of skills would be relieved through training, and the wages of specialists would conform to the wages of unskilled labor suitably augmented to compensate exactly for the cost of training. This type of adjustment requires, of course, competition.

exist. For instance, maximizing the rate of growth of consumption or the discounted sum of future consumption may be alternatives. More realistically, a large number of objectives may be pursued simultaneously. However, reaching full employment at the fastest rate is certainly one important goal and under certain circumstances it could be a dominating one.

If capital is the only constraining factor, the rate of growth of national income and employment depends on the rate of saving. This assumes an efficient use of resources which cannot, however, be taken for granted. If conditions favorable to competition prevailed, the market mechanism could reach the right decisions. The function of government planning would then be no more than to facilitate the mobility of factors, provide certain social services, improve the information available to decentralized decision-makers and otherwise diminish risk. But competitive conditions cannot be expected to prevail in developing economies, at least not to the extent operative in more industrialized countries. (For instance, the establishment of new industries in thin markets may directly result in monopolization.) For this reason and sometimes for ideological reasons, the governments of most underdeveloped countries directly participate in many types of market decisions.

Under ideal circumstances, government control of pricing and investment could be as efficient as competitive enterprise, and even more so, if long-run increasing returns and external economies existed. However, government enterprises would have to be operated competitively, requiring decentralized decision-making by administrators who would act as competitive (social) profit-maximizing entrepreneurs. Competition (real or simulated) requires pricing and investment autonomy; however, politicians may feel that development is too important to leave to competitive determination.

Among the primary areas of conflict between politician and economist is the problem of regional economic development. Each regional political unit within a nation wants to develop as fast as possible. Yet, in all likelihood each one is differently endowed; hence, its pattern of development and growth should be different from the point of view of national efficiency. But the political body will seldom accept such facts of life. Regional and other pressure groups exercise their frequently very considerable influence to introduce policies they hope will work in their favor, whether or not the same policies are also in the nation's interest. Thus, unemployment may be decreased in some areas at the cost of creating more unemployment elsewhere; urban food prices may be depressed at the cost of discouraging farm production; excess capacity in transportation may be created in some regions while critical bottlenecks develop in others; and the price system can be distorted to protect the nonviable at the expense of hampering the efficient. All these examples represent situations where efficient patterns of pricing and investment are violated and where, as a consequence, the nation's economic development is unnecessarily impeded.

In this paper some models demonstrating the relationship between national and regional economic growth will be constructed. Though the models are simple, they nevertheless can yield patterns of efficient price relationships, the violation of which may retard the growth of national income and employment.

Furthermore, the models are computable for many sectors and with nonlinear production functions. This is important because they can be used for the numerical evaluation of the effects of alternative patterns of consumption, investment, and other growth factors. They can also be employed for projecting the demand for those productive capacities which will not be provided by the private sector in sufficient quantities—such as transportation and social overhead capital—and which must be planned for by the government if the desired rates of economic growth are to be sustained.

Simple Models of National and Regional Growth[2]

Assume that the production of investment goods and other non-farm activities are located in well-defined urban industrial regions. All goods are produced with labor and capital, and production is subject to the law of constant returns to scale. Furthermore, the country is

[2] The models given in this section were computed with a nonlinear maximand and six sectors (including a transport sector) by Mssrs. M. Datta-Chaudhuri of the Massachusetts Institute of Technology and Frank Levy. For models of this type a very general and readily computable solution involving m sectors and nonlinear production functions is given in L. Lefeber and S. Chakravarty, "Wages and Growth," Center for International Studies, Publication No. C/64-27.

endowed with agricultural land used only partly by commercial farming. The rest is occupied by a subsistence sector which for lack of capital is unable to increase its output beyond the immediate consumption needs of its workers. Commercial agriculture can draw unimproved land from the subsistence sector and produce, with the application of capital and hired labor, farm goods for commercial disposal.

The subsistence sector is also the source of labor in unlimited amounts; the supply of labor in the classic manner of Lewis is infinitely elastic at some minimum real wage rate.[3] The rate must be such as to permit labor employed in the commercial sectors to satisfy certain basic needs at institutionally determined minimum levels as well as to provide some motivation for seeking employment outside subsistence agriculture.

To determine this wage rate one must make the simple assumption that the services of labor in the commercial sectors are "manufactured." In other words, every unit of labor employed outside the subsistence sector requires a given amount of housing, food and manufactured goods. These needed inputs are not necessarily the same in urban and rural areas; for instance, urban housing requirements may be much more elaborate than rural housing and they may, in addition, include a number of urban services.

Under these assumptions, labor is nothing but an intermediate good, and the wage rate must equal the value of the bundle of goods needed to maintain the last unit of labor employed in a particular activity.[4] Given homogeneous first order demand relationships for these maintenance services, the income of commercially employed labor must exactly match the total cost of the goods and services needed for its maintenance.

If labor is an intermediate output and its wage income exactly

[3] W. A. Lewis, "Development With Unlimited Supplies of Labour," *The Manchester School*, May 1954.

[4] I. M. D. Little made a basically similar assumption in his article, "The Real Cost of Labor, and the Choice Between Consumption and Investment," *Quarterly Journal of Economics*, February 1961. He included, however, his "consumer good" produced exclusively for labor's maintenance in the maximand of his system so that an intermediate good, for which there is no final demand, is arbitrarily weighted and maximized along with his final good. More important is his assumption concerning the savings of labor to which I shall return later.

corresponds to the cost of its consumption, then it follows that the value of the final goods and services must correspond exactly to the rents accruing to the owners of capital. I shall assume that the latter save their entire profits.[5] Hence, in any time period final demand exists only for investment goods. The output of the latter is then used in the next period to augment the capital stocks in the different sectors.

The growth process can be summed up as follows: By maximizing final output or savings one can simultaneously determine the allocation of investment, the amounts of labor needed in each occupation, and the amount of goods and services needed for their maintenance. Given the value of the maximand, i.e., final output or savings, one can repeat the process for the next year and subsequently for following years, thereby generating the growth of the economy. This can go on as long as labor is available in unlimited quantities, and forever if the rate of growth of the potential labor force is equal to or exceeds the rate at which actual employment can increase.

Economy with an Urban Industrial Center and an Agricultural Region

Assume then that investment goods are produced in the urban area with the help of capital and labor. The urban labor force requires housing and manufactured, as well as agricultural and consumer goods, for its maintenance. The rural labor force in agriculture requires similar services but possibly in different quantities. Furthermore, the production of goods and services, as well as the movement of farm goods to the urban region and of manufactured goods to rural areas, require transportation. All relationships are first order homogeneous.

Investment goods and transportation services are denoted by X^1 and X^2, and the total output of agricultural goods, manufactured consumer goods, and housing services by C^1, C^2, and C^3 respectively. Then the demand for consumer goods by urban labor (L_U) and rural labor (L_R) can be represented as follows:

$$1]\qquad D_U{}^j(L_U) = C_U{}^j, \qquad j = 1, 2, 3;$$

[5] Capitalists, of course, also present demands for consumer goods, but for simplicity's sake I abstract from them. They could be shown, for instance, by a proportionate augmentation of labor's consumption. Thus the essential structure of the framework would remain unchanged.

and

2] $$D_R^j(L_R) = C_R^j, \qquad j = 1, 2, 3.$$

The demand for transportation can be written as a function of the diverse outputs and the movement of consumer goods between rural and urban areas:

3] $$T(X^1, C^1, C^2, C^3, C_U^1, C_R^2) = X^2.$$

The demands for different goods and services must be met by production. In the consumer goods industries we have

4] $$C_U^j + C_R^j = C^j = g^j(K_C^j, L_C^j), \qquad j = 1, 2, 3;$$

and for the investment goods and transportation

5] $$X^i = f^i(K_X^i, L_X^i), \qquad i = 1, 2.$$

The distribution of the capital stock corresponds to

6] $$\sum_j K_C^j + \sum_i K_X^i \leq K(t),$$

where $K(t)$ denotes the total reproducible capital in the economy. The latter, in turn, corresponds to the capital stock augmented by investment from the previous period:

7] $$K(t) = K(t - 1) + X^1(t - 1).$$

Finally, urban labor consists of the sum of labor employed in the production of all activities excepting agriculture:

8] $$L_U = L_C^2 + L_C^3 + L_X^1 + L_X^2,$$

and rural labor corresponds to employment in commercial agriculture:

9] $$L_R = L_C^1.$$

As long as the assumption of an unlimited supply of labor holds, employment in commercial urban and rural occupations taken together must be less than the potential labor force. Denoting the latter by $L(t)$ and assuming that it is growing at an annual rate n, it follows that

10] $$L_U + L_R < L(t) = L(t - 1)(1 + n).$$

The system is solved by maximizing the output of the investment good industry, X^1, subject to relationships (1) to (10). Given the maximal value of $X^1(t)$, one can immediately proceed to the next period as described under (7). Maximizing investment implies that the economy will grow at the maximum attainable rate and, because of constant returns to scale, all other activities, including employment, will grow at the same rate. This balanced growth is attained because homogeneous capital is the only scarce factor.[6]

The exact maximal rate of growth is readily deduced. The investment good being the only final output, it follows from the principle of product exhaustion that

$$11] \qquad\qquad X^1(t) = rK(t),$$

where r denotes the rate of return to capital. Hence, the percentage rate of growth, i.e., the ratio of investment to total capital, must be equal to the rate of return itself. Thus,

$$12] \qquad\qquad \frac{X^1(t)}{K(t)} = r.$$

Since employment also grows at the maximal rate r, it follows that the time needed to attain full employment is minimized. In turn, r depends on the amount of different consumption goods which must be made available for the maintenance of labor. Hence, lower maintenance requirements will lead to faster growth and a more rapid attainment of full employment.

It is to be noted that the higher the maintenance demands of labor, the greater must be the capital intensity (capital-labor ratio) in different lines of activity at any moment of time. This is so because labor must earn its keep; i.e., it must have a sufficiently large marginal productivity to make up for its consumption. The capital intensities will differ from sector to sector; however, in a state of balanced growth, they will remain constant over time. This is so because in a first order homogeneous system the optimal capital-labor ratios are independent of scale.

If the initial distribution of the capital stocks is unbalanced, the allocation of investments will be correspondingly uneven and the rate of growth of the diverse activities will not be equiproportionate. But the

---

[6] In fact, the above model is but a special case of von Neumann type growth models and possesses all the efficient and maximal properties of the latter.

optimizing mechanism will adjust to an initial imbalance by offsetting changes in the capital-labor ratios. Then, in the allocation of investments, those activities will be favored where capital is scarce relative to the balanced distribution. In this process the capital-labor ratios adjust over time and growth of all outputs and employment approach the balanced path.

The growth path—the optimum solution in each time period—is supported by a set of competitive prices. These can all be expressed in terms of the price of the final good, which is arbitraily assumed to be unity.

As far as the use of capital is concerned, its marginal product in any one nonzero activity must equal its rent. If it is less than the rent, the activity would not be performed. Furthermore, in all activities where new investment takes place, the rent of capital must be identical and, in equilibrium, it must also be equal to the interest rate.

To ensure the optimal use of labor in either urban or rural employment, the value of its marginal product must equal its competitive or shadow wage rate. As long as unemployment exists, the shadow wage rate cannot exceed the sum of the value of goods and services needed to sustain the last unit of labor employed, i.e. the marginal cost of producing labor services. Thus, if W_U denotes the shadow wage of urban labor and $P^j{}_U$ the shadow prices of the consumer goods needed for the maintenance of urban labor, we can write

13]
$$\sum_j P_U{}^j \frac{\partial C_U{}^j}{\partial L_U} = W_U.$$

A similar relationship, which need not be spelled out, applies to the allocation of rural labor.

The above conditions relating to the optimal use of labor hold as long as its supply is infinitely elastic. Once full employment is attained, i.e., after relationship (10) turns into an equality, labor will receive an additional wage signifying its relative scarcity value. Once this stage is reached, labor is free to increase its consumption and to save; hence, the savings rate will be affected. This analysis, however, is not concerned with growth beyond the attainment of full employment.

Several Urban Industrial Centers and Agriculture

A multiregional analysis is closely analogous to the previous case, and it is not necessary to write out detailed relationships. It is worth-while, however, to point out certain problems which are introduced by the assumption of more than one urban center.

If the rate of saving from the returns to capital is less than one, there may be regional variations in the rate of saving. Hence, for the maximum attainable national rate of growth, one would have to maximize the sum of the total returns to capital in each region suitably weighted by the regional savings rates. Thus, in the allocation of investable resources, a technologically less efficient region may be pre-ferred if its savings rate is sufficiently higher than the savings rate in more efficient regions. This is a Galenson-Leibenstein type conflict between maximizing output and savings as it applies to regional al-location of resources.[7]

The solution of the multiregional system may or may not be unique. If it is unique, a simple extension of the above analysis to many regions but with different regional patterns of consumption and technology, may lead, in a state of balanced growth, to capital ac-cumulation and development only in one of the regions. With more complex extensions, such as those which involve interregional factor and commodity movements, i.e. systems where the feasibility surface is more than a simple linear combination of the final outputs of the producing regions, one can reasonably expect that a unique solution would indicate growth in more than one region. This is certainly so if homogeneous first order but nonlinear production relationships define an interregional feasibility function which in terms of commodity transformation demonstrates diminishing returns to scale.[8]

In the case of nonunique solutions there is no price system that could sustain a growth path. In such cases, within the range of indeter-minacy, it is immaterial whether investments are made in only one or, in some suitable proportion, in any of the regions. The introduction of

[7] W. Galenson and H. Leibenstein, "Investment Criteria, Productivity and Economic Development," *Quarterly Journal of Economics* (August 1955).

[8] For the derivation of such interregional feasibility functions, see my *Allocation in Space*, Contributions to Economic Analysis (North Holland Publishing Company, Amsterdam: 1958), particularly Chapter 2.

a decision function showing political or other preferences can yield unique solutions and a determinate growth path.

Policy Problems

What does the model show that is helpful for economic development policy? The most important conclusion is that deviations from the norms of the optimum will slow down the rate of economic growth and the attainment of full employment. An efficient price policy must be maintained, and economic planning must respond to the signals of the price system. This has particular relevance for the problems of regional economic development because regionalism breeds extraordinary political pressures. But an efficient price mechanism must also incorporate an adequate wage policy.

Wage Policy

For a given rate of savings from the share of capital and for given demands for the maintenance of employed labor there will be a unique growth rate. An upward shift in the demand functions will decrease the rate of growth of outputs and the rate of growth of employment. This does not mean, however, that the *level* of employment could not be increased in any one time period in response to increasing labor demands. For instance, this would be the case if wage goods were relatively more labor intensive than investment goods. But the *rate* of unemployment absorption would diminish. This may be the case in several underdeveloped countries where politically powerful urban labor obtains increasing benefits from growth while underemployment continues and frequently worsens. It is important to realize that these conclusions do not depend on ideology. The Manchester slums and the Soviet housing squeeze both contributed to the speed of industrialization.

The shadow wage rate as previously defined in relationship 13 contains the rate of change of the demand for the consumer goods weighted by their shadow prices. Inasmuch as the goods are marketable commodities and the demand relationships are homogeneous of first order, the money or market wage rate can exactly account for the shadow wage. It is possible, however, that with an increase in employment, the demand for food per unit of labor will fall (as Little has argued) perhaps because of a more favorable ratio between employed labor and unemployed dependents.[9] This may also be true for industrial goods or housing. The situation is, of course, incompatible with constant returns to scale; in fact, scale economies are implied. Under these circumstances the shadow wage rate would have to be below the market wage rate and a payroll subsidy would be required to ensure optimal hiring.[10]

The goods and services which enter the determination of the shadow wage rate may not be marketed, however, for political reasons or because they are not readily marketable. Typically, urban services would come under these headings. Many governments establish gigantic housing programs (and, in the extreme, build new cities) charging less than efficient rents to users. Furthermore, the cost of social overhead services and disservices, such as urban transport, sewerage, etc., cannot be charged directly to the wage recipient. Nonetheless, the value of the marginal product of labor in urban occupations should be high enough to cover these costs also. If the market criterion for hiring is in terms of money rather than shadow wage rates, the damage done to resource use by hiring more than the efficient amounts of labor will not be registered and the social marginal product of labor will be less than the real wage cost. In other words, urbanization, instead of aiding economic growth, may retard it. Under these conditions a payroll tax may be the proper solution, i.e., a tax which has the effect of holding down urban employment to a level where the value of the social marginal product of urban labor is not less than the sum of its money wage and the tax.

Finally, we must reiterate the fact that the optimal capital intensity (capital-labor ratio) in all occupations is a function of technology *and* of the maintenance needs of labor. It is important to recognize that

---

[9] I.M.D. Little, *op. cit.*

[10] I.M.D. Little, *op. cit.*, correctly argued the need for a subsidy under such circumstances. But he erroneously based his argument on the assumption that labor saves as the rate of employment increases—an assumption incompatible with his mathematical framework. If competition exists, the market wage must correspond to the subsistence cost as long as a reserve army of unemployed hovers in the background. Hence, if there are savings by labor, they must be due to wage rigidity or some monopolistic elements.

labor-abundant economies, in the interest of rapid growth, must not push indiscriminately in the direction of labor-intensive methods. Competition, if permitted to operate under suitable conditions, will select the most efficient capital intensities. But where the government provides goods and services, such as transportation, the danger of choosing excessively labor-intensive techniques may well be present, perhaps as a political response to underemployment.

Regional Policy Problems

Balanced regional growth is the dream of politicians. Unfortunately, the conditions under which equiproportional regional growth can also be efficient for any and all political regions are limited to constant returns to scale in all activities, as well as a suitable distribution of resources in all regions. Forcing investment into economically inefficient areas may result in equiproportional growth, but only at the expense of diminishing the rate of national growth. The level of employment may be increased in the retarded regions, but as a consequence, the rate at which national unemployment is absorbed must also decrease.

Given an efficient price mechanism, investment will not be attracted to locations where economic activity is less profitable. It can be forced to do so, however, if investment is licensed. Furthermore, if prices do not reflect marginal costs, producers will not be able to seek out locations that are also desirable from the social point of view. This may be the case if they are, for instance, unaware of the relationship between urban overhead expenditures and their location decisions.[11]

It should be quite clear that the assumption of constant returns to scale may not be the best one in the context of urban or regional development. How will urban development react to increasing and diminishing returns to scale? Increasing returns may emphasize the

[11] For instance, Paul Rosenstein-Rodan of the Massachusetts Institute of Technology has contended that the social profitability of investment in North Italian industrial regions is inferior to its private profitability. The Italian government offers incentives of direct and indirect subsidies to industrial migrants to the South; however, offering a choice between two carrots is not quite the same as a carrot and stick policy. Perhaps, if entrepreneurs would also be penalized (taxed) for the external diseconomies in their Northern location, they might be less reluctant to move to the South.

need for concentrating investment in one or a few regions. In the case of increasing returns to scale, free competition, of course, cannot bring about optimal resource allocation. But, sooner or later, diminishing returns may set in and growth may respond by spreading urban development to other geographic locations. Investment will be diverted by the gradual erosion of profitability in the older region.

Transportation Policy

Transportation is the link between geographically separated markets, whose growth can maintain a balance only if transportation is provided in efficient amounts and at efficient rates.

Efficient pricing of regionally separated activities requires that the difference between the prices of homogeneous goods at different locations should not exceed the marginal cost of transporting these goods. In other words, if the difference equals the marginal cost of transportation, an interregional commodity flow will take place. If the rates charged for transport services do not reflect long-run marginal costs, interregional trade will not be efficient. If they are larger, socially profitable trade will be diminished; if they are smaller, socially unprofitable movements will be induced. In the first case, inefficiencies of the autarchic type must result. In the second case, there will be excessive demand for transportation services, the satisfaction of which results in the waste of scare resources. In either case economic growth must suffer.

Decentralized decision making, if applicable, should bring about efficient transportation development. But there may be reasons to assume that private enterprise cannot push transport investment to an efficient level. First, there are the technical economies which are external to transportation. These undoubtedly exist, but because of lagged responses and usually high interest rates I do not attach much importance to them. Second, and this I consider more important, the private risk of investing in the fixed transportation plant (but not rolling stock) is very high. This is so because the initial capital needed is usually large, while the estimation of potential demand is very difficult. Faced with higher risk, private capital may shy away from investing socially efficient amounts. Third and equally important, is the possibility of monopoly control in transportation.

The force of the underinvestment and monopoly argument disappears if the government provides the fixed plant, and decentralized units invest in rolling stock as well as provide the services. This is, of course, not feasible with railways but can be the case with road and water transport. Then competition can ensure an efficient utilization of the plant as well as efficient pricing of the services.[12] All other things being equal, this is a powerful argument for basing development on road and water transportation rather than on railways.

In contrast with private enterprise, public transportation investment may be excessive. Paradoxically, this can happen even in instances where transportation appears to be a bottleneck. Underpricing of transportation services induces an unbalanced increase in the demand for transportation. This is so because entrepreneurs base their market decisions on monetary rather than real costs. If the price of transport services does not reflect long-run marginal costs, the choices of industrial location will not reflect the true costs with respect to transported inputs and goods. Also, the efficient use of locally available inputs may be by-passed in favor of less efficient substitutes which require transportation.

For a monopolist, discrimination by value may have justification if excess capacity exists. But it is undesirable from the social point of view.[13] Because it encourages excessive flows of bulk commodities and distorts the choice of location, it induces in the long run a greater demand for transportation than required to maintain efficiently a given rate of economic growth. Hence, increased amounts of scarce resources must be allocated to transportation or a bottleneck must develop. In either case the rate of growth will be adversely affected.

---

[12] The fixed plant should have zero rent if excess capacity prevails. Crowding —measured in terms of time and accident costs—indicates the need for a user's tax which is the rent of capital. If this rent is comparable to that of other investment, expansion is in order. If expansion is lumpy (excess capacity is created), the rent or user's tax after expansion must again be zero (cf. Harold Hotelling's bridge case in "The General Welfare in Relation to Problems of Taxation and of Railway and Utility Rates," *Econometrica*, 1938, p. 242). The actual financing must be based on neutral taxation. From this point of view, technologies which more readily permit capacity graduation are preferable. (Conversations with transportation engineers indicate to me that highways, in this respect, are more flexible than railways.)

[13] Discriminatory pricing is justified only in directional terms: the marginal cost rate on backhauls may be lower than on movements in the forward direction.

Distortions caused by inefficient transport policies are to some degree irreversible. Badly located plants are there to stay and may attract further ill-located investments to their neighborhood. The longer the inefficient policies are maintained, the greater will be the geographical and technical distortions and the heavier will be the burden on the transportation system. But irreversibility has a meaning only in the short run. Introduction of efficient policies should motivate regional growth toward balanced development. The demand for transportation is inelastic in the short run; hence, rate adjustments are feasible. If necessary, temporary subsidies can be used to mitigate the shock. In the long run, however, more efficient choices of location and improved selection of inputs and technology will tend to correct initial distortions.

Conclusions

Regional economic growth has been analyzed in the context of a labor surplus economy and with an emphasis on the criteria for efficiency. Efficiency is not a goal in itself; it is a requisite companion of the highest attainable rate at which a national economy can grow and unemployment can be absorbed. Competitive pricing and investment policies will lead, if conditions are favorable, to efficient patterns of national and regional growth.

Regional economic policies can be subject to heavy political pressures and the conditions for competitive pricing may not be present. This absence can be remedied by implementing the pricing mechanism with suitable subsidy and tax programs. This should typically be the case with transportation development and in other instances where increasing returns, risk, and external economies may be important.

As to politically motivated distortions in investment and pricing policies, the economist can do no more than warn about the excess costs of inefficient methods of subsidization. Disregard for efficient pricing and investment policies slows down the rate of growth of the economy and the attainment of full employment; hence, the goals of a program for economic development may be jeopardized.

VII

Transportation in Soviet Development

HOLLAND HUNTER*

In the long drama of Russian modernization, trans-
portation has played a leading role. Her rivers, and later her railroads,
have been on stage throughout Russian history. In this review, however, only a few scenes of the play can be sketched, as seen from only
one of several possible vantage points. Transportation under Soviet
auspices, especially during the 1928-1940 period of forced-draft industrialization under Stalin, will be the subject. These were the years of the
Soviet "big push." The economy was given the strength to withstand
Nazi invasion and a base was laid for subsequent maturation. While no
other country is likely to duplicate exactly the circumstances that
faced Soviet decision-makers in these years, the Soviet record is
nevertheless illuminating. It may suggest a few general lessons, both
positive and negative, concerning the role of transportation in economic development. At the least, it can identify a few questions that
will bear reflection as programs are formulated for the development of
other economies.

This chapter focuses on three major policy issues. The first and
broadest is: how much transportation capacity is needed to promote
rapid economic development? The second concerns the forms of transportation to be expanded: which did the Russians choose, and why?
The third issue relates to the demand for transportation: what regional
pattern of industrial expansion is best from a transportation—and
overall—point of view? In discussing these issues, I draw on the
evidence in my 1957 study of Soviet transportation policy, to which
the reader is referred for underlying detail.[1] Here only summary judg-

* Haverford College.
[1] *Soviet Transportation Policy* (Harvard University Press, 1957). The analysis
is carried further in Ernest W. Williams, Jr., *Freight Transportation in the Soviet
Union* (Princeton University Press, 1962).

ınents are offered. After some background for the three issues is
filled in, section II sets out ten lessons from the Soviet record. Section
III goes on to a series of linked reflections growing out of Soviet experience. Since the reciprocal relations between the transportation
sector and the development process extend over space and over time
in a variety of intricate ways, our judgments must match them in
complexity. What follows is a first approximation to a connected set
of observations, each placing limits on the others.

Issues on Which Soviet Experience Sheds Light

A familiar Western view places low-cost transportation at the very
center of the forces that have stimulated Western economic growth.
The rise of Great Britain, the expansion of Western Europe, and the
growth of the United States are all ascribed in no small degree to
innovations in cheap maritime and overland transport. This historical
experience has led to an impression that the provision of low-cost
transportation capacity is both a necessary and a sufficient condition
for economic development. During the nineteenth century and up into
the 1920's, Russian leaders followed precisely in this accepted tradition
of economic policy. Railroads had acted as the bellwether of the
Russian drive toward industrialization.

How Much Transportation for Development?

Since the mid-1920's, however, the U.S.S.R. has made transportation a secondary sector of the economy. Its share of national investment funds has been cut drastically in favor of heavy industry.
Transportation capacity has been expanded only in response to actual
or impending traffic bottlenecks. Except for railroad lines built to tap
specific resource deposits, few Soviet transportation projects have been
built ahead of demand to stimulate subsequent economic development. Soviet efforts were focused on heavy industry; resources were
diverted into expanding transportation capacity only when this was
clearly necessary for expanded industrial production.

Was this Soviet policy for transportation a sensible one? Has it
proved successful? The questions are deceptively simple, and answers

are not easy to find. Yet the effort is surely worthwhile. Today countries do not feel able to wait for the leisurely unfolding of economic development consequent on the provision of generalized transportation capacity in advance of demand. For one thing, rapid population growth calls for rapid expansion of production if per capita living standards are not to fall. Many other sectors besides transportation lay claim to investment funds, and the grandiose visions of nineteenth century railway promoters are now replaced by a decidedly frugal approach in plan-making and aid-giving circles. All this suggests that the Soviet record should be of considerable interest to those concerned with current economic development policies.

Which Modes of Transportation Should Be Expanded?

The choice of carriers for transportation expansion of course reflects each country's geographic potentialities. It also depends on technological possibilities and their relative costs at the time that basic decisions are taken. One forgets, perhaps, that the fundamental decisions which have shaped Soviet industrial growth were taken almost forty years ago, when several modern forms of transportation were in their infancy. On both counts, Soviet experience may have only limited relevance for other economies. Yet reflection on Soviet experience is valuable for its demonstration of railroad potentialities not exploited in the West, and for its evidence on the relation between specific policy purposes and specific modes of transportation.

Engineers and politicians in developing countries appear to look for tested methods in technological advances, and the Russians were no exception. Specifically, Soviet advisors in the 1920's paid relatively little attention to long-distance trucking as a means of freight transportation. Their outlook was still that of the nineteenth century, when railroads were contending with inland and coastal waterways as the chief means of freight transportation. Forty years ago intercity truck movement would have been prohibitively expensive. Political leaders seem to have had even more antiquated tastes, as symbolized by Stalin's fondness for canal building. In 1952, two and one-half centuries after Peter the Great proposed the project, Stalin finally completed a canal joining the Volga and Don Rivers (its traffic since then has not matched expectations). But in so northern a country, freezing cuts the availability of internal waterways to an extent that cripples their competitive standing. In practice, except for canals, Soviet policy has favored railroads over waterways for transportation expansion, with relatively minor attention to highways and pipelines. Countries developing in the 1960's have open to them very different technological possibilities.

Soviet expansion of transportation capacity was also shaped by the regime's concern for freight traffic rather than passenger movement. The general public understandably focuses on conditions of passenger travel, but in the Party's scheme of priorities, heavy industry ranked far above consumer welfare, including passenger transportation. Clearly any economic development program must give primary attention to the movement of raw materials and fabricated output, though regimes less Draconian than Stalin's may be less willing than he was to skimp on expansion of passenger transportation capacity. But a stress on heavy industry narrows the emphasis still further. Neglect of diversified light industry means that fuel, ores, building materials, and a handful of similar freight categories will dominate the flow of traffic. These are precisely the kinds of freight for which railroads have pronounced advantages over intercity trucking. Moreover, as we shall see, Soviet location policy tended in the same direction, since it generated concentrated flows of heavy freight among a limited number of industrial complexes. (See map on page 141.)

How Should New Industrial Capacity Be Regionally Distributed?

The Soviet regime launched its industrialization drive with several concrete locational objectives. The first was national self-sufficiency. Russia's previous links with Western Europe were to be severed so that the U.S.S.R. could be economically independent of hostile capitalist powers. In harsh and extreme form, this approach was a continuation of Count Witte's aims some three decades earlier.[2] The second objective was also a continuation of Tsarist dreams: to develop the "fabulous riches of Siberia." The Trans-Siberian railway had opened large territories to development; now dozens of projects for extracting minerals, felling timber, and using the arable land awaited implementation. There was also a strong political consideration. Industrial development in the Urals, Siberia, Central Asia, and the Caucasus

[2] Theodore H. von Laue, *Sergei Witte and the Industrialization of Russia* (Columbia University Press, 1963).

would, it was argued, speed the advance of the peoples of outlying regions who had previously suffered exploitation or neglect at the hands of St. Petersburg and Moscow. These predominantly non-Russian ethnic groups were the special concern of the Commissar of Nationalities, J. V. Stalin, whose rise in the 1920's drew much of its Party support from the provinces.

Prerevolutionary industrial growth had centered in the north around St. Petersburg and Moscow, based on imported machinery and raw materials, combined with a nascent urban labor force, to supply local markets. In south European Russia an iron-and-steel complex had taken shape in the eastern Ukraine and an oil industry had appeared in the Transcaucasus. Now the thrust of Bolshevik objectives was still further extended beyond the established centers in European Russia. The Party's eyes were directed toward northern European Russia, toward the Caucasus, toward Soviet Central Asia, and especially toward the frontier domain stretching from the Urals some 4,500 miles to the Pacific. Pioneer railroad lines had already been extended into these territories, but many additional lines were projected to support their industrial development.

The effect of expanding industrial capacity in Siberia and other outlying areas was initially—and perhaps paradoxically—seen as relieving rather than increasing the pressure on transportation capacity. Industry would develop at or near the sources of its fuel and raw materials. These heavy, weight-losing inputs would thus not have to be shipped for thousands of kilometers from the East or South to St. Petersburg (renamed Leningrad in 1924) and the factory towns around Moscow. Instead, fabrication would take place where the rich natural resources were located, and only the manufactured product would require shipment back to the current centers of population. Analytically, the approach was entirely consistent with the location theory of Alfred Weber, whose views carried great weight in the 1920's.[3]

Thus Soviet locational intentions when the era of Five-Year Plans began were summed up in slogans that called for developing industry more evenly throughout the U.S.S.R. and for moving industry closer to the sources of raw materials and fuel. Readers familiar with the development programs of countries in Asia, the Middle East, Africa, and Latin America will recognize the ubiquity of both notions. To the

[3] Alfred Weber, *Theory of the Location of Industries*, translated with an Introduction and Notes by Carl J. Friedrich (University of Chicago Press, 1929).

extent that minerals and coal tend to be found in mountains rather than arable plains, the geographic tendency is necessarily bound up with an expanding share of nonagricultural activity in a formerly agricultural economy. Since the locational problem appears to have these universal aspects, the fate of Soviet locational objectives in the period since 1928 may serve to point up certain general implications.

Ten Lessons Suggested by the Soviet Record

In dealing with the issues sketched above, Soviet authorities have produced a most interesting record. Though times change and countries differ, Soviet experience can illustrate both dangers and opportunities for countries now seeking rapid development. The complex record is of course subject to varying interpretations; the following summary judgments are not yet part of a tested structure of accepted historical analysis. Undogmatically asserted and cautiously pondered, however, the lessons may prove instructive.

1. *Traffic Bottlenecks Are a Danger During a Takeoff.*

The first lesson, in time if not in importance, arises out of the freight transportation crisis that hampered Soviet industrial expansion for three or four years in the early 1930's. It is that traffic bottlenecks are a danger during a crash program to develop heavy industry. Traffic increments running beyond expectations might logically be associated with growth in a decentralized market economy; it is perhaps discouraging to note that the same phenomenon can arise under central planning. Soviet transportation officials gave ample advance warning of the danger, and the crisis was minutely studied as it progressed. Despite both foresight and understanding, however, the freight traffic bottleneck of the early 1930's seriously hampered Soviet industrial expansion, contributing not a little to the disorganization and turmoil of the period.

With the benefit of hindsight one can readily visualize a reallocation of current and capital inputs that would have reduced or eliminated the freight traffic bottleneck and generated instead an orderly sequence of output expansion. Whether such a rearrangement of policies would have been practicable or not is a rather intricate issue in Soviet economic history. In either case the implication for all who are concerned with economic development planning is clear: the freight traffic requirements of a growth program deserve careful scrutiny. On Soviet railroads the backlogs of unshipped freight were especially large in building timber, coal, iron ore, and (occasionally) grain. The planners evidently underestimated the amounts of basic inputs that would be needed, being overly optimistic regarding rates of utilization, and thus underestimated the demands that would be placed on the carriers. In a specific future situation the commodity groups involved might well differ from those under special pressure in the U.S.S.R. thirty years ago, but the prospect that input coefficients will be higher than planned, thus leading to unplanned freight traffic demands, is worth careful review.

The difficulties that have developed in moving coal and iron ore on Indian railroads evidently reflect unanticipated traffic increments perhaps somewhat reminiscent of Soviet experience. While the underlying operating details may in fact be substantially different in the two cases, the appearance of the phenomenon after a decade of careful Indian planning evidently reinforces the view that the danger of traffic bottlenecks should be called to the attention of all planning officials.

2. Transportation Growth Requires Efficiency Gains and Added Capital.

A second lesson of Soviet experience concerns the way the transportation crisis was overcome. For several years the regime had insisted that the railroads could handle sharply increased traffic mainly through more efficient use of their existing plant and equipment. Notable gains in operating efficiency had in fact been achieved. But the unshipped backlogs were not worked off, and the system's capacity was not brought up to match overall demand, until substantial additions had been made to the railroads' plant and equipment. Simultaneously the railroad labor force was enlarged and upgraded. Major efforts were made, not only to retrain railroad workers, but to reorganize railroad administration, break out of traditional operating routines, and stimulate a spirit of competitive vigor at all levels of railroad operation. If the record shows that more intensive utilization, without large additions to capital plant and equipment, could not meet enlarged demands, Soviet experience also suggests that large-scale capital expansion would not have achieved the desired results without these simultaneous gains in labor productivity and operating efficiency.

Improvements in the way motive power, rolling stock, and line capacity were utilized had a great deal to do with Soviet success in mastering rapidly growing freight traffic. Potential gains in this direction were, however, overestimated for the first few years. With large injections of more advanced locomotives, freight cars, and line equipment, further marked advances in operating effectiveness became possible. Precise transfer of this experience to other railroad systems is unlikely, yet the important lesson is that progress in the transportation sector results from reciprocal interaction between improvements in capital and improvements in all the human and organizational factors that combine to determine its effectiveness.

3. Transportation Capital-Output Ratios Need Not Be High.

A third lesson of Soviet transportation experience is that capital-output ratios in this sector of the economy need not be high. Western records have made it appear that transportation capital is very expensive in relation to its annual output of service; average capital-output ratios around 6 or 7 to 1 have been reported.[4] The experience of Soviet railroads shows conclusively that with intensive utilization, both average and incremental capital-output ratios can be in the neighborhood of 3 or 2 to 1. This should be welcome news for planners seeking to allocate scarce capital funds and conscious of the need for enlarged transportation capacity.

The key to the contrast between Western and Soviet experience lies in the intensity with which transportation capital plant and equipment is utilized. Western railroads in recent decades have typically operated with substantial excess capacity compared to theoretical engineering maxima. In addition, operating practices in relation to shippers and receivers, railroad labor, and the traveling public all reflect a willingness to use capital lavishly where convenience and safety could thus be served. Under Soviet conditions, by contrast, the existing railroad plant, together with reluctantly provided capital additions, was made to supply a huge volume of freight traffic service at the expense of both convenience and safety. Mass railroad shipments often meant higher production costs for shippers and receivers forced to handle intermittent bulk consignments. Intensive operations on crowded lines

---

[4] See, for example, the figures in Wassily Leontief and others, *Studies in the Structure of the American Economy* (Oxford University Press, 1953), p. 215.

raised the frequency of accidents and wrecks. Clearly, other countries might not wish to pursue measures of this sort as far as Stalin did. Customer convenience and labor safety are important. Nevertheless, where development capital is exceedingly scarce, it would seem that capital plant and equipment in the transportation sector should be more intensively utilized than they have been in the West.

Recent studies by the National Bureau of Economic Research have shown that capital-output ratios in the American economy have generally declined substantially compared to their level in, say, the 1880's. The average capital-output ratio for United States railroads, in particular, has declined from around 16-to-1 in 1880 to less than 3-to-1 in the 1950's.[5] High ratios in the early years arose from building expensive indivisible plant ahead of traffic; as the volume of freight traffic grew, the average capital-output ratio fell rapidly. Still, the contrast between Soviet and American railroad practice persists. An economic development planner might well argue that pioneering transportation investment in a preindustrial economy must necessarily resemble late nineteenth century U. S. railroad investments more than it can resemble Soviet transportation investments of the 1930's. If so, one could expect a ratio above 10, say, instead of a ratio below 3. For some projects this will surely be true. The planning issue, however, concerns the extent to which railroads (or roads) should be built ahead of traffic, and the extent to which less expensive and indivisible forms of plant and equipment can be used. Here Soviet experience is clearly relevant and, on the whole, encouraging.

4. Rapid Industrial Growth Conflicts with Industrial Dispersion.

For reasons both political and economic, Soviet leaders in the middle 1920's sought to develop industry in the outlying portions of the U.S.S.R., especially in the East. The so-called Ural-Kuznetsk Kombinat, designed to join the rich iron ore of Magnitogorsk in the southern Urals with the coking coal of the Kuznetsk Basin in Western Siberia, was a central feature of the first Five-Year Plan.[6] Growth in Soviet

[5] Melville J. Ulmer, *Capital in Transportation, Communications, and Public Utilities: Its Formation and Financing* (Princeton University Press, 1960), especially chapters 4 and 6.

[6] Franklyn D. Holzman, "The Soviet Ural-Kuznetsk Combine: A Study in Investment Criteria and Industrialization Policies," *Quarterly Journal of Economics* (August 1957), pp. 368-405.

Central Asia was to be spurred by construction of the Turkish-Siberian railway, which would bring Siberian wheat to districts which could then specialize in growing irrigated cotton, thus freeing the U.S.S.R. from dependence on imported cotton. Copper, bauxite, tin, nickel, and gold deposits in various parts of non-European Russia were slated for large-scale development. In this way the outlying areas would be brought up to the level of the Center, their share of the nation's industrial output would rise, and industry would be located more equitably and rationally over the whole territory of the U.S.S.R.

The record since 1928 has demonstrated, however, that rapid industrial growth as a policy objective conflicts with spatial dispersion of industrial activity. During the 1930's, and again since World War II, industrial capacity has grown rapidly in European Russia. In the Eastern Ukraine, around Moscow, and around Leningrad, existing plants were enlarged and new facilities were built. Evidently planning and production officials, charged with bringing additional capacity into operation quickly and cheaply, found decisive advantages in old locations as against pioneer territories on the edge of the economy. Existing social overhead capital, together with a more attractive climatic and social environment (better able to hold a labor force than the harsh conditions of the East), proved an irresistible magnet. After 1937 the Party and government sought to forbid further industrial expansion at major centers in European Russia, but with little success. The pressure for quick results was evidently stronger than the ostensible hopes of the authorities. This aspect of Soviet experience would appear to provide an instructive confirmation of the dilemma that Albert Hirschman has identified as "the North-South problem."[7]

5. Net Regional Shifts in Economic Activity Come About Slowly.

A fifth lesson of Soviet experience concerns the consequences of this conflict between rapid industrial development and regional dispersion. Under these conditions, net regional shifts in economic activity take place rather slowly. Absolute growth in outlying regions has of course been impressive and percentage gains over time have been remarkable. Simultaneous growth in European Russia, however, has meant that its preponderant share of total Soviet industrial production has de-

[7] Albert O. Hirschman, *The Strategy of Economic Development* (Yale University Press, 1958), pp. 187-195.

clined very gradually. Even today, after thirty-five years of planned growth, European Russia continues to account for over 70 percent of Soviet industrial production, as shown in the accompanying table. Moreover, major efforts have been made in recent years to enlarge the fuel and resource base in European Russia, close to existing industrial concentrations, thus demonstrating a partial collapse of the early ambitions.

TABLE VII-1. *The Changing Pattern of Industrial Production, 1927-28 and 1960*

(In percent of total USSR industrial production, by region)

	1927–28	1960[a]
Northwest RSFSR and Belorussian SSR	16.1	11.6
Central RSFSR	41.6	22.1
Ukrainian SSR	19.1	22.2
Volga Valley and Caucasus	13.9	17.6
Subtotal, "West"	90.7	73.5
Urals	4.1	10.8
Kazakh SSR	0.9	2.7
Soviet Central Asia	2.9	3.5
Siberia and Soviet Far East	1.4	9.5
Subtotal, "East"	9.3	26.5
TOTAL USSR	100.0	100.0

Sources: 1927-28 estimates from Gosplan SSSR, *Piatiletnii plan narodno-khoziaistvennogo stroitel'stva SSSR*, 3rd ed., Vol. III (1930), p. 584. 1960 estimates from Paul K. Cook in U.S. Congress, Joint Economic Committee, *Dimensions of Soviet Economic Power* (1962), pp. 704-731. Approximate matching and aggregation of regions carried out by Alan Abouchar, making use of IA. G. Feigin, *Razmeshchenie proizvodstva pri kapitalizme i sotsializme*, 2d ed. (1958), pp. 407-408 *et passim*.

[a] Within pre-1939 boundaries (approximately): that is, excluding the three Baltic SSR's and the Moldavian SSR, but including annexed parts of Ukrainian SSR, Belorus SSR, and RSFSR.

Western observers, and geopoliticians particularly, might learn from this record to attach a substantial discount to the glowing publicity that continues to embellish Soviet plans for eastward expansion. Ever since 1928, plan documents have read as though the Soviet East were about to equal or surpass the old centers. Uncritical Western commentary has retailed these glowing visions without anticipating the extended time lag that occurs before pioneer installations are completed, and without noticing the intervening growth of long-established centers. Perhaps the lesson has broad applicability to all developing areas: raising the share of outlying regions in an economy's overall output is likely to be a gradual process.

6. Politicians Need Slogans; Economists Need Rules.

The experience of the Soviet transportation sector, especially the railroads, under central planning suggests an important procedural lesson for development planners. Soviet plans have been hortatory. They exhort and goad all participants to improve their performance and achieve demanding targets. To this end, the guidelines issued by the Party have been slogans embodying the rallying cries of the moment.

In Soviet experience, moreover, the Party's slogans have frequently obscured the real issues of efficient resource use. Wise planning decisions and rational operating methods require coherent rules addressed to the unavoidable need for hard choices. Yet properly qualified statements may be insufficiently galvanizing, and may provide excuses for those resisting change. In that case, the urge for change will override the need for precision. For example, the basic Soviet principle for location decisions has been: place industry closer to raw materials *and* to markets, blandly ignoring the intricacies involved in seeking an optimum where markets and raw materials are geographically scattered. In the first two Five-Year Plans, the Party espoused huge new plants, whose production costs would be low, but when the third plan was issued, this policy was condemned as "gigantomania," and the men who had carried it out denounced as "wreckers." Railroad traffic planners have had the Party's backing for 25 years in a campaign against "irrational, excessively long, and cross hauls," though the conditions under which such shipments might be desirable for the economy have never been carefully specified. Perhaps the lesson is that efficiency criteria for economic performance must be somewhat blurred and distorted by the political requirements of campaigning for rapid progress.

7. Taut Plans Require Jaundiced Insight.

A similar lesson emerges from comparisons between Soviet operating plans and actual events. The annual plans which govern production and transportation generally stretch each producing unit between ambitious output targets and stringent input supplies. In the case of Soviet railroads, freight traffic targets were in fact optimistically *under*stated. The regime regularly hoped that other carriers would assume an increased share of the traffic, and that traffic growth would only be modest. At the same time the plans regularly promised substantial additions to railroad plant and equipment to handle the added traffic. In practice, however, the railroads have generally been forced to carry more traffic than the plan called for, and to carry it, moreover, without all the promised additions to their capacity. The lesson is therefore not only that events will not conform exactly to plan, but that harried production administrators will probably need to develop jaundiced insight into the degree to which their "internal reserves" are likely to be exploited.[8]

8. *State Ownership Will Not Automatically Unify a Transportation System.*

The eighth lesson of Soviet transportation experience is that state ownership does not automatically bring unified operation of the transportation system. It was expected that the rivalry and duplication that have marred the Western transportation record would give way to a smoothly coordinated system under Bolshevik management. In particular, it was hoped that joint shipments, using river or canal or coastal vessels wherever possible, would somewhat relieve the hard-pressed railroads and make full use of each carrier's inherent advantages. In practice, shippers and receivers have shown what one railroad official ruefully called "hydrophobia" in their reluctance to use water transport where railroads were available. The reasons are not far to seek. In latitudes matching those of Canada, internal waterways are frozen from three to nine months each year. Water movements are frequently much slower than rail shipments. For some commodities, water shipment requires more careful packing than rail shipment does. Most important, transshipment involves delays and expenses that can be avoided through all-rail movement. For all these nonideological reasons, three decades of exhortation have failed to prevent a decline in the share of total freight traffic carried by water carriers, and failed to promote the joint use of rail and water carriers.

As freight-carrying automobiles became available in the U.S.S.R., they displaced horse-drawn vehicles in local cartage and took over

[8] For further discussion, see my "Optimum Tautness in Development Planning," *Economic Development and Cultural Change* (July 1961), pp. 561-572.

some of the railroads' local traffic around major junctions. Trucks also came to play an important role in bringing agricultural produce to a nearby rail station. Intercity trucking, however, has not developed. Thus the great issue of modern freight transportation in countries like the United States, the United Kingdom, and India, has not yet been confronted in the Soviet Union. The reasons are not entirely clear, though one can identify several relevant considerations.

First, the regime has not permitted a latent desire for passenger automobiles to stimulate a national program of highway construction. Without adequate roads and adequate supplies of fuel distributed over the countryside, industrial enterprises could rarely use trucks to obtain or deliver even their highest-priority supplies. Second, under these conditions truck shipments over any appreciable distance have been very much more costly than rail shipments. The typical Soviet truck is still a two-and-one-half ton or five-ton open-top vehicle, and, for shipments of any appreciable size, it cannot compete with a railroad box car over long distances. Third, the relative neglect of agriculture, light industry, and consumer goods has brought with it a neglect of the intercity trucks that carry such freight in other countries. Resourceful Soviet citizens have for some time carried oranges from the Caucasus to Moscow in passenger aircraft, or vegetables from collective farms to nearby cities in passenger cars, for lack of a developed long-distance trucking service.

To date, therefore, rail-highway competition has been averted in the U.S.S.R. A perennial campaign to shift short-haul shipments in major centers from railroads to trucks continues, but long-haul traffic (if it cannot be shifted to internal or coastal waterways) will remain on the rails. State ownership, it must be admitted, has to this extent succeeded in preventing duplication of facilities, and thus made a step toward a unified transportation system.

9. The Soviet Tight-Rations Policy Has Succeeded, and Yet . . .

Since 1928 Soviet authorities have, as we have seen, consistently kept the transportation sector of the economy on tight rations, squeezing a maximum of services from it with grudging allocation of inputs to it. The policy has been designed to promote the rapid development of heavy industry and national defense. Has the policy succeeded? Crude historical evidence suggests that it has. The Nazi invasion was repulsed. Industrial and military power have attained massive dimensions. In the three decades since the transportation crisis was overcome, Soviet transportation (meaning essentially the railroads) has contributed impressively to Soviet success. The lesson would therefore appear to be that other countries would do well to imitate the Soviet tight-rations policy toward the transportation sector.

A refinement of this tentative judgment would, however, be desirable. Soviet methods of intensifying the use of railroads laid appreciable costs on shippers and receivers. It may well be that the U.S.S.R. went too far, that some of the cost-reducing benefits to railroads were more than counterbalanced by cost-raising difficulties for shippers and receivers. Clearly more generous allocations to the railroads between 1928 and 1934 would have prevented the capacity bottlenecks of 1930-1934, with consequent benefits to heavy industry and the economy at large. But even since 1934, it is possible that the provision of transportation to industry on more generous terms would have more than paid for itself in contributing to industrial expansion. Intricate research will be required to test the hypothesis, but even now the rough record suggests that other countries should exercise caution in probing the limits of a tight-rations policy toward the transportation sector.

10. *Soviet Regional Development Appears to Have Been Sensible, and Yet . . .*

A final lesson of Soviet experience grows out of appraising Soviet location policy. Here the U.S.S.R. found it expedient to develop industry around established centers though ostensibly the Party was calling for a decisive shift toward the East. The "second iron and steel base" in the Southern Urals and Western Siberia grew more slowly than intended, and a host of projects for outlying areas remained on the shelf. Nevertheless by 1941, when Hitler attacked from the west, the Soviet economy proved able to withstand the invasion. Roughly one-third of Soviet industrial capacity was occupied by the Nazis, yet stocks and facilities in unoccupied European Russia and farther east (along with supplies from the United States and the United Kingdom) were able to turn the tide. In recent years outlying regions have seen the regime's long-standing promises being fulfilled.

The indicated lesson is thus that a springboard policy of developing old centers in order to gain the wherewithal for launching new regions has demonstrated a certain practical success. This unintended Soviet practice developed despite doctrinal rhetoric to the contrary. One notes also that pragmatic Soviet actions have been roughly consistent with the stern logic of allocative efficiency as expounded, for example, by Professor Lefeber in Chapter VI of this book. Where resources are very scarce and speed is important, "Marxist" practice and "capitalist" theory may actually occupy common ground.

Evaluation of Soviet industrial location and transportation policy requires further research. It is true that the Soviet approach has shown itself to be a viable one. We have no assurance, however, that alternative policies for regional allocation of investment in expansion of industrial and transportation capacity might not have led to smaller transportation requirements associated with the observed bill of goods, or produced a larger bill of goods than had been obtained by 1940. Planners in other countries seeking an optimum development path can learn more from the Soviet experience if it is subjected to systematic numerical comparison with alternative paths. Research designed to throw light on this issue is currently under way at Brookings.

Further Reflections on Soviet Transportation

Three lines of speculation extend beyond the conclusions that have been briefly set forth in the preceding section. One concerns the influence of transshipment costs in determining industrial location and the fate of various carriers. The second involves the possible future influence of containers on an integrated transportation system. The third relates to the impact of population density on transportation and location policy in a developing economy. Each is in the nature of a tentative comment arising out of an attempt to discern the broad relevance of Soviet transportation experience to the role of transportation in economic development.

Multi-carrier Movement, Transshipment Costs, and Industrial Location

Why are multi-carrier shipments difficult? The answer, I believe, is that transshipment is expensive. Line haul movement is cheap in comparison. The costs of transshipment are not merely those of unloading freight from one carrier and loading it on another. The time required for the journey is likely to be noticeably increased, and speed may be very important to the consignee. Not infrequently the dangers of pilferage rise notably as commodities pass from one carrier to another. Fabricated commodities may suffer breakage, and raw materials may suffer attrition in one form or another during transshipment. The paperwork covering a shipment becomes more complex as more than one carrier gets involved. For all these reasons, joint shipments are likely to be at a disadvantage in competition with through service if one carrier can provide it.

One response to the problem historically has been to take advantage of the necessity for transferring freight between carriers by processing the commodity at transshipment points. Manufacturing has tended, for this reason among others, to develop at transshipment points. Transshipment costs have thus had an important bearing on past industrial location. But perhaps the appearance of the container will remove this constraint. An interchangeable sealed container can be readily transferred from one carrier to another without the difficulties listed above. It follows that some types of industry, at least, can to this extent become footloose by comparison with earlier days. Other locational factors, like water supplies, can have more influence.

The Attractiveness of Containers

Recent developments in container technology appear likely to contribute to a unified transportation system whether it is under state or private ownership. The universal container is an extremely flexible transportation instrument.[9] It can pass rapidly from a highway truck to a railroad flat car, a river barge, the hold of a trailer ship, or even a large aircraft. The cost of rolling or lifting containers from one carrier to another is very low in comparison with the costs of older transshipment methods. Sealed containers are relatively nonpilferable, well protected against moisture, and easy to handle gently. They make it somewhat easier than before to handle a consignment over several carriers by a single bill-of-lading.

For all these reasons, containers may go far to solve the transshipment problem. In the U.S.S.R., experimental use of containers for railroad shipment of consumer goods began in the 1930's along the lines

[9] See descriptive analyses in *Railway Age* (July 22, 1963), pp. 16-26, and (August 26, 1963), pp. 19-27.

then being followed in the United Kingdom. In the postwar period the stock of containers has grown and handling facilities equipped with cranes, storage depots, etc., have been enlarged. As yet the use of tractor-trailer or semitrailer units is only in an experimental stage. Instead of trailer-on-flat-car service, the Russians may develop a container service that would shift containers from a flat bed truck trailer to a railroad flat car and back (or lift it into a ship or aircraft). For certain kinds of traffic, then, a unified transportation system would emerge.

Technological solutions to the transshipment problem would of course help other countries too. American railroads can display their inherent advantages in long-haul freight carriage, letting trucks handle the initial and final steps in a door-to-door transportation sequence. Bulk commodities already move between water and rail, or pipeline and water, with increasing efficiency. Thus from raw materials up through highly fabricated output, modern technology enables development planners to contemplate a multicarrier transportation development program to an extent not heretofore practicable.

Population Density and Industrial Location

The record of Soviet economic development contains much evidence of interest for all students of development. Nevertheless we should remind ourselves of its peculiarities. We are not here concerned with its special political features. A purely geographic point deserves emphasis, however, especially in relation to location and transportation issues.

The U.S.S.R., like the United States, has been relatively sparsely settled, with ratios of population to natural resource supplies that have been highly favorable for economic development. On the other hand, many low-income countries are, like India, densely settled, with unfavorable ratios of population to arable land and other resources. The contrast may have decisive significance for location and transportation policies.

Densely settled regions can get economies of scale in production with plants whose output will be distributed over a relatively short radius in the surrounding territory. This can be true especially for activities related to agriculture. By contrast, the giant Soviet plants built between 1928 and 1937 often distributed their ouput from one

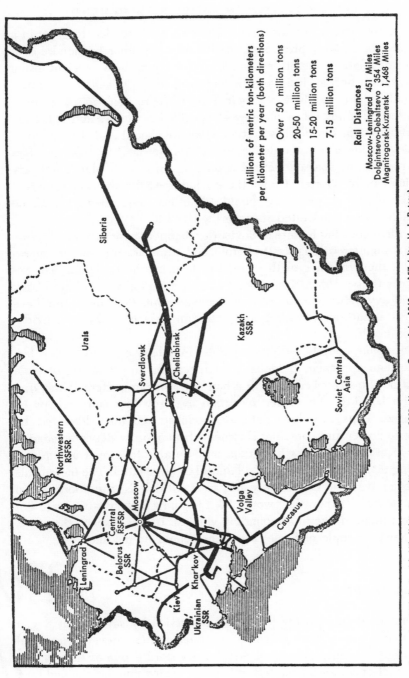

Millions of metric ton-kilometers
per kilometer per year (both directions)

▬▬▬ Over 50 million tons
▬▬▬ 20-50 million tons
▬▬ 15-20 million tons
▬ 7-15 million tons

Rail Distances
Moscow-Leningrad   451 Miles
Dolgintsevo-Debaltsevo 354 Miles
Magnitogorsk-Kuznetsk 1,468 Miles

Siberia

Urals

Sverdlovsk

Cheliabinsk

Kazakh
SSR

Northwestern
RSFSR

Soviet Central
Asia

Central
RSFSR

Moscow

Volga
Valley

Leningrad

Belorus
SSR

Caucasus

Khar'kov

Kiev

Ukrainian
SSR

DENSITY OF FREIGHT TRAFFIC ON THE RAILROADS IN 1955

Source: Igor' Vladimirovich Nikol'skii, *Geografiia transporta SSSR*, Moscow: Geografgiz, 1960, p. 157 (after V. I. Petrov).

end of the country to the other. Soviet industry tended to grow in a handful of major centers, separated from each other by hundreds of miles of relatively empty economic space. Where heavy weight-losing inputs are not a decisive consideration, densely settled countries should be able to distribute their industry more uniformly over their territory. For any set of plants with specified capacities and unit costs of production, the densely settled economy should find it possible to achieve a lower average delivered cost for finished commodities than is open to the sparsely settled economy, since each plant's delivery radius can be shorter. Under these conditions the share of resources used up in transportation should, all other things being equal, be smaller than in the United States or the U.S.S.R.

A distinguishing feature of Soviet development policy for thirty years was a singular willingness to permit and stimulate rural-urban migration without much growth in urban social overhead capital. The resources thus withheld from social overhead capital were plowed back into heavy industry. Only recently have attempts been made to relieve intense urban overcrowding and catch up on a large list of long-deferred needs.

But again, densely settled economies may have open to them a less Draconian approach. If factories with reasonable economies of scale need not be so concentrated in a handful of major centers as was true in the U.S.S.R., the degree of urban overcrowding can perhaps be reduced. Especially for relatively footloose activities, liberated by electric power and container shipments from narrow dependence on a few locations, countries like India may be able to spread new plants among many towns instead of a handful of large cities. The increments in social overhead capital necessary to avert Stalinist conditions would then be smaller than they would be if the new factory labor force did not continue to live in surrounding villages. In this respect, therefore, the harsh example of Soviet experience could be modified.

Conclusions

One could sum up the preceding discussion by saying that Soviet experience shows how frugality in transportation development can contribute to rapid industrialization. The record is one of success, not failure. Respect for Soviet performance is, if anything, heightened by a recognition that planning has not proved to be a magic key to optimum solutions. Furthermore, nationalization, while it may have shifted questions to different offices, has not provided elegant and efficient answers to the basic questions in this field. Soviet planning methods and operating procedures in the 1928-1940 period were crude. Advances in programming techniques should enable currently developing economies to plan and manage the development process with less cruelty and waste of resources than the U.S.S.R. has experienced. Moreover input-output and linear programming methods are receiving extensive development at present in the U.S.S.R.; their application to the Soviet economy can thus facilitate (though it cannot guarantee) more humane and efficient economic performance in the U.S.S.R. as well.

VIII

Regional Development Policy

MITCHELL HARWITZ*

Extreme inequalities of personal income and
wealth are familiar problems in underdeveloped countries. Almost
equally well known are differences in the rates of return on various
activities.[1] In many underdeveloped countries these differences express
themselves geographically, too. For instance, the phenomenon of the
dual economy, so often discussed in the literature on economic development, can result in an enclave of relatively high incomes that is just as
distinct geographically as it is industrially. In physically large countries,
like Brazil or Nigeria, the past economic growth of the nation frequently
involved the imposition or reinforcement of sizeable regional differences in income and wealth.

The political systems of underdeveloped economies have not been
insensitive to these inequalities. Short-run considerations of equity and
the simple facts of political life in representative governments have led
politicians to try to equalize incomes geographically. Their policies often
take the form of transport investments and/or preferential rate policies.
Such policies may be justifiable on their economic merits. Whether
they are or are not often seems immaterial to the political leaders who
formulate them.

The subject of the present paper will be a method of implementing
an equalization policy that does as little harm as possible—in a sense
to be clarified later—to the general economic interests of the country
fostering the policy. The approach assumes that an equalization policy,

* State University of New York at Buffalo.
    [1] The form of the statement is deliberately loose. One hesitates to attribute the
return to the factor income of some specific factor, in view of present debates
as to the relative importance of human versus nonhuman capital and the importance of the extent of the market.

144

in more or less explicit form, is being pursued. It also takes as given that the statistical information available in the developing economy is rather limited. Specifically, it is assumed that the data are insufficient to provide a basis for a long-run, dynamic optimizing model in regional form. Thus, a useable short-run approach that relies not upon time-series data but mainly upon observations in a single year will be presented. The statistical assumption is of first importance as a justification for the entire procedure.

Another rather specialized feature of this approach is the treatment of the role of planning by government. Aside from the obvious limitations imposed by the presumed lack of data, the author takes a view that apparently—though not actually—assigns a more limited role to government than is usual in the literature on economic development. Very broadly, the government: (1) produces public goods which cannot be priced in the market (e.g., defense) and "political" goods such as education; (2) produces other goods and services on a competitive basis, as if its enterprises were private; and (3) produces transportation services, which are neither public nor, necessarily, produced on a competitive basis. Finally, the government may have reason to regulate the prices of certain primary commodities, as will be suggested later.

Otherwise, the government is assumed to be a "price taker" in the specific sense that, in the absence of a dynamic, optimizing program of some sort, it does not presume to impose prices on capital and other durable goods. It takes domestic or world market valuations as given in these cases, except insofar as tariffs are imposed on imports or taxes on exports *without* specific justification from a dynamic program. Such a procedure can be faulted on the grounds that the results might not be "optimal." But since this approach is based on the assumption that an "optimal" result is not available because of lack of information, the point is moot.

The fundamental idea of the approach taken herein is to obtain a characterization of the "productive" sector of the economy; that is, both the private sector and state producing agencies acting "privately." The assumption is that this sector either is, or should be, competitive so that the characterization involves the basic assumption that any equilibrium of the productive sector is, or should be, a competitive equilibrium. The final assumption is that the technology of the productive sector (other than that of the transportation "industry") is linear and, therefore, exhibits constant returns to scale with no internal or external economies or diseconomies. This is an assumption that would be hotly debated by many economists. However, one is forced to it on computational grounds. The model is rather large-scale, and all such models are probably forced by limitations of data and computing equipment into a constant-returns, no-externalities format. Later, this paper will explore briefly the implications of assuming that there is an error in this specification of the model.

Broadly, then, the desired model may be described as follows: a linear, many-commodity, many-region model of the productive sector of the economy, that can be compiled from one year's data and then computed. The purpose of the computations is to evaluate the responses of the productive sector to the government's transportation policies, on the assumption that "competitive" equilibrium is maintained in the sector. The problem is to learn, with the limited data at hand, whether or not there is a tendency to regional income equalization, and, if there is not, to learn which government policies, if any, will change the current trend. If political considerations dictate that some such changes *must* be made, what is the "cheapest" way to accomplish them? The present model is a step toward an answer.

On Regions in Underdeveloped Countries

One of the great insights of theoretical economics is the idea that, when a commodity is not produced in a particular place, the reason is that it is unprofitable to produce it there and not necessarily that it is impossible to do so. This notion is central to the approach to regions and regionalization used here. Several other assumptions are made: (1) In characterizing the technology of the productive sector, there is but one output from each productive process. (2) There is but one way to produce each output. This last assumption is not necessary in the formal analysis and is actually made only because it is difficult to obtain enough data to characterize alternative processes. (3) Finally, many resources (that is, nonproduced goods and services) are immobile between regions. Given these three assumptions, one can expect that some areas of a multiregional economy will be highly specialized in production as a consequence of differences in resource endowments among the regions. The degree of regional specialization at any moment in time will then depend on the degree of variation in resource endowment, and the change in specialization over time will depend on the ways in which the passage of time renders resources mobile between regions.

As a consequence of this point of view, there is another assumption that might seem flatly unrealistic: namely, that the same productive processes *could* be used in all regions if it were profitable to do so. For example, one could argue on this basis that the reason for the present heavy concentration of industry in southeastern Brazil lies in its relatively abundant stocks of natural and produced resources, in comparison with those of other regions of the country. This "common technology" assumption is associated with another, less obvious, one: that firms in the productive sector are national in scope in the sense that they can locate in any region and buy and sell in any region. It follows from this assumption that single regions need not have zero balances on current account in their trade with other regions, since there is a built-in mechanism for the transfer of indebtedness within the country.

A final group of assumptions relates to the sectors engaged in foreign trade. Since most underdeveloped economies are very much "open" economies, foreign trade is possible. However, only some of the regions can engage in such trade—namely, the regions with ports. The movement of imports into other regions and the movement of exports into the "port" regions will be subsumed under internal interregional trade. Further special aspects of trade, in particular the pricing of imports that are not produced domestically, will be dealt with during the exposition of the model.

The Model and Its Setting

In an underdeveloped country with a significant foreign trade sector and limited statistical resources, one can expect that the strongest sources of statistical information are those connected with the pricing and production of exports and with importation. Time-series information on the behavior of demand for consumption goods and capital goods and on the national income may be very limited. In such a case, one can expect that a "convulsive" statistical effort could produce sound national income figures for a base year, the rudiments of an input-output table for that same period, and various special kinds of current price data in addition to those produced by the foreign trade sector. A certain amount of additional effort can probably generate data from government and private sources on the costs of moving various classes of commodities from place to place in the economy. Finally, information on current rates of output by region in nonagricultural activities should be relatively easy to compute from such government sources as tax returns and the raw materials of the investigation into the national income. This, then, is the statistical setting of the model.

The goal of government planning, in this situation, is to use these limited data in such a way as to be able to consider intelligently the feasibility and soundness of proposals to equalize regional incomes. The central idea of the examination is this: by assuming that the "productive" sector and the transportation sector operate as if they were competitive and have a "linear" technology (constant returns to scale), one can use computers to describe "efficient" relationships between the prices of "final" goods and those of resources and transportation. This allows one to examine the relative prices of various resources in different regions, to predict in a loose way the responses of the productive sector to these relative prices and, finally, also to predict (loosely) the effects of changing various prices and costs that are under government control, e.g. transport. The approach used here amounts to the substitution of assumptions ("competitiveness," "linearity") for information, in the hope that many assumptions plus some data will yield hints about actions that can be taken while more data accumulate.

The goods and services that enter the model fall into two categories of use and two of source: final and intermediate use and produced and nonproduced by source. In any fixed period of time, a good or service may have both uses but not both sources. As a matter of terminology, I shall refer to goods and services generally as "commodities." Nonproduced commodities will be called primary commodities or "resources." Labor is a resource, as is coal in the ground. Consumption goods and capital goods have final uses, but capital goods may also have intermediate uses. Transportation, insofar as it is considered a distinguishable commodity, would have intermediate uses when it is used to transport other commodities and final use when it is used for pleasure trips. The distinction between resources and other commodities, it should be noted, depends on the time period under consideration. Capital goods, for example, are primary commodities in the very short run, since the available quantity cannot be changed within a brief period. Ultimately, however, they are producible. Exportation is an intermediate use, and imported goods may have final or intermediate uses. Neither type of commodity is primary. Imports can, in fact, be regarded as "produced" by exports, which provide the foreign exchange needed to buy the imports.

The final uses of produced goods are the *raison d'etre* of the productive sector. They are the items that enter Gross National Product (gross national income at market prices) in a standard income accounting framework. In planning terminology, they are also the items that enter the "objective function" that is to be maximized. The underlying idea in the assumption of competitive behavior in the productive sector is that a competitive productive sector, given the prices attached to final uses of commodities, operates so as to maximize the value of its final outputs at the given prices, within the limits imposed by the technology and resource availabilities. In more traditional utilitarian language, the competitive productive sector acts as if it were a computer designed to maximize a social utility index. This index is a linear function of the quantities of each commodity available for final use, the coefficients of the linear function being the given prices.[2]

Before describing the model, one last point should be clarified. Why deal with a model in which the objective is apparently to maximize the value of net output of the *productive* sector? Surely, a more reasonable approach would be to maximize the national product, including the value of output of "public goods" and other goods, such as education, that do not enter the market. This more general approach may be logically acceptable, but application of the general optimizing condition requires an evaluation of education and other "politically controlled goods relative to outputs of the productive sector. The evaluation must be independent of the cost of producing the "political" goods. Thus, it would be necessary to have prices for such goods and services in order to include their values in the objective function. These prices are seldom measurable in underdeveloped countries, but, even if they were, political realities probably would not allow for the use of such

[2] Robert Dorfman, Paul A. Samuelson, and Robert Solow, *Linear Programming and Economic Analysis* (McGraw-Hill, 1958), Chapters 13, 14; T. C. Koopmans, "Analysis of Production as an Efficient Combination of Activities" in T. C. Koopmans (ed.), *Activity Analysis of Production and Allocation* (Wiley, 1951).

measurements. Instead, one must assume that the government is prepared to produce certain quantities of these commodities and to purchase the necessary inputs on the open market out of tax revenues. On such an assumption, the model predicts the behavior of the productive sector in response to changes in government policies about "political" commodities and certain prices.

To make some of the basic economic ideas as clear as possible, the discussion will proceed in two stages. It will begin with a simple model dealing with the production of a single homogeneous final commodity in various regions. Then the useful intellectual "juice" will be abstracted from this case, and the general model will be considered. In this way, the use of a programming model as a *predictive* device can be made more clear.[3]

The data needed to develop and use the transportation model for the single good are as follows:

a. division of the economy into producing and consuming regions;
b. money costs of producing and transporting a unit of the good from each producing region to each consuming region;
c. demand per unit of time in each consuming region;
d. capacity to produce, per unit of time, in each producing region.

For this application, demand is fixed and independent of delivered price. The assumption will be abandoned later, so there is little need to discuss it. The introduction of "capacity," a concept that will be used a good deal, requires more extensive examination.

A linear economic model of the sort used here can be envisaged as a collection of "activities" each of which can be operated at any desired level of intensity. The word "linearity" embraces the assumption that one can learn everything there is to learn about an activity (except its absolute scale) by observing it at a representative level of intensity. Consider, for example, the activity of producing one unit in region 1 and shipping it to region 2. In this very simple model, all that is required to carry out the activity is the ability to produce in region 1. In more general models, one would of course require various inputs of other goods and services. But in either case, there is ap-

[3] Reference to the technical aspects of the models can be found in the works already cited and in Harold W. Kuhn and Albert W. Tucker (eds.), *Linear Inequalities and Related Systems* (AMS 38, Princeton, 1956), especially pp. 183-193.

parently nothing intrinsic to the process that limits the level of output. Intuition suggests that, at least in the short run, there is something wrong with this view. One might suggest that in the short run (by definition) certain required factors of production are available to an industry only in limited quantities. For example, a certain kind of capital equipment may be a "limitational factor." This essentially technical limitation is embodied in a limit on the level of intensity of the given activity. The limit is expressed as a constraint on the capacity to produce. Insofar as the constraint is binding, it will generate a quasi-rent above and beyond any factor payment embodied in the money cost of production and transportation that is used in the criterion.

The criterion to be minimized is the total money cost of production and transportation. The problem is to deliver at least enough to each region to cover demand, without requiring more than any region can supply, at total minimum cost. The dual of minimizing the criterion is to maximize the total value of deliveries less quasi-rents (which I shall henceforth call "rents") attributable to capacity limitations. Each activity operated at the unit level of intensity requires as input one unit of capacity in the region of production and delivers as output one unit at the region of consumption. The formal model is presented and discussed in Appendix I.

In essence, the model can be used to compute production in each region and reveal the entire pattern of trade among regions by using data on costs, demands and capacities, all under conditions of the short run equilibrium of a perfectly competitive industry. The initial responses of the productive sector to possible government policies can also be computed. Insofar as government policies have predictable effects on such parameters as production costs, transportation costs, and regional demand, the ranking of regions according to rents can be computed on the basis of a given set of policies. It is demonstrated in Appendix I that this ranking corresponds to a private industry's ranking of sites in terms of profitability, so that the movement of new capacity can be predicted on this basis. This will serve as an indication of the kinds of policy the government ought to follow, given a criterion such as maximizing the value of the output of the productive sector.

The one-commodity transportation model is clearly too limited to be used as an approach to the calculation of valid development policies or to the evaluation of transportation's role in these policies. Even a generalization in the direction of many final goods is insufficient. For example, the possibility that it would be profitable to make apple sauce in a region leads also to other possibilities that need to be considered: the making of apple sauce machines and the raising of apples, for example. A model that is general enough to be really useful ought to consider intermediate uses of commodities as well as purely final uses. Furthermore, capacity limitations are really not the only constraints on output that ought to be encompassed by the model. Even though there is some interregional mobility of primary factors, limits on factor supply are very important in many industries. Finally, exports and imports for the whole economy have to be considered.

The first step in the generalization is to note that activities that produce a unit of output in one region for delivery to any region (different or not) will use various quantities of nonproduced and produced goods in the process. The economy of a region can thus be visualized as a collection of activities that produces goods for final or intermediate use, either within the region or in another region. It requires goods for final or intermediate use that may be supplied from the region itself or from another region. It follows from this characterization that limitations on total output will arise not only from short-run capacity constraints but also from the requirement that sufficient inputs must be available in a region to support its total level of output.

The computation of costs of production and transportation presents difficulties in a general model that simply did not arise in the single-commodity example. In the simpler case, it was correct to assume that the cost of production was independent of the pattern of trade. This is clearly not the case in a general model. The cost of a unit of output that uses ten different inputs, eight of which can be imported, depends on the prices of the inputs in the region where they are made and the cost of transporting them to the region where they might be used. On a more general level, one could conceive of the observed money cost figures in a one-commodity model as representatives of real social costs, while such a conception may be invalid in a model that is supposed to embrace all the activities of an economy. In such a model the costs of produced goods cannot all be given from outside the system.

These problems suggested two different approaches to generalization. The first, which is due to A. P. Hurter and is discussed in detail elsewhere,[4] develops a cost-minimization model that minimizes the total cost of primary input requirements at observed prices of these inputs. Thus, observed prices of certain nonproduced goods are assumed to measure the social costs of production of all other goods in terms of their direct and indirect requirements of primary goods. The prices of all goods produced in the economy are actually computed in the course of solving the dual linear programs associated with the model.

The second approach takes the view that the prices of commodities in final uses are to be taken as given, all other prices being computed by the model. Actually, since the economy is open, I assume that world market prices for both imports and exports are given, along with domestic prices for the final uses of commodities. However, these export and import prices function less as money prices than as "production coefficients" specifying the terms on which units of exports can be converted into units of imports. For this reason, I speak of "given prices" only with reference to the final uses of commodities. The maximand of the primal problem, therefore, is the value of domestic production for productive sector consumption and investment (including desired inventory change), plus imports for these uses, plus given government requirements. The formal model is presented and discussed in Appendix II.

Interpretation and Use of the Model

To see the ways in which the larger model can be used to examine government policies, recall first the basic principle of interpretation given in the small, single-commodity example. The model provides a relatively convenient, detailed description of the short-run equilibrium of the economy; not, in this instance, of a single industry, but of the entire productive sector, which is made up of private competitive firms and government enterprises behaving competitively. The equilibrium is stated in terms of an observable set of prices given from outside the problem: in particular, domestic and foreign prices are given, and the equilibrium is described with these as the prevailing prices. This is

[4] M. Harwitz and A. P. Hurter, "Transportation and the Economy of the Appalachian Region" (Transportation Center Report No. 66, Research Division, The Transportation Center at Northwestern University, August 1964), pp. 47-59.

the technical meaning of my earlier remark that in using this model the government acts essentially as a "price taker" rather than as a price maker. One exceedingly important consequence of taking observed prices as given is that the relative valuations of consumption and investment implied in the observed price system are taken as given. It is practically a cliche in development literature that the free market may produce the wrong relative valuation in such cases. But there appears to be no way to compute an alternative set of prices in the statistical circumstances specified earlier. So the analysis proceeds on what may be an incorrect "equal-ignorance" hypothesis.

Another important characteristic of the short-run equilibrium described by the model (a characteristic that has very important effects on its comparative-statical properties) is that the transportation sector is "linear." Whether the sector is assumed to be run by the government, by private firms, or by both, a crucial aspect of the description is that there are no economies of scale in transportation. There are various other features normally associated with the relation of unit transportation charges to size of shipment (mixture of items in the shipment, number of stops to discharge, etc.) that are also slighted, but these are hard to specify at the statistical level of this model. They are not nearly as important as scale economies in any case.

What if there are economies of scale in transport? What effect has this on the usefulness of the model as a predictor of the effects of government policies? Assuming that the description of the initial short-run equilibrium state is reasonably accurate, the effect will be that the costs of transportation should vary from the initial figures as the pattern of shipments changes, simply because of changes in the volumes shipped. Since growth is of primary concern here, the particular error that may be introduced is that the current unit costs of transportation, which should decline as shipments increase, will be assumed in the computation of the results to remain constant. This would amount to saying that the model will give conservative estimates of the increase in productive-sector output achievable through increases in capacity to produce or in resource availability. At the same time, an attempt to compute the capital costs of given improvements in the cost of transportation would give too high an answer unless the scale economies were accounted for.

There are various ad hoc ways to make adjustments for these inaccuracies. However, these methods tend to require considerable special knowledge and research into the cost structure of the transportation sector. Perhaps the best that should be done at an early stage is to note that the results of the computations would tend to be conservative and to allow for this in evaluating policies. Finally, the presence of economies of scale means that, even if the description of the current pattern of costs and shipments is fairly accurate, the transportation sector cannot break even at the computed prices. If the model were an entirely satisfactory linear approximation to a nonlinear technology in all other regards, it must necessarily produce a total income for the transportation sector less than the total costs of the sector. This simply reflects the fact that an efficiently run, increasing returns industry ought to be losing money in an (otherwise) efficient competitive equilibrium.

With these two provisos very much in mind, I turn finally to a listing of the policy problems that can be put to the model and, hopefully, answered for the short run. The basis of the analysis is the fact that the model provides prices for immobile resources and productive factors, and, therefore, points to those regions where the long run should see inflows of factors of production seeking high returns. The result of the initial computation is a description of the activities of the productive sector, by region, on the assumptions listed in so much detail about technology, competition, etc., and on the assumption that the government has made up a budget for its activities that involves purchase of factors of production and other commodities in open, competitive markets. There will presumably be considerable regional inequality in level and type of economic activity.

The goal of government planning is that the income of the productive sector is to be maximized provided that current government plans for the production of public goods and "political" goods can be carried out. The first thing that can be checked is the regional distribution of government purchases. The rate of change of productive-sector income with respect to a change in some government requirement can be calculated, as can be the rate of change of income with respect to a change in government purchases of a produced commodity. Using these results, government planners can try to distribute the total of government requirements among regions in such a way as to interfere as little as possible with the achievement of maximum output by the productive sector.

The second step is to observe the rents on capacities by region and the rates of remuneration of resources by region. If areas of relatively low income show relatively high returns to certain kinds of capacity and certain resources compared to other regions, it may reasonably be expected that the productive sector itself will produce movements tending to reduce the regional inequalities. However, some of these scarcities will not be of the kind that private initiative can correct easily in underdeveloped countries. In that case, the model provides a suggestion as to the particular resources that need to be supplied in relatively backward regions to induce the productive sector to initiate new activities in the regions. It may be discovered in the course of such an analysis that the regional inequalities of income cannot easily be reduced by these methods. It is possible that relatively backward regions are so disadvantaged by a combination of meager resources and costly transportation that the model suggests that they should simply empty out. This means that the government planner will try to raise income in the particular region only at the cost of running counter to the short-run tendencies of the productive sector. Since the model can provide no justification for such a policy, the best that can be expected from applying it to this situation is the "least unfavorable" method of raising income by subsidizing, directly or indirectly, those activities least unprofitable to the productive sector. It should not be hard to see that the entire thrust of the model is in the direction of requiring a very strong justification for such a procedure.

Finally, the role of changes in transportation costs and tariffs (positive or negative) must be considered. The short-run increase in productive-sector income arising from changes in transportation costs can be computed, at worst by solving the model anew and at best by a step-by-step procedure of the kind suggested earlier. The question then is whether the change is worthwhile in terms of connected necessary changes in government requirements for commodities and resources. The model gives a conservative estimate of the comparison between the costs and the income benefits of the change. If such an estimate passes a minimum "rate-of-return" test, then I should judge that the actual results will be more profitable even than the model predicts. If the test is not passed, the situation might be examined further. In the spirit of the model, the first approximation to the correct rate of return is the prevailing rate of return on capital investment. It is important to note that this test does *not* require that the return accrue to the transportation sector. The effects of changes in tariffs and export taxes can also be computed, since these represent changes in prices. There are various ways for the government to obtain a given level of revenue from such taxes. The purport of the model is to choose the way that maximizes the value of productive-sector output.

On Sources of Data and Other Problems

All the previous discussion of the interpretation and use of this efficiency model has been based on the implicit assumptions that the model was completely disaggregated and that the input coefficients were strictly technical relations. Needless to say, there is not enough data available to estimate the coefficients at this level of disaggregation and no computer big enough to handle the model if the data were available. The coefficients that could be estimated would necessarily be in the "dollar's worth" form used by Wassily Leontief and his associates in their studies of the American economy:[5] estimates of the value of purchases from each industry group per dollar of the value of output of each industry group. Fortunately, aggregation does not apparently make any difference in the use of the model. It simply means that the model undergoes a special transformation based upon the price parameters given from outside the model. If there are any doubts about the results, they would then arise in terms of the accuracy of the estimated prices. This is a familiar problem to economists, one they have learned to live with if not to solve. The appropriate operational principle would seem to be that disaggregation should be pursued where error is most costly. The application of this idea will be noted below.

Once it is assumed that there must be considerable aggregation, the remaining problems are those of collecting enough information to use the aggregated model. The research budget of any agency likely to apply the technique will be limited, so certain broad principles of allocation of expenditure on research have to be laid down beforehand. The most obvious rule is the one mentioned just above: allocate any given budget in such a way as to minimize the cost of error. If one knew at the start the relative importance of the various kinds of data, the rule would be easy to apply. But of course one cannot have such prior knowledge. The best that can be done a priori is to make an intelligent guess about the relative importance of the data and then proceed as if the guess were correct.

[5] *Studies in the Structure of the American Economy* (Oxford University Press, 1953), pp. 150-152.

The data actually needed to use the model fall into four broad categories:

1. prices;
2. input-output coefficients related to production;
3. input-output coefficients related to transportation;
4. capacity and availability measurements related to production, transportation, and primary goods.

The relative importance of these categories as areas of research depends on one's assumptions about the importance of the factors determining each region's trading position. If it were assumed that technological advantages and disadvantages are paramount, the most important requirement would be input-output coefficients for each region. If it were assumed that costs of transportation are most important, accuracy in these measurements would be required. Finally, if capacities and resource availabilities were assumed to be the dominant short-run influence, measurements of these parameters would take precedence. My own belief is that the second and third of these three assumptions are generally of far more interest than the first, and that the third is most important for many underdeveloped countries.

There has been no mention of problems connected with the measurement of prices mainly because this kind of measurement has been the subject of more successful effort than any of the other areas of interest. Price data are surely available on a regional basis if the other data are.

The measurement of capacities is especially difficult. In principle, resource requirements and the input costs of movement are observable, and in practice one may expect reasonably good approximations if one is prepared to spend money. But it may be argued that capacity, though observable, cannot be measured reliably even in principle. It may be asserted that the maximum flow rate of output from any process (the definition of capacity that is used in this model) is determined only on the basis of depreciation, maintenance, and other policies that vary so much from firm to firm and time to time that any estimate is necessarily unstable. That is to say, even a firm-by-firm survey will necessarily produce an estimate subject to influences that cannot be measured, like "the business atmosphere." To the degree that this argument is true, the hypothesis that capacities are empirically important would be a most difficult one to test. On the other side, the limited size of the industrial sector of many underdeveloped countries may make it possible to obtain better estimates of "capacity" for the purposes of this model than are available at similar cost in more developed economies.

Another area of interest is the measurement of "resource availability." There are problems of definition here. Since resources are assumed to be immobile in the short-run, coal below the ground is a resource while coal at the minehead is not. This point is an example of a case in which the technical definition of resource is too narrow. An industry like coal mining, which surely seems to be an industry exploiting a resource, might have to be classified as an industry with a capacity limit instead, because of the mobility of its raw product and the vertical integration of its productive processes. More important than the problems of definition are gaps in data that might be crucial.

One of the major shortages of many underdeveloped countries is a scarcity of "human capital." The use of a model of the kind suggested herein properly directs the attention of statistical agencies in underdeveloped countries to a really serious effort to evaluate the character of the labor forces in various regions. It is a shocking fact that no agency in the United States collects such information on the U.S. labor force. No poor country can really afford this kind of gap in its information.

Conclusion

A static general equilibrium model which could be employed to evaluate programs of regional economic development has been presented. While the use of this system involves substantial data acquisition requirements, these are not so burdensome as to invalidate this approach to development planning. Certainly more formal techniques than those currently utilized merit consideration, since the present methods permit the planner neither to evaluate the efficiency of past decisions nor the potential effectiveness of future ones. Models like this one represent systematic attempts to enforce evaluation of the over-all effects of policies and to pinpoint important areas of ignorance. Hopefully, this type of model will help to ease the burdens of those responsible for planning and those who must suffer the consequences of poorly conceived development programs.

Appendix I. One Commodity—Many Regions Static Equilibrium Model

Notation used:

$_{ij}C$ = money costs to produce a unit of the good in the i-th region (I producing regions) and move it to the j-th region (J consuming regions);

$_{j}B$ = demand per unit of time in each consuming region;

$_{i}A$ = capacity to produce in each producing region;

$_{ij}X$ = level of intensity of the activity of producing in region i and delivering to region j, or, quantity produced in region i and delivered to region j per unit of time;

$_{j}P$ = delivered price in region j;

$_{i}R$ = rent of capacity in region i.

The minimizing problem (usually called the "primal" problem in this case) is

(1) minimize $C = \sum\limits_{i=1}^{I} \sum\limits_{j=1}^{J} (_{ij}C)(_{ij}X),$

subject to

(2) $\sum\limits_{j=1}^{J} {}_{ij}X \leq {}_{i}A,$ $\qquad i = 1, \cdots, I$

(3) $\sum\limits_{i=1}^{I} {}_{ij}X \geq {}_{j}B$ $\qquad j = 1, \cdots, J$

and

(4) $_{ij}X \geq 0$ $\qquad i = 1, \cdots, I$
$\qquad\qquad\qquad\qquad j = 1, \cdots, J.$

The nonnegativity requirement on each $_{ij}X$ is simply a requirement of meaningfulness. It is assumed implicitly that total capacity

$$\sum\limits_{i=1}^{I} {}_{i}A, \text{ exceeds total demand, } \sum\limits_{j=1}^{J} {}_{j}B,$$

so that there is at least one real solution.

The maximizing problem that is dual to this minimizing primal is:

(5) maximize $V = \sum\limits_{j=1}^{J} (_{j}P)(_{j}B) - \sum\limits_{i=1}^{I} (_{i}R)(_{i}A)$

subject to

(6) $_{j}P - {}_{i}R \leq {}_{ij}C$ $\qquad i = 1, \cdots, I$
$\qquad\qquad\qquad\qquad j = 1, \cdots, J$

and

(7) $_{j}P, {}_{i}R \geq 0$ $\qquad i = 1, \cdots, I$
$\qquad\qquad\qquad\qquad j = 1, \cdots, J.$

160

Expression (6) requires that there be no positive profit on any activity, after rent is deducted.

The important feature of this construction is that it allows one to compute production in each region and the entire pattern of trade from data on costs, demands, and capacities. Furthermore, the dual variables, which also arise from the computation, can be given an interesting and useful interpretation. To make this quite clear, let us review a few theorems on linear programming. Suppose the dual problems (1)–(4) and (5)–(7) have been solved for certain numbers, $_{ij}\overline{X}$ $_j\overline{P}$, and $_i\overline{R}$. Then:

(8) (a) $\overline{C} \equiv \sum_{i=1}^{I} \sum_{j=1}^{J} (_{ij}C)(_{ij}\overline{X}) = \sum_{j=1}^{J} (_j\overline{P})(_jB) - \sum_{i=1}^{I} (_i\overline{R})(_iA) \equiv \overline{V}$;

(b) If $\sum_{j=1}^{J} _{pj}\overline{X} < {_p}A$ for $i = p$, say, then $_p\overline{R} = 0$;

(c) If $_q\overline{P} - {_p}\overline{R} < {_{pq}}C$ for $i = p$ and $j = q$, then $_{pq}\overline{X} = 0$.

Thus, if one regards $_{ij}C$ and $_i\overline{R}$ as unit costs that are, respectively, paid out by firms and attributed to limitational factors as rent, (8a) states that total revenues must be completely allocated to costs or rents. Proposition (8b) says, essentially, that no activity carried out in a region with excess capacity should generate positive rent. Proposition (8c) is the sensible theorem that if revenue, $_q\overline{P}$, is less than all costs, $_{pq}C + {_p}\overline{R}$, then the "unprofitable" activity must be operating at zero intensity. It should therefore be clear that these dual programs can legitimately be interpreted as a description of the short-run equilibrium of a perfectly competitive industry with inelastic industry demand curves.

Furthermore, the direction in which the equilibrium should change can also be suggested. It can be shown that the saving of total cost (the change in $\overline{C}$) that would result from a small increase in one capacity (say, $_pA$) occurs at the rate of $-{_p}\overline{R}$ per unit of increase in capacity. This theorem has to be stated in "rate-of-change" terminology because its validity requires that the contemplated change in capacity be strictly less than the *smallest* quantity shipped in the optimal solution. Using this version of the theorem, one can rank the regions according to the rents accruing to capacity in the region.

Consider the situation of the industry when it can shut down capacity already in existence and add new capacity wherever it is profitable to do so. If demand in each region remains constant, then the first units of new capacity will be placed in the region where the highest rent is being recorded. In effect what is happening is that units of capacity that have no locational advantage or are relatively old are being shut down in favor of units that are newer or better located with respect to a given demand pattern. As capacity is shut down in a region, its shipments are reduced by the same amount.

One may visualize this process in terms of the addition of new capacity one unit at a time. Eventually, the number of units of new capacity must be large enough to reduce to zero the shipments from a region where capacity is being shut down. Until this happens, the rents, $_i\overline{R}$, remain fixed, even though the shipments, $_{ij}\overline{X}$, are changing. However, once one of the shipping links between regions falls to zero, a new pattern of shipping links has to be computed (technically, a new basis has to be found), and when this is done there will be new values for $_iR$ and $_jP$ in the new solution. As the industry continues to seek a long-run equilibrium, new capacity will be placed in the region with the highest rent generated by the new shipping pattern.

Note how this procedure is useful as a device for predicting the behavior of the productive sector. Suppose that the government plans to improve the transportation system linking one region to various other regions. What consequences can be expected to flow from this act? First, a theorem dual to the one just stated can be used. If the cost of transportation from region p to region q is reduced, from $_{pq}C$ to $_{pq}C'$, the saving in total cost will be $(_{pq}C - _{pq}C')$ times $_{pq}\overline{X}$, if the basis is unchanged by this change in the cost parameters. However, the ranking of regions according to rents accruing to capacities located in the region may change. The new ranking can be computed by solving the problem with the new cost, $_{pq}C'$, taken as a datum, and one can then predict the direction of change in capacity according to this new ranking.

One must point out at this stage that there are several unsettled mathematical questions connected with the analysis suggested above. The theorems actually stated therein are true, and have been proved. However, certain other questions of great interest for computational or planning purposes are quite unsettled. For example, suppose one asks: "What is the largest cost-saving achievable from the addition of a given number of units of capacity?" The problem is soluble in a finite number of computations simply by solving the dual programs a sufficient number of times. But it is not possible at this point to prove whether or not the step-by-step process outlined earlier will arrive at a correct solution, though it is believed that it will. Furthermore, suppose one were to construct a graph of cost-savings as related to number of units of capacity added, starting from the solutions $_{ij}\overline{X}$, $_i\overline{R}$, and $_j\overline{P}$. It is known that the initial rate of saving is the highest of the $_i\overline{R}$. As noted above, the basis must change eventually, and new rents, say $_iR'$, will arise. It is not known whether or not the largest of the $_iR'$ is necessarily smaller than the largest of the $_i\overline{R}$. As a result, computationally convenient attacks, using step-by-step procedures, are not yet available for questions of the sort raised earlier in the paragraph. All these matters are being studied now.

Appendix II: Many Commodities—Many Regions Static General Equilibrium Model

Notation used:

i) There are I internal regions (indexed by subscripts i, j, p, and q). The outside world is the zero-th region, and region 1 has all the ports and therefore all imports and exports. (This can be generalized, but it is not necessary to do so.) There are K commodities with final and intermediate uses (indexed by subscripts k and m.) There are R primary, nontransportable commodities (indexed by the subscript r).

ii) ${}_iY_k$ denotes the total quantity of commodity k available in region i for final use.

iii) ${}_{10}E_k$ denotes the export of the k-th commodity from region 1 to the rest of the world.

iv) ${}_iP_k$ denotes the price of the k-th commodity in final use in region i.

v) ${}_1e_k$ denotes the world market price of the k-th commodity at the port in region 1. Hence, it is an f.o.b. export price or a c.i.f. import price at the port, adjusted for export taxes or tariffs on imports.

vi) ${}_ia_{km}$ denotes the quantity of the k-th commodity required to produce one unit of commodity m in the i-th region.

vii) ${}_ib_{rk}$ denotes the quantity of the r-th primary commodity required to produce one unit of commodity k in the i-th region.

viii) ${}_{ij}X_k$ denotes the quantity of commodity k shipped from the i-th region to the j-th region. In particular, ${}_{01}X_k$ is an import of the k-th commodity into region 1.

ix) ${}_iL_r$ denotes the available quantity of the r-th resource in the i-th region.

x) ${}_iA_k$ denotes the capacity of the i-th region to produce the k-th commodity.

xi) ${}_{ij}l_{rk}$ denotes the quantity of the r-th primary commodity required to transport one unit of commodity k from the i-th region to the j-th region. This item could be added to item (vii) to derive a "unit requirement" coefficient for production *and* movement. It is assumed that the shipper buys resources in the i-th region.

xii) ${}_{ij}v_{mk}$ denotes the quantity of commodity m required to transport one unit of the k-th commodity from the i-th region to the j-th region, assuming that the shipper provides transportation.

xiii) ${}_iR_k$ denotes the rent accruing to the capacity to produce good k in the i-th region.

xiv) ${}_iW_r$ denotes the value of a unit of the r-th resource in region i.

xv) ${}_i\pi_k$ denotes the value of a unit of the k-th commodity in intermediate use in region i.

163

xvi) λ is a variable associated with a restriction on the balance on current account in external trade. It is, basically, a factor of proportionality between foreign and domestic price systems.

xvii) $_iG_k$ and $_iG_r$ denote government requirements of commodity k and resource r, respectively, in the i-th region. An intolerably complex extension of notation could derive these fixed numbers from a "technology" for the production of political and public goods, but this is unnecessary.

The quantities mentioned ($_iY_k$, $_{10}E_k$, $_{ij}X_k$, $_iL_r$, $_iA_k$, $_iG_k$, and $_iG_r$) should be thought of as flows per unit time, not as stocks. In accordance with the earlier discussion, the input coefficients, the parameters $_iP_k$, $_1e_k$, $_iL_r$, $_iA_k$, and the requirements $_iG_k$ and $_iG_r$ are fixed numbers in the problem. The variables to be evaluated in a solution are $_iY_k$, $_{10}E_k$, $_{ij}X_k$ (including $_{01}X_k$), $_iR_k$, $_iW_r$, $_i\pi_k$, and λ.

The primal problem is to maximize

(9) $\quad V = \sum\limits_{i=1}^{I} \sum\limits_{k=1}^{K} (_iP_k)(_iY_k)$

subject to

(10) (a) $\quad _iY_k + \sum\limits_{j=1}^{I} \sum\limits_{m=1}^{K} (_ia_{km} + _{ij}v_{km})(_{ij}X_m) - \sum\limits_{j=1}^{I} _{ji}X_k \leq - _iG_k$

$$i = 2, \cdots, I$$
$$k = 1, \cdots, K$$

(b) $\quad _1Y_k + \sum\limits_{j=1}^{I} \sum\limits_{m=1}^{K} (_1a_{km} + _{1j}v_{km})(_{1j}X_m) - \left(\sum\limits_{j=1}^{I} _{j1}X_k + _{01}X_k \right)$

$\quad + _{10}E_k \leq - _1G_k$

$$k = 1, \cdots, K$$

(11) $\quad \sum\limits_{j=1}^{I} \sum\limits_{m=1}^{K} (_ib_{rm} + _{ij}l_{rm})(_{ij}X_m) \leq _iL_r - _iG_r$

$$i = 1, \cdots, I$$
$$r = 1, \cdots, R$$

(12) $\quad \sum\limits_{j=1}^{I} _{ij}X_k \leq _iA_k$

$$i = 1, \cdots, I$$
$$k = 1, \cdots, K$$

(13) $\quad \sum\limits_{k=1}^{K} _1e_k(_{10}E_k - _{01}X_k) = 0$

and

(14) $\quad _iY_k, \; _{ij}X_k, \; _{10}E_k, \; _{01}X_k \geq 0$

$$i, j = 1, \cdots, I$$
$$k = 1, \cdots, K.$$

The maximand is the value of the output of the productive sector available for final use. Recall that this means all domestically produced goods plus all imports. In view of the condition of current trade balance given by Expression (13), this amounts to defining the maximand as the value of "productive sector" consumption and "productive sector" investment expenditure, at market prices, including expenditure on imports for these uses. I shall interpret this in terms of national income after writing the dual. Expression (10a) states the requirement that, in all regions except the one with foreign trade, the final, intermediate, and governmental uses of each commodity not exceed the total quantity available from local production plus import into the region. Expression (10b) states the same requirement for the region with foreign trade, extending total utilization of each commodity to include exports and total availability to include imports. Expression (11) is the requirement that the need for primary products in each region not exceed their availability in the region, the latter quantity being total supply less government purchases. Expression (12) expresses capacity limits in each region imposed by short-run limits on plant and equipment not produceable in the period of analysis. Expression (13) is the requirement that current trade be balanced. It could easily be extended to cover several regions with facilities for foreign trade, in which case no one region would necessarily have balanced external trade. It could also specify any fixed level of external imbalance on current account. Expression (14) is the sensible requirement that the solution values of all variables be nonnegative.

The dual problem is to minimize

$$(15) \quad Z = \sum_{i=1}^{I} \sum_{r=1}^{R} (_iW_r)(_iL_r - {}_iG_r) + \sum_{i=1}^{I} \sum_{k=1}^{K} (_iR_k)(_iA_k) + \sum_{i=1}^{I} \sum_{k=1}^{K} (_i\pi_k)(-{}_iG_k)$$

subject to

$$(16) \quad {}_i\pi_k \geq {}_iP_k \qquad\qquad\qquad i = 1, \cdots, I$$
$$k = 1, \cdots, K$$

$$(17) \quad \sum_{k=1}^{K} (_i\pi_k)(_ia_{km} + {}_{ij}v_{km}) - {}_j\pi_m + \sum_{r=1}^{R} (_iW_r)(_ib_{rm} + {}_{ij}l_{rm}) + {}_iR_m \geq 0$$

$$i, j = 1, \cdots, I$$
$$m = 1, \cdots, K$$

(18) (a) $\quad {}_1\pi_k + \lambda(_1e_k) \leq 0$ for imports

(b) $\quad {}_1\pi_k + \lambda(_1e_k) \geq 0$ for exports $\qquad k = 1, \cdots, K$

and

$$(19) \quad {}_iW_r, {}_iR_k, {}_i\pi_k \geq 0 \qquad\qquad i = 1, \cdots, I$$
$$k = 1, \cdots, K$$
$$r = 1, \cdots, R.$$

The data for this problem are the same as those for the maximizing problem. The solution gives nonnegative values of the variables listed in Expression (19). Because the variable λ is associated with Expression (13), an equality, its solution value is unrestricted in sign. Indeed, Expressions (18a) and (18b), which are associated with imports and exports respectively, are jointly associated with the variables $_{10}E_k - {}_{01}X_k$, which are unrestricted in sign, too, since they are the *differences* of non-negative variables. Expression (18) is actually the requirement that each computed price $_1\pi_k$ must be proportional to each external-trade price $_1e_k$, the factor of proportionality being λ in all cases. Expression (16) requires that the computed value of the k-th good in the i-th region, which is a value of the commodity in intermediate use, cannot be less than the value of the commodity in

166 REGIONAL DEVELOPMENT POLICY

final use. If the value in intermediate use strictly exceeds the value in final use, all production will be directed to intermediate use ($_iY_k$ will be zero if $_i\pi_k > _iP_k$). Expression (17) states the requirement that the computed values $_i\pi_k$, the value of primary commodities $_iW_r$, and the rents to capacity $_iR_k$ must be so chosen that there is no positive profit on the sale of the m-th good in the j-th region, whether it is produced there (in which case $i=j$ in (17)) or elsewhere (in which case $i \neq j$). The minimand is the value of payments to owners of primary commodities ("factors of production") and capacity ("other limitational factors") *less* the value of government purchases.

Since the fundamental theorem of linear programming guarantees that a solution of V, say $\overline{V}$, equals a solution value of Z, say $\overline{Z}$, the equality $\overline{V} = \overline{Z}$ says that the value of total sales of the productive sector (including sales of imports) to domestic buyers equals in equilibrium the total value of buyers current incomes. These values both differ from net national product by a quantity

$$\sum_{i=1}^{I} \sum_{k=1}^{K} (_i\pi_k)(_iG_k) + \sum_{i=1}^{I} \sum_{r=1}^{R} (_iW_r)(_iG_r),$$

which is the value of government purchases and therefore also the usual estimate of the value of government "output". It is assumed here that the government does not participate in foreign trade directly, and that no primary goods move in international trade.

This entire construction exploits two well-known and rather deep theorems of welfare economics.[6] The first says, in effect, that a set of outputs for final use, such as a list of values $_iY_k{}^*$ in a solution of (9)–(14), is "efficient" if it is produced by the kind of competitive productive sector I have described. The second theorem, after defining efficiency, establishes that it exists if and only if the "efficient" set of outputs satisfies a pair of dual linear programs, such as (9)–(14) and (15)–(19), for which the prices $_iP_k$ are given and are positive. The operating definition of efficiency is this: a list of outputs $_iY_k{}^*$ (covering all values of i and k) is efficient if and only if there is *no* other set of quantities available for final use from the same resources, for which the inequalities

(20) $_iY_m{}^{**} > _jY_m{}^*$ (for $i = j$ and $k = m$)
and
(21) $_iY_k{}^{**} \geq _iY_k{}^*$ (for all other values of k and all values of i)

all hold. These inequalities translate into the simple statement that no set can be efficient unless it is impossible to have more of the m-th commodity available for final use in the j-th region *and* at the same time at least as much of all commodities in all other regions and all other commodities in the j-th region available for final use. In geometric terminology, efficients sets are "points" on a Pareto-optimal production-possibility locus.

It is very easy to introduce variations into the formal scheme at this stage. Since several of them are worth considering at the stage of application, they should be available for analysis. First, it may be noted that there are no consumption requirements analogous to Expression (3). They can be included. The efficiency model provides a point on a production-possibility locus for each set

[6] See Dorfman, Samuelson, and Solow, *op. cit.*, Chapters 13 and 14.

of prices for final use, as illustrated by point A in Figure VIII-I. The demand constraints restrict the points that can be called efficient to the area northwest of Point B. The primal problem will have an additional constraint, of the form

(22) $\quad _iY_k \geq {_iB_k} \qquad i = 1, \cdots, I$
$$k = 1, \cdots, K$$

and the dual problem will have a new nonnegative variable $_i\beta_k$. The minimand of the dual will then be modified by the addition of the term

(23) $\quad \sum\limits_{i=1}^{I} \sum\limits_{k=1}^{K} (_i\beta_k)(-_iB_k),$

while Expression (16) will become

(16′) $\quad _i\pi_k - {_i\beta_k} \geq {_iP_k} \qquad i = 1, \cdots, I$
$$k = 1, \cdots, K$$

The effect of this modification is to guarantee that a solution such as point C cannot arise. This is accomplished by changing observed market prices to virtual

FIGURE VIII—1

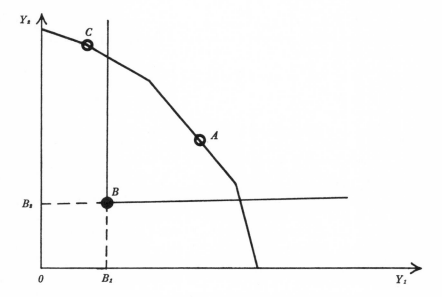

prices equal to $_iP_k + {_i\beta_k}$, and evaluating the prices and rents $_i\pi_k$, $_iW_r$, and $_iR_k$ as if the virtual prices were the observed ones. It follows that the activities that produce commodities for which $_i\beta_k$ is strictly positive will show an accounting loss, since the virtual revenue to the process, on which payments to factors are based, exceeds actual revenue.

A second modification that might be needed consists in treating the cost of transportation not as a cost in terms of goods and resources generally. but as a cost in terms of a single resource called "transportation." This approach would mean setting all the coefficients $_{ij}t_{rk}$ and $_{ij}v_{mk}$ equal to zero, with the resulting obvious modifications in Expressions (10), (11) and (17). In addition, three new concepts would have to be introduced:

1) $_iT$, the capacity of the i-th region to transport;
2) $_{ij}t_k$, the transportation input required to move one unit of the k-th good from the i-th region to the j-th region;
3) $_is$, the rent of a "unit" of transportation capacity in the i-th region.

These enter the model in the following way. Assume that exporters always pay the cost of transportation, in the sense that it is their capacity to transport that is used in carrying out a movement. A new set of constraints then appears in the primal model:

$$(24) \quad \sum_{j=1}^{I} \sum_{k=1}^{K} (_{ij}t_k)(_{ij}X_k) \leq \, _iT \qquad i = 1, \cdots, I.$$

This is the requirement that transportation capacity not be overutilized. The minimand of the dual problem, (15), then must contain an additional term

$$(25) \quad + \sum_{i=1}^{I} (_is)(_iT),$$

which is the total of rents to transportation capacity. Finally, the constraints of the dual problem must be changed in order to account for the new variables, $_is$, and the new constraints, (25). Expression (17) will thus become

$$(17') \quad \sum_{k=1}^{K} (_i\pi_k)(_ia_{km}) - _j\pi_m + \sum_{r=1}^{R} (_iW_r)(_ib_{rm}) + _iR_m + (_is)(_{ij}t_m) \geq 0.$$

$$i, j = 1, \cdots, I$$
$$m = 1, \cdots, K.$$

It can be seen that this expression includes the same "elements" of cost as did (17), namely, costs of intermediate inputs, primary inputs, and capacity. In addition, transportation is included only in the final term, in the form of a payment by the shipper from region i to region j. Expression (19) must be changed to include the obvious restriction that the rents, $_is$, be nonnegative.

Having introduced the formal modifications for purposes of reference and discussion, I shall carry through further formal arguments in terms of the original version of the dual programs, leaving to the interested reader the obvious modifications necessary to apply these arguments to the modified forms. To summarize the position, I shall manipulate a model consisting of:

Primal problem	*Dual problem*
Expressions (9)–(14)	Expressions (15)–(19)

The other versions available are:

Modification 1

Primal problem	*Dual problem*
Expressions (9)–(14) and (22)	Expressions (15) modified by (23), (16'), (17), (18), and (19) extended to cover $_i\beta_k$.

Modification 2

Primal problem	*Dual problem*
Expressions (9), (10) and (11)	Expressions (15) modified by (25),
modified, (12), (13), (14), and (24).	(17'), and (19) extended to cover $_is$.

Still other changes—such as a combination of the first and second modifications—are formally possible, though not necessarily of great interest.

What have I available now, in the way of theoretical manipulations and insights? First, there are certain basic price and cost relationships that give a certain economic insight. For instance, consider an imported good not produced at home. How is it to be priced? Obviously, it cannot arise through domestic manufacture, and its price will be based somehow on its c.i.f. import price, say $_1e_k$. From Expression (18) we may learn that the relevant domestic price is $_1\pi_k$. If the good is in fact imported, it will command a price in intermediate use in region *1* equal to $_1\pi_k$, which is proportional to $_1e_k$. Prices in intermediate use in other regions will be equal to $_1\pi_k$ plus the costs of shipment to other regions. The import will be restricted to intermediate uses only if the given prices in final use, $_1P_k, \cdots, _1P_k$ are less than $_1\pi_k, \cdots, _I\pi_k$. Otherwise, there will be both uses. A similar line of reasoning will clarify the pricing of exports for which there is no home demand (e.g., iron ore shipped from Liberia). It is worthwhile to note that a good can be produced at home and imported at the same time in this model. If this occurs, however, it means either that there are positive rents on domestic capacities (the relevant $_iR_k$ is non-zero) or that there happens to be exact indifference between domestic and foreign production of the particular good.

Aside from these basic equilibrium relationships, there are a number of questions of "comparative statics" that can be examined, using what are essentially generalizations of the theorems referred to on pages 161-62 above. The basic technique is to examine the effects on the equilibrium values $\bar{V}$ and $\bar{Z}$ of changes in various parameters. Among those changes whose effects are easy to check are changes in $_iG_k$, $_iG_r$, and $_iA_k$. A little less easy computationally but still fairly direct are changes in such coefficients as $_{ij}v_{km}$ and $_{ij}l_{rm}$, the input costs of transportation of the k-th commodity from the r-th to the j-th region. The ability to carry out these analyses directly on a computer makes possible the evaluation of government policies referred to in the first part of the paper.

It should be noted that the convenient step-by-step calculating procedures are no more sure to converge in this large model than they are in the small example; hence, the solutions are available for some of the computations only by recalculating the entire problem. Consider also the following example, which is meant to remove the impression that systems of this kind apply only in developed economies. Consider the problem of improving the relative income of a purely agricultural area. Would industry, where there was none before, help? The model will give the virtual rent on industrial capacity in the agricultural area. It may show that a little is "too little," in the sense that several capacities may be needed at once to raise virtual rents to a tolerable level. How about new crops? If the data are good enough to distinguish between different outputs of the agricultural sector, and input coefficients on the new crop are available, then the model can be used to test the new crop as well.

IX

Economic Evaluation
of Transport Projects

HANS A. ADLER*

THE ECONOMIC ART of evaluating transport projects in less developed countries is still primitive, but whether the discrepancy between theory and application is greater than in medicine, for example, is difficult to judge. This article describes the generally prevailing status of the art among those who have perhaps the greatest experience with it, discusses some of the major problems, and makes a number of suggestions for further improvements. The main emphasis is on the evaluation of highways because they usually present greater difficulties for economic evaluation and because in the future their expansion is likely to be more important in most developing countries than that of other modes of transport. However, the methods and techniques discussed are of general applicability.

The economic evaluation of public works projects has been developed most extensively in connection with water-resource measures, such as flood control, navigation and soil conservation. It received its initial impetus in the United States in the 1930's when legislation required the Bureau of Reclamation, the Army Corps of Engineers and other agencies to measure costs and benefits and to use such measurements in the selection of particular projects. There have been many of these studies in the last 10 years, with particular emphasis on water resources.

In the transportation field, the evaluation of railway projects and to some extent also of shipping and port projects, was usually limited

* The author is a transportation economist with the World Bank. While the article is based in large part on the Bank's experience in project evaluation, the views expressed do not reflect any official views of the World Bank.

to a financial analysis to determine whether future revenues could cover costs. In recent years a few railroads have adopted more formal capital budgeting methods. Economic evaluations, however, became a necessity with highways since they do not generally produce direct revenues. The first ones were made by engineers in state highway departments in the late 1930's. Their use in less developed countries did not become extensive until a few years ago under the impetus of various foreign aid programs.

There is, of course, no causal relation between the backwardness of the economics of transport evaluation and the fact that until a few years ago it was virtually the exclusive domain of engineers. On the contrary, this condition is to a considerable extent due to the failure of economists to interest themselves in this area even though it is one in which close cooperation between economists and engineers is especially important. As a result, some of the most common mistakes in project evaluation result from the failure to apply economic criteria correctly or at all; a few of these, such as the failure to distinguish between private and public costs and benefits and between average and marginal costs, are discussed below.

A very special problem in less developed countries is the absence of basic statistics; this is frequently decisive for the degree of accuracy and refinement possible in the analysis. Most of these countries have, for example, initiated only very recently the collection of highway traffic data. Where statistics are available, they are usually limited to simple traffic counts; information on origin and destination of traffic or on the types of commodities carried on highways is hardly ever available. Little is usually known about vehicle operating costs on different types of highways or about road maintenance expenditures on different types of surfaces. As a result, most new investments and the allocation of maintenance expenditures have usually been made virtually without any detailed economic analyses of priorities. It is no doubt true that, within limits, some of the most obvious investments can be made simply by looking at a map and at the location of major industries and population centers. But this is not true after the most obvious highways have been constructed, nor does such a simple approach permit an adequate judgment about priorities over time, among the modes of transport, or between transport and investments in other fields. The absence of basic statistics, however, is not only a cause of the backward status of much analysis in this field but also an effect: because until recently economists have not focused on the right questions, there has been little incentive for collecting the right statistics.

Preliminary Steps

Before a specific transport project can properly be evaluated, two preliminary steps are highly desirable and usually essential in order to gradually reduce the consideration of alternatives to the project. The first step consists of a general economic survey of the country. Such a survey has two major functions. The first is to establish the country's overall transportation needs by exploring, for example, the rate of economic growth and the resultant expansion in traffic. The second is to provide a basis for appraising the transport needs as against the requirements of other sectors of the economy. This is not something that can be done very precisely, and it depends heavily on qualitative judgments. It is interesting that several such surveys have suggested that too much was being spent on transport investments. A recent survey of Colombia, for example, found that investments in education, housing and health deserved a greater priority than the marginal investments in transport.[1] Such surveys are also needed to help decide whether by changes in the location of industries, the total demand for transport can be reduced, and at what cost. The failure to make such surveys has led to transport investments, as well as recommendations for additional investments in some countries, which are out of line with the total investment resources of the country and with the priorities of other sectors.

The second step should be a detailed transportation survey of the country in order to determine the priorities within that sector. Examples of this are transportation surveys made recently in Argentina, Colombia, Ecuador and Taiwan under World Bank auspices. Such surveys, if they are to be of maximum usefulness, should not only establish the broad framework of priorities for each mode of transport, such as the listing of highways in order of their importance, but should also indicate the proper role for each mode and the priorities among them. Such a transport program will be subject to

[1] Cases mentioned in this chapter are products of research by the World Bank, much of it unpublished. Published material that is available is listed in the Bibliography.

later revision when specific projects are analyzed in detail. Unless both a general economic and a transportation survey precede the evaluation of a specific project, there is a considerable risk that the evaluation may be sufficiently incomplete as to lead to a misallocation of resources.

Problems of Project Evaluation

The basic purpose of the economic evaluation of a project is to measure its economic costs and benefits in order to determine whether its net benefits are at least as great as those obtainable from other marginal investment opportunities in the particular country. There are, of course, many costs and benefits other than economic ones, such as the cultural opportunities from greater travel and the military and administrative advantages, and sometimes disadvantages, from greater mobility. These are not considered here because they have been excluded by definition, and also because, for better or for worse, they are not a main consideration for lending by most sources of foreign finance whose primary purpose is to stimulate economic development. Nevertheless, these other benefits and costs are quite real and should be taken into account by the country involved.

It is sometimes stated that the value of a project should be measured by its contribution to the growth of national income as conventionally measured. This is not inconsistent with the above formulation, but it is not a practical approach. For one, it would exclude certain benefits altogether, such as greater comfort from an improved highway, or the time saving used for more leisure, which would not be reflected in national income. More important, the national income approach is too complicated and indirect and in underdeveloped countries is simply not possible. For example, if transport costs are reduced, an analysis would have to be made on how the freed resources are used in the future in other sectors of the economy to determine the resultant increase in national income. However, the national income approach is useful in focusing on costs and benefits from the point of view of the economy as a whole and not merely of the parties directly involved. In this way it helps in selecting the benefits to be included and those to be omitted and in avoiding counting the same benefit twice in different forms, such as when an improved highway reduces transport costs and increases land values. It is helpful in identifying economic costs and benefits, but not in measuring them.

In evaluating a project which consists of a number of separable and independent subprojects, separate economic analyses should be made of each subproject. Otherwise it is quite possible that the extra large benefits of one subproject may hide the insufficient benefits of another. For example, in the case of a port expansion project in Central America, the engineers recommended the construction of two new wharfs. The economic justification indicated an economic rate of return on the investment of about 12 percent, which was a satisfactory rate in the particular country. However, when separate analyses were made for each wharf, it turned out that the rate of return on one was nearly 20 percent, while that on the other was only about 4 percent even after allowance was made for the extra costs of building it separately; the second wharf was clearly not justified. The same principle applies especially to various degrees of highway improvements and frequently also to different highway sections.

In order to measure economic benefits and costs and to compare them with other investment opportunities, they must be expressed in monetary terms, which is the only practical common denominator. This presents a problem since market prices do not reflect real costs to the extent that workable competition does not prevail in major sectors of the economy. In addition to any generally applicable limitations on competition in less developed countries, there are two special problems in the transport field. The first one arises from the fact that some transportation services by their very nature are oligopolistic or even monopolistic so that the prices charged for these services frequently have no direct relation to costs. The most obvious example is the historic pricing of railway services whereby freight rates for particular commodities are not based on the costs of transporting these commodities but on the value of the commodity. A second related problem arises from the direct and indirect subsidization of many transportation services by governments. A generally applicable example is the provision of highways. In most developing countries gasoline taxes and other charges on the beneficiaries do not cover the costs of highways (including maintenance, depreciation, interest, and administration); even where they may cover overall costs, there is usually no direct relation between specific user charges and the differing costs of the various transport services, such as those of trucks, buses and passenger cars.

In spite of these difficulties, monetary terms are the only practical common denominator, and they can be made substantially more useful by the use of "shadow prices" to reflect real economic costs and benefits more closely.

Measuring Economic Costs

Measuring the economic costs of a project is substantially simpler than measuring its economic benefits and can usually be limited to making adjustments in the actual expenses to the extent that they do not adequately reflect real economic costs. Three classes of costs for which such adjustments are usually necessary, i.e., for which "shadow prices" must be determined are discussed below.

The Use of Shadow Prices

The first example is sales and other indirect taxes. The tax on gasoline, for example, is a cost to those who pay the tax, but it does not necessarily reflect economic costs to the country as a whole in the sense that an increase in the tax does not mean that more economic resources are required to produce a given volume of gasoline. It is interesting that the famous report *Road User Benefit Analyses for Highway Improvements* by the American Association of State Highway Officials erroneously includes taxes in its measurement of fuel costs and thus fails to distinguish between private and public costs (and benefits).[2] Similarly, license fees and import duties should be excluded, and adjustments should be made for the costs of imports at artificial exchange rates including a subsidy.

A second example is wages. In most countries minimum wage laws and other regulations and inflexibilities have the result that some wages actually paid do not correctly measure the real costs of labor. Where an economy is marked by extensive unemployment or underemployment, the real costs of the type of labor involved are much

---

[2] Washington, D.C., 1960. Reprint of 1952 report without basic change except for use of 1959 unit costs.

less than actual wage rates. When this is a widely prevailing condition and is likely to remain so for some time, as in many less developed countries, the cost of labor, especially unskilled labor, should be calculated at substantially less than actual wage payments. On the other hand, it would also appear that the real costs of skilled labor may be greater than the wages paid. The same considerations are also applicable on the benefit side. In measuring the benefits of labor-saving equipment, the real benefit is substantially less if the replaced labor remains unemployed for a significant period during the economic life of the equipment.

A final example is interest. Interest actually paid is the financial cost of capital, which frequently has no relation to its economic cost, i.e. the opportunity cost of capital. Investment funds provided by governments for transportation are often made available at rates below the cost to the government; and even if they cover the government's costs, the latter do not reflect economic costs if the funds were obtained by the government under direct or indirect compulsion, such as by taxation or by requiring banks to lend to the government below market rates. Funds obtained from foreign sources very frequently carry interest rates substantially below the opportunity cost of capital in less developed countries.

The economic cost of capital is very difficult to determine in the absence of free markets, especially since prevailing interest rates also reflect such factors as inflation and risk. The World Bank has made a number of studies attempting to measure the opportunity cost of capital in selected countries. While they do not permit any definitive judgments, they do indicate a range from about 6 to 12 percent for the particular countries selected, and there is reason to believe that in most developing countries the rate is at least 8 percent and frequently more than 10 percent. Whether market interest rates or a lower (or perhaps higher) social rate should be used in discounting costs and benefits is beyond the scope of this article. As a practical matter, however, investments in less developed countries with rates of return below 8 percent deserve very special scrutiny.

The problem of the appropriate interest rate can be minimized somewhat in the evaluation of many projects by expressing the results in terms of an internal rate of return on the investment, rather than in terms of benefit-cost ratio. This is discussed further below in the final section.

Other Types of Adjustments

In addition to the use of shadow prices, there are other types of adjustments which are frequently necessary for an economic evaluation. The three examples given below are selected primarily because they illustrate mistakes which occur frequently.

In calculating the costs of a project, engineers usually include a contingency for unforeseen expenses. These are of two types. First, costs may be greater than anticipated because the work turns out to be more difficult or more extensive; for example, more earth may have to be moved or the soil conditions may be less favorable than indicated by the sample data on which the cost estimate was based. In another case, costs may be greater because generally prevailing inflationary conditions increase wages and prices. For the purpose of economic analysis, this second element of the contingency allowance should not be included under costs, nor should a general inflation in the prices of benefits be taken into account. However, changes in relative prices should be allowed for to the extent that they are foreseeable and are likely to affect costs and benefits differently.

A second common error involves the treatment of interest during the construction period. Such interest is usually included in the costs of those projects which are financed by loans, such as new equipment for a railroad or the construction of a toll road, but it is frequently excluded where the project is financed by grants from general revenues, as in the case of most highways. This important financial distinction has no significance as far as the economic costs of the project are concerned since the real resources used—labor, material, equipment, etc.—are the same regardless of the source of financing. Money is the means of procuring these real economic resources, so that interest should not be included in the economic costs of the project.

However, interest is relevant in a quite different sense. Since the benefits of a project do not begin until sometime after the project has been started and costs have been incurred, it becomes necessary to compare costs and benefits beginning in different years and having different time streams. Regardless of the financing method, the timing of costs is an important element since a cost incurred this year has a different economic value than the same cost incurred sometime in the future. To measure the difference, future costs can be expressed in terms of present values by discounting them at an appropriate interest rate. The proper method of comparing benefits and costs with different time streams is, therefore, to discount all future costs *and benefits* as of the time a *cost* is first incurred. Under this method, interest (as well as depreciation) is implicitly allowed for, so that adding interest to the costs would involve double counting.

An alternative method which is sometimes used includes interest during construction and discounts benefits as of the first year they begin, which is generally sometime after the first costs are incurred. This tends to confuse the financial with the economic analysis since usually the interest included in costs is the interest actually paid. In most cases, this has no direct relation either to the opportunity cost of capital or the internal rate of return by which the benefits should be discounted, so that, in effect, the costs are discounted by a rate different from that used for benefits. It should also be noted that this method actually overstates costs where benefits begin before the project is completed, which occurs quite frequently in highway construction. There seems to be no particular advantage to discounting costs and benefits to a year other than the year in which the project starts, which is nearly always the first year in which costs are incurred.

A third mistake, which only deserves mention because it occurs quite often, arises from the failure to define properly the scope of the project with the result that project costs do not include all relevant costs. For example, a toll road authority in a developing country included in the costs of a new road only the expenses for which it would be responsible. This, however, failed to take into account the necessity for improving access roads. Since the improvement of access roads was essential for the effective utilization of the toll road, the costs involved should have been included in the project costs for the purpose of economic evaluation, even though they could properly be excluded for an analysis of the authority's financial position. In this particular instance it was probable that the access roads would have been improved in time in any case. Therefore, it became necessary to establish the additional costs of making the improvements earlier than would otherwise have been the case and of the higher design standards needed for the greater volume of traffic caused by the toll road.

Measuring Economic Benefits

Measuring the economic benefits of transport projects is usually much more difficult than measuring their economic costs. There are a number of reasons for this. First, some benefits, even though quite direct—such as the increased comfort and convenience from an improved road—are difficult to express in monetary terms since there are usually no market prices for such benefits. Second, monetary benefits, such as reduced transport costs, benefit a great number of people over a long period of time, requiring difficult long-range forecasts. Third, many benefits are indirect, such as the stimulation to the economy from improved transportation; and for these benefits to materialize, investments in fields other than transport are frequently necessary.

The most important benefits from transport projects include: (1) reduced operating expenses initially to the users of the new facility and also usually to those who continue to use the existing facilities; (2) lower maintenance costs; (3) fewer accidents; (4) savings in time for both passengers and freight; (5) increased comfort and convenience; and (6) stimulation of economic development. Not all of these benefits exist in all projects, and their respective importance differs from project to project. At the present state of the art of project evaluation, those listed near the beginning can frequently be measured in monetary terms more easily than the others. This article will not deal with the measurement of maintenance costs and of comfort and convenience. The former offers probably the least difficult conceptual problems, and the latter would seem to have a relatively low social value in developing countries, even though to judge by differences between first- and second-class railway service, it has a considerable private value.

Before discussing the problems of measuring the remaining benefits, it may be useful to refer to a matter which is rarely considered in their evaluation, i.e. the distribution of benefits among the beneficiaries. For example, if the improvement of a port reduces the turnaround time of ships, much of the benefit might go initially to foreign ship owners; the degree to which they pass it on to the country paying for the investment depends largely on the degree of competition in shipping. Similarly, the improvement of a scenic highway may initially benefit foreign tourists primarily or those from other areas of the country. A government could, of course, adopt a policy of recouping some or most of these benefits by appropriate user charges. The matter of the distribution of benefits is important therefore in the selection of a policy of user charges which will channel the benefits to the desired recipients.

Perhaps even more important is the fact that the distribution of benefits affects their overall size. For example, if a railway maintains previously existing freight rates even though a transport improvement has lowered costs, the consumers would not benefit directly, but the railway might have higher profits; a determination of the net benefits to the economy would depend on weighing what the railway would do with its higher profits (or the government with its "savings" from reduced losses) as against the benefits from lower freight rates. An important consideration is that if the rates are not lowered, the transport improvement would hardly stimulate new traffic. Where there is reason to believe that the likely distribution of benefits either reduces their overall size or is inconsistent with other public policies, the problem deserves greater attention than it now usually receives, with special emphasis on appropriate user charges.

Reduced Operating Expenses

The most direct benefit from a new or improved transport facility, and frequently also the most important one and the one most easily measurable in monetary terms, is the reduction of transport costs. While this benefit accrues initially to the users of the facility, competition or the desire to maximize profits leads them to share it in various degrees with other groups, such as producers, shippers and consumers. The cost reduction therefore benefits the nation as a whole and not merely the users of the facility.

Traffic Growth

The first step in measuring the benefit from reduced costs is to estimate the future use of the facility, i.e. the future traffic during its useful life.[3] This traffic can be broken down into three main types:

[3] The useful life of a facility is limited primarily by economic change and tech-

the "normal," the "diverted" and the "generated" traffic. The "normal" traffic growth is that which would have taken place on the existing facilities in any case, even without the new investment. This type of traffic benefits by the full reduction in operating costs made possible by the new facility, since, by definition, this traffic would otherwise have traveled even at the higher (and perhaps steadily increasing) costs of the existing facility.

The proper standard for measuring the savings in vehicle operating costs is provided by the "with and without" test: what will the costs be with the new facility and what would they have been without it? In numerous project evaluations, however, a quite different standard is mistakenly applied—the "before and after" test: what were the costs before the new facility was constructed and what will they be afterwards? As shown below, this test usually leads to a serious underestimate of economic benefits.

For example, in connection with the evaluation of a new expressway in Japan, the responsible authorities measured the operating costs of a truck on the existing highway in 1958; they were about U. S. 15 cents equivalent per kilometer, excluding taxes. The costs on the new expressway, which is scheduled to be opened in 1969, were estimated at 11 cents, or a saving of 4 cents per truck/kilometer. This saving was then applied to the estimated truck traffic for the years 1969 to 1979; no increase in traffic was assumed thereafter because the so-called design capacity of the expressway would then be reached and vehicle operating costs would thereafter begin to increase. This approach, which is based on the "before and after" test, illustrates a number of common mistakes. The first is that the comparison of costs on the existing highway in 1958 with those on the new expressway in 1969 fails to take into account the important fact that the increasing congestion on the existing highway will have increased operating expenses considerably by 1969 over those prevailing in 1958. Secondly, the operating costs on the existing highway would have continued to increase after 1969, while those on the new expressway are likely to remain relatively stable for 10 years and the

---

nical obsolescence, such as new or improved processes and changes in markets. These are much less predictable than the facility's physical life. While forecasts of service life are therefore to some extent inevitably speculative, the discounting of far-off periods makes these relatively unimportant. In many cases, for example, it will make little difference whether the life of a highway is taken at 25 or 30 years.

increase thereafter is likely to be less sharp than on the existing highway. The situation is illustrated by Figure IX-1.

FIGURE IX–1

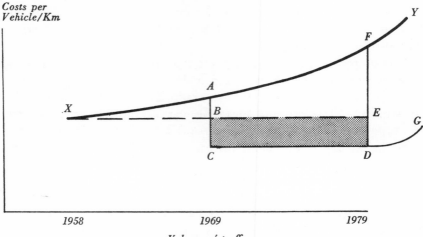

XY represents the truck operating costs on the existing highway, assuming the expressway is not built. It slopes upward in time because of increasing congestion. By the time the expressway is opened in 1969, they have already increased somewhat over the 1958 level. The reduction in operating costs per truck, according to the "before and after" test is BC throughout the life of the new investment and the benefits (until 1979) are represented by the shaded area BCDE. Actually, the reduction is AC when the facility is opened in 1969, DF by 1979, and the benefits are at least ACDF. Also, it is questionable whether no increase in traffic should be assumed after 1979. The concept of highway capacity is hardly a scientific one and the traffic on the existing highway is more than double the design capacity. The real issue is at what point new investment is justified in order to increase capacity further. Since such investment is likely to be lumpy, the decision involves weighing the costs of increased congestion on the existing highway as against the net benefits of additional capacity. Depending on the lumpiness of the investment, traffic increases substantially beyond design capacity may be justified before expanding the capacity further.

It is sometimes stated that when the increasing costs of growing congestion are properly taken into account, i.e. the difference between the *CG* and the *AY* curves, the growth in vehicle operating savings tends to be twice as great as the growth in traffic. While such generalizations have to be treated carefully, a few actual cases indicate that it may sometimes serve as a rough approximation. For example, a study of a road improvement in Jamaica indicated that it would reduce operating costs by about £40,000 in 1963. If this benefit is increased by the estimated annual traffic growth of 12 percent, it would reach £70,000 in 1968 and £120,000 in 1973. If, however, the increasing costs of further congestion are allowed for, the benefit would be £90,000 in 1968 and £250,000 in 1973. The difference would become even greater in the following years.

The application of the erroneous "before and after" test can lead to curious results. In connection with a proposed highway improvement in Syria, investigation showed vehicle operating costs on the existing highway to be quite reasonable; it had a fair surface and a satisfactory width. Unfortunately, the highway was not constructed to carry the prevailing heavy loads, and engineers advised that it would break up in about two years and that (even with heavy maintenance expenditures) a complete reconstruction would be necessary. However, vehicle operating costs would not be significantly lower thereafter. The "before and after" test indicated that the reconstruction would bring only modest benefits and would not be justified, at least not at that time. The "with and without" test, however, indicated that without the new investment, vehicle operating costs would go up very sharply, to say nothing of maintenance costs; the avoidance of this increase should in this case have been the proper basis for the economic evaluation of the benefits.

The above examples have been limited to highways, but the analysis is in principle identical for railways or ports. For example, in 1963 the Spanish Railway developed a 10-year modernization and expansion program estimated to cost about U.S. $1 billion equivalent. In addition to evaluating the benefits from individual components of the program, it was also desired to measure the return on the program as a whole. Analysis showed that the program would reduce operating costs by about 25 percent between 1963 and 1973. When this benefit was measured against the investment costs of the modernization part of the program, it showed an internal rate of return of about 15 percent. This "before and after" approach, however, understated the benefits significantly since in the absence of the new investments, operating costs would not have remained at the 1963 level, but would have increased. When allowance was made for this, the rate of return on the investment became about 18 percent.

The second type of traffic is that which is diverted to the new facility either from other modes of transport or from other routes.[4] The benefit for diverted traffic is measured by the difference in transport costs on the old route or mode of transport and on the new facility. There are, however, two special problems which should be kept in mind in measuring this benefit. The first one is that the relevant costs in this connection are not the average costs of transport, on both facilities, but the avoidable costs, i.e. the amounts that would be saved. If, for example, traffic is diverted from a railway to a new highway, the benefits cannot be measured by comparing the transport costs on the new road with either railway charges or even average railway costs, but by comparing them with the marginal costs of carrying the diverted traffic by railway. If, for example, the diverted traffic is only a small part of the railway's total traffic and if the railway has excess capacity, the marginal savings would be substantially less than indicated by a comparison of average costs; this is probably the usual case. While the available data in most developing countries do not permit precise estimates of marginal costs, the understanding of the correct concepts is essential for making the best use of the data which are available.

Comparing costs of different transport modes presents a further practical problem in that the transport services provided by each mode usually differ substantially and must therefore be reduced to a common denominator. Total distribution costs are the primary concern, not just the cost of shipment. For example, comparing the costs of coastal shipping traffic diverted to a highway must take into account not merely shipping costs, but also such additional costs as loading and unloading, storage, insurance, breakage, delays, etc. These additional costs may readily add 50 percent to the basic shipping costs.

[4] Another type of diverted traffic consists of a change from one type of conveyance to another on the same route, such as passenger trips previously made by bus but now made by private car. In this case, the higher relative operating costs of a private car are evidently outweighed by its qualitative advantages, especially the greater convenience and comfort; it is usually not possible to measure this difference in monetary terms.

Similarly, in comparing the costs of railway and highway transport, adequate allowance must be made for the fact that trucking is a door-to-door service, while railway service will generally require two loadings and unloadings, which, in addition to the direct costs, frequently involves delays and breakage.

While the benefits to the economy are measured by the reduction of social costs (e.g. excluding taxes), it is not the social but the private costs which are relevant in estimating the amount of traffic diversion. In fact, since many people make decisions on driving largely on the basis of out-of-pocket costs, it is the difference between these and railway rates actually charged (regardless of cost) which will largely decide the amount of passenger traffic which will divert from a railway to a highway.

The third type of traffic is that which is newly generated as a result of the lowering of transport costs and which previously did not exist at all. This includes traffic both from increases in industrial or agricultural production caused by the cheaper transport as well as transport not involving an increase in production, such as the transport of commodities previously sold locally but now transported to markets where a better price can be obtained.

As far as reductions in transport costs are concerned, it would not be appropriate to apply the total reduction in unit operating costs to this traffic since it would not have materialized without the reduction. If there is reason to believe that in a particular situation the traffic would have been generated with a transport cost reduction of only a quarter the actual reduction, it would be appropriate to apply three-quarters of the unit cost reduction to the generated traffic. In the many situations where the available data do not permit a judgment on the relationship between the degree of transport cost reduction and the volume of generated traffic, perhaps the most reasonable assumption is that this traffic would have developed in proportion to the reduction in transport costs; if so, it would be appropriate to apply approximately one half of the unit cost reductions to this traffic.

To the extent that the main purpose of a new transport facility is to open up new lands for cultivation or to otherwise make possible new economic development, reductions in transport costs for generated traffic are not a significant measure of the economic benefits of the project. In this situation, the benefit consists of the new production made possible; the problems of measuring this benefit are discussed later.

Accident Reduction

Accident reduction is clearly an economic benefit, but not every transport improvement reduces accidents; whether it does or not must be investigated in each case. For example, it is quite possible that an improved highway may initially increase not only the number of accidents, but, more importantly, the accident rate per vehicle/km and the severity of each accident. This could happen where the increased speed is not offset by additional safety factors, especially in a country where automobile driving is still in its initial stages and the discipline required for safe driving is equally underdeveloped. Accident reduction is apparently most significant for expressways with divided lanes and controlled access.

Measuring the economic benefits involves two main steps. The first is to estimate the reduction in accidents, which entails, for example, comparing the accident rate on the existing highway as it would be in the absence of the improvement with the rate on higher standard highways within the country or, if necessary, in other countries (but making allowance for national differences).

The second step is to estimate the value of the accident reduction. For this purpose, it is useful to consider three types of damages. The one most readily measurable in monetary terms is property damage, usually to the cars involved in the accident. Police statistics in Japan, for example, indicate that the average property damage per accident is about U.S. $600 equivalent; this may not be an unreasonable figure —though it should be adjusted for excise taxes, for example—since about two-thirds of the traffic is accounted for by trucks and buses, with a relatively low average age. The cost of injuries is more difficult to measure. In the Japanese studies this was estimated at about U.S. $100 equivalent per accident, which includes an allowance for both loss of earnings and the cost of medical treatment for the injured who were over 14 years of age.

Finally, to measure fatality reduction, there is the problem of putting a value on life. In the Japanese case, this was calculated by capitalizing the average annual income per worker over a 30 year period. This is obviously a highly controversial proposition. At a minimum there should be deducted from gross income the resources needed to produce that income. It would be too callous to suggest that if a country is overpopulated, the social and the private values of the fatality reduction would be quite different. On balance, it would seem preferable not to express fatality reduction in monetary terms.[5] In any case accident reduction in the less developed countries is likely to be of minor significance compared to other benefits, and the reduction of fatalities is only a small part of accident reduction. Fatalities can either be neglected in most cases or simply expressed in terms of the number of deaths involved.

Time Savings

Even though most transport improvements reduce travel time, the value of time for passengers and freight is frequently omitted from project evaluations. This may lead to a serious underestimate of benefits since time savings can be substantial.

As far as persons are concerned, time can be money, but it need not be. Whether it is, depends primarily on how the opportunities made possible by the increased availability of time are used—whether for increased production or voluntary leisure, on the one hand, or for involuntary idleness, on the other. Unfortunately, in **many** developing countries there is extensive underemployment, so **that** time savings may merely make the situation worse. But even here, time savings for entrepreneurs, for example, may be very valuable.

What can be done to measure the value of time may be illustrated by a recent study in Japan, where a new expressway was to reduce travel time very substantially. All travelers were divided into two classes: the relatively few who can afford to travel in private cars, and the many who travel in buses. As a first step, the average value of time was related to the per capita income of the two classes. This showed that in one hour, travelers in cars could earn at least U.S. $1 equivalent, while those in buses at least U.S. 20 cents. Since there are ample employment opportunities in Japan, this calculation was not unreasonable.

However, to check on its validity, these average values were com-

[5] However, if the purpose of a project is to reduce accidents, such as safety measures in the aviation field, for example, it becomes quite essential to express fatality reduction in monetary terms.

pared with the amounts people are actually willing to pay for time. For this purpose, a study was made of surcharges imposed by the railway for different types of trains running between the same cities. On the Tokaido line, for example, travelers have a very ample choice between different trains, ranging from slow, local trains to very fast expresses. While between some of these trains speed is not the only difference, convenience and comfort being others, it is the most important one and between at least two of them it is probably the only difference. An analysis of these surcharges indicates that travelers are willing to pay at least U.S. $2 equivalent in first class and U.S. $1 equivalent in second per hour saved. These findings and those based on the earnings method give a clear indication of the range of values that might be given to time savings of passengers. They suggest that in Japan, at least, many individuals prefer to take these time savings in the form of leisure even if they could devote them to income producing activities. This is probably not true in most underdeveloped countries. In any case, since the time savings will presumably exist for the life of the project, allowance should be made for the increasing value of time as per capita income grows.[6]

Time saved on the shipment of freight may well be more valuable in the less developed countries than those already more advanced. Freight tied up during transit is in fact capital, and is therefore of particular importance where capital is in short supply. This saving can be measured by the price of capital; i.e. the rate of interest. In addition, faster delivery which is usually accompanied by more reliable delivery reduces spoilage and makes possible lower inventories, which in turn is an additional form of capital saving. Beyond this, where larger inventories are not possible, a delay may immobilize other resources, as where the absence of a spare part may prevent the utilization of expensive equipment.

As in the case of time savings for travelers, a study was made in Japan on the prices shippers are willing to pay for different types of transport services, where time is by far the major and in some cases perhaps the only difference. The study covered a dozen important

---

[6] Time savings for truck and bus drivers are generally allowed for under calculations of vehicle operating savings.

commodities and indicated, for example, the following prices actually
paid for a saving of one ton/hour (in U.S. cents):

Dairy products	35
Fresh fish	21
Vegetables	20
Fruit	14
Minerals	1

The relative importance of time savings as against other benefits
depends of course on the nature of the particular project. That it can
be very significant is indicated by the project for which the above
studies were made. In this case, the value of time savings was nearly
half as great as the benefits from lower vehicle operating costs.[7]

Economic Development

It is frequently assumed that all transport improvements stimulate
economic development. The sad truth is that some do, some do not,
and that even some of those that do may not be economically justified
in the sense that there may be better investment opportunities. Each
project must therefore be investigated individually and no helpful
generalizations appear possible until more research may show that
certain definite correlations do exist.

Before any transport improvement can be said to have stimulated
economic development at all, a number of conditions must be met.
The most important is showing that the economic development would
not have taken place in any case even without the transport improvement. A second is that the resources used in the new development
would otherwise have remained unused or used less productively.
Finally, it is essential that the economic activity stimulated does not
replace activity which otherwise would have taken place.

These conditions may be obvious, but it is surprising how often they
are forgotten in practice. In the sophisticated Japanese studies previously referred to, extensive research was undertaken to measure the
growth in industrial output in the area of influence of a new highway,
and there were strong reasons to believe that the highway and the
output were indeed causally related. While this was very useful from
a local point of view, it had much less significance for the economy as
a whole. Further inquiry indicated that most of the resources used

---

[7] The time saving for the vehicles is usually covered in the lower depreciation
allowance made in vehicle operating costs.

in the new production would not otherwise have remained unemployed and that the firms responsible for the new output had planned to expand in any case and picked a location near the new highway because of its advantages. From a national point of view, therefore, the highway cannot be regarded as having contributed significantly to stimulating new economic development. This is not to say that the locational shifts caused by the highway involved no economic benefits other than lower transport costs; they may have facilitated more efficient production, but this benefit can only be a fraction of the total net output.

Where a transport facility does lead to increased output and the above conditions are met, the net value of this additional output is the proper measure of the economic benefit.[8] In many situations, however, the transport facility is not the only new investment needed to achieve the increased production. This raises the problem of allocating the benefit, i.e. the increased production, among the transport and the other investments. For this there exists no correct theoretical answer but there are at least three practical approaches. One would be not to make an allocation at all and relate the total benefits to the total investments. A second would be to annualize the other investment costs and deduct them from the benefits. And a third would be to allocate the benefits in the same ratio as the transport investment has to the other needed investments.

Each of these solutions is appropriate in different situations. For example, in the actual case of new coal mining in Sarawak, it was necessary to build a road to transport the coal from the mine to a port. The estimates indicated that the coal would account for more than 90 percent of the total traffic using the new road. The road was an integral part of the coal mining scheme—just as integral as the mining equipment—and had virtually no other use. In this case an allocation of benefits between the road and the investments in the mine would be meaningless. On the other hand, where a road is being built to facilitate new agricultural as well as industrial development which, however, will also require other major investments, an allocation of benefits might be more useful.

Where the transport facility enlarges the market for commodities previously produced, the economic benefit consists of the difference in

[8] The net value of output and the vehicle operating savings for generated traffic are, of course, not additive.

value of the commodity in the old and the new market, minus the new costs of transport. For example, the price of a commodity in the old market may be 10 cents; in a second market it is 20 cents, but because transport costs are 12 cents, shipment to this market is uneconomic. Assuming a transport improvement that cuts transport costs in half, to 6 cents, the commodity can be delivered to the second market for 16 cents and there be sold for 20 cents. The benefit from the new investment (assuming resources before and after the change are fully employed) would be 4 cents. Account must be taken of the fact that the increased supply may affect prices in both markets; if so, the benefit is usually valued at prices prevailing after the transport improvement is completed.[9]

What can be done in practice to measure the net value of increased production or of wider markets differs from case to case. For example, in the Sarawak illustration given above, detailed studies were made by various experts of the supply of coal, the costs of production and transport, and probable market prices. The problems are usually much more difficult for agricultural development because its success depends on the willingness and ability of a large number of people and the development potential of large areas. In the Sarawak case, the likely agricultural output as a result of the highway could be estimated within a satisfactory margin of error since only two commodities were involved and experience from previous transport improvements on land with a similar agricultural potential could serve as a reasonable guide on probable future output and the other investments needed to achieve it.

This is an area where only very little research has so far been done. But it is clear that if the main purpose of a transport facility is to stimulate economic development, greater efforts must be made to measure this benefit—efforts similar to those now made for an irrigation scheme, for example. And if the economic development can be achieved only if the transport improvement is supplemented by such measures as other investments, extension service to farmers, land reform, etc., then these other measures become an essential condition of the project. This, too, has been recognized in the field of irrigation, but unfortunately not yet fully in transport.

[9] For passenger traffic, this benefit, i.e. the difference between staying at home and traveling, minus the transport costs, can usually not be measured in monetary terms.

Comparing Costs and Benefits

Once costs and benefits have been measured in monetary terms to the full extent meaningful, the results can be put into at least three different forms: the rate of return on the investment, the benefit-cost ratio, or the pay-back period. A great deal has been written about these alternatives, so that the discussion here is limited to a few salient points.

There is unfortunately no uniformity in the application of these forms. In some benefit-cost ratios, for example, gross costs are compared with gross benefits, while in others, some costs are first deducted from the benefits; this can affect the ratio very substantially. Sometimes—and more correctly—it is the difference between benefits and costs which is used. In the case of rate of return calculations, the benefits are sometimes measured against the investment costs (with or without allowance for depreciation), or sometimes by the internal rate of return. It is essential to know exactly what formula is used if the final result is to be correctly interpreted.

While the basic ingredients—the value of the costs and benefits—are the same regardless of the final form in which they are expressed, the usefulness of the various forms is different, depending on the purpose. A short pay-back period is important where the future is unusually uncertain, where better investment opportunities are likely to arise soon, or where funds are not available on a long-term basis. These considerations are much more important for private businesses than for governments. Also, the fact that the benefits of an investment are large in the beginning may give no indication of what they are over the life of the investment, so that this method is a particularly poor one for comparing investments having a different time stream of benefits. Furthermore, there are superior techniques for incorporating uncertainty into investment analysis.

Discounting benefits and costs by the opportunity cost of capital is theoretically the best way of comparing different projects. The most important disadvantage of this approach is that a particular interest rate must be chosen for discounting. In practice, the interest rate mistakenly selected is frequently the one being paid, which may or may not have any relation to the opportunity cost of capital in the country. Unfortunately, the opportunity cost of capital is frequently not known or can be estimated only with a considerable margin of error. This is particularly crucial since the discount rate chosen is one of the major determinants of the benefit-cost comparison.

This disadvantage can be minimized somewhat by expressing benefits and costs in terms of the internal rate of return on the investment, i.e. the rate which equalizes discounted costs and benefits. In this case, the opportunity cost of capital becomes important only in the marginal cases where the internal rate of return is not clearly above or below the area within which the opportunity cost of capital may be estimated to be. For example, it would be virtually certain that an investment in Japan with a rate of return of 12 percent is justified, since the opportunity cost of capital is less, probably between 6 and 10. But even where the two rates may be relatively close, the internal rate of return formula has the advantage of focusing directly on the crucial question: how the particular investment compares with other investment opportunities. The benefit-cost ratio tends to hide this crucial point in assuming a certain interest rate.

On the other hand, the internal rate of return formula also has its disadvantages. While, as a practical matter, it usually leads to a correct choice of projects, it may sometimes be misleading in comparing projects having different lives and different time streams of benefits. In practice, however, transportation nearly always involves long-term investments and the time streams of benefits do not tend to vary drastically. Even where they do, the margin of error involved in an internal rate of return calculation may be less than discounting by the opportunity cost of capital, which is usually known only within a wide range. Also, where a project is compared not with a direct alternative but with investment opportunities in general, the internal rate is generally a perfectly satisfactory formula.

Another disadvantage of the internal rate of return is that the answer may be ambiguous in that more than one rate may equalize costs and benefits. In practice this is rare in the case of transport projects since the costs are predominantly incurred in the early stages and the benefits arise later, in which case the solution would be unique.

Finally, the rate of return formula has the practical advantage that economists, financial experts, and many businessmen have some concept of what an interest rate is, so that a rate of return is probably more meaningful to many audiences than a benefit-cost ratio. On balance, therefore, the internal rate of return on the investment is usually, but not invariably, the most satisfactory form in which to express benefits and costs of transportation projects in the less developed countries.

X

Pricing Transport Services

JAMES R. NELSON*

. . . It should be noted at the outset that in raising the problem of an optimum transport policy we are perforce becoming engaged on the terrain of *normative* considerations. It is not what *is,* but what *ought to be,* that is fundamental. If we wish to avoid a series of unproductive discussions, we must clearly determine the norms we are setting for ourselves. Indeed, in the absence of agreement on normative principles, any discussion directed toward rules of behavior ultimately based on these principles can, at best, only lead to a prudent compromise but never to a truly satisfactory solution.[1]

THIS ESSAY BEGINS with a brief exposition of the "classic" normative prescriptions for transport pricing. It continues with a critique of these prescriptions from the standpoint of the theoretical and institutional environment in which they arose: the theory of comparative statics, within the framework of micro-economic analysis, in relatively developed economies. It then proceeds to examine what might be the consequences of relaxing these traditional features of transport analysis. Then, in the rest of the discussion (1) comparative statics is supplemented by certain dynamic aspects of transport problems; (2) micro-analysis is pursued beyond the usual enclosure in order to investigate possible interactions between the transport sector and the economy as a whole; and (3) the special institutional structure of developed economies, with full-fledged railroad systems often work-

* Amherst College.
[1] C. J. Oort, *La Théorie Marginaliste et les Prix de Transport* (Fondation Verkeerswetenschappelyk Centrum, 1960), pp. 9-10; also published in German as *Der Marginalismus als Basis der Preisbildung in der Verkehrswirtschaft* (Stichting Verkeerswetenschappelyk Centrum, 1961). My translation.

ing below short-run capacity, as well as elaborate highway systems and possibly even articulated inland waterways, are put to one side so that we may examine the economic implications of transport networks which are initially less extensive and possibly not as thoroughly coordinated.

Transport Investment and Pricing: Classic Comparative Statics

The relationship between economic theory and normative prescriptions for transport has been reciprocal during the historical development of both. The theory of demand and consumer surplus was to a considerable extent the product of analyses of transport economics as well as a tool developed for investigation of these special problems. Jules Dupuit was a pioneer in developing most aspects of modern normative prescriptions, although he did not foreshadow Pareto's general equilibrium analysis. He was also a pioneer in developing the concept of the demand curve and the related concept of consumer surplus as the area below the curve and above the price, or prices, charged consumers.[2]

More specifically, he both originated the doctrine of marginal cost pricing of transport services and, long after his death, was cited as one of the progenitors of the modern controversy that is centered on the subject of marginal cost pricing. An explanation of the controversy will serve to explain the doctrine as well.

Dupuit's position with respect to a proper base for investment policy was that:

1. A new investment should be undertaken—in, say, a bridge—if the

[2] Dupuit's first major article, which was originally published in 1844 in the *Annales des Ponts et Chausées* (Mémoires et documents . . . Second Series, Vol. 8, pp. 332-375), appeared in 1952 in an English translation under the title "On the Measurement of Utility of Public Works," in *International Economic Papers*, No. 2, pp. 83-110. This article has been republished as the first of a series of Dupuit's articles which appeared under the general title *De l'Utilité et de sa Mesure*, edited by Mario de Bernardi (La Riforma Sociale, 1933).

The modern vogue of Dupuit in English-speaking countries may be dated from the appearance of Harold Hotelling's "The General Welfare in Relation to Problems of Taxation and of Railway and Utility Rates," *Econometrica*, Vol. 6 (1938), pp. 242-269.

summation of the maximum amounts that each potential user would pay for each use of the bridge yields an amount of money in excess of the "cost of maintenance and interest on the capital expended in construction" of the bridge.[3]

2. "To the extent that the toll increases, the utility of the bridge diminishes."[4] This is true because of the "loss of the utility derived from the . . . passages of the bridge which would have taken place without the toll."[5] This is the familiar "dead loss" of English-speaking economists: to the extent that demand curves depart from the vertical, any increase in the price of the product will induce consumers to forego some consumption (and thereby whatever net utility this consumption previously had for them) without contributing to the revenue of the seller.

Dupuit himself used his second argument as a step toward conclusions about price structure. Asking rhetorically whether the inverse relationship of bridge utility to the height of the toll meant "that tolls must be very low, or even that there should be none at all?" He went on:

> This will not be our conclusion, when we occupy ourselves with rates; but we hope to make plain that rate levels require study, and on rational principles, to produce, simultaneously, the greatest possible amount of utility, and receipts which repay the cost of maintenance and interest on the capital expended.[6]

> If a tax is gradually raised from zero to a prohibitive figure, its yield starts at zero, reaches a maximum, then decreases and again becomes zero. It follows from this, that when the state needs to raise a fixed sum through a tax, there are always two taxes which satisfy its requirements, one above, the other below, that which gives the maximum return. Between these two taxes which yield the same revenue there can be an enormous difference in the utility lost.[7]

> When . . . one begins to graduate the rate of the toll, in such fashion as to demand a price which is not proportional to weight, to volume, to distance, but more and more closely related to the importance of the service rendered, the utility lost by the toll becomes less and less.[8]

[3] *De l'Utilité* . . . , p. 50. My paraphrase and translation.
[4] *Ibid.*, p. 51.
[5] *Ibid.*
[6] *Ibid.*
[7] *Ibid.*, p. 60.
[8] *Ibid.*, p. 162.

It is evident that Dupuit saw no contradiction between investment policy and price policy: if a transport improvement could be supported by *any* system of charges, then build it, and adopt the system of charges which would produce the maximum net utility to users ("maximize consumer surplus") *subject* to the constraint of recovering costs. Given differing demand elasticities, this system of charges would involve "value-of-service" pricing within the overall cost constraint.

In 1938, when Dupuit's presentation was almost a century old, Harold Hotelling opened up some new terrain:

> . . . we shall bring down to date in revised form an argument due essentially to the engineer Jules Dupuit, to the effect that the optimum of the general welfare corresponds to the sale of everything at marginal cost. This means that toll bridges . . . are inefficient reversions; that all taxes on commodities, including sales taxes, are more objectionable than taxes on incomes, inheritances, and the site value of land; and that the latter taxes might well be applied to cover the fixed costs of electric power plants, waterworks, railroads, and other industries in which the fixed costs are large, so as to reduce to the level of marginal cost the prices charged for the services and products of these industries.[9]

As a revision of Dupuit's argument, this passage came close to demolishing it. The process of modernization ended by turning the whole Dupuit structure back-to-front:

> Determination whether to build . . . [a] bridge by calculation of the revenue . . . obtainable from tolls is always too conservative a criterion. Such public works will frequently be of great social value even though there is no possible system of charging for their services that will meet the cost.[10]

The damage to Dupuit was not, however, quite as great as these passages seem to indicate, because Hotelling added that a bridge or similar improvement should be free to the public only as long "as the use of it does not increase to a state of overcrowding."[11] In an expanding industry with constant long-run costs, prices which prevent overcrowding will also provide the wherewithal to cover total costs, including capital costs. Thus the Hotelling argument does not really apply to fixed costs, as such, but to *decreasing* costs.

[9] Hotelling, *op. cit.*, p. 242.
[10] *Ibid.*, p. 248.
[11] *Ibid.*

Three variants of decreasing cost will be considered in increasing order of probable importance. The first is the special case of indivisibility or lumpiness attendant on decreasing long-run and intermediate-run costs for the smallest size of plant that is technically possible.[12] This emerges in its clearest form (see Figure X-1) only if (a) the demand curve intersects the intermediate-run cost curve (which represents the first lump of costs and, thus, is also the long-run cost curve) while the cost curve is still declining, or (b) the demand curve lies below the cost curve throughout, but an average revenue curve may be lifted above the demand curve by the use of price discrimination to intersect the cost curve.

Thus, in Figure X-1, DD represents any demand curve intersecting the average total unit cost curve, BAC, before this reaches its minimum point; $D'D'$ represents any demand curve which falls below BAC throughout but which can be converted, by price discrimination in place of a uniform price charged on all units sold, into an AR' curve which lies above BAC at very low outputs and intersects it while it is still declining. In both cases, the meaning of "decreasing cost" is unambiguous.

If, however, both D' and AR' lie below the BAC curve throughout and if this can be taken to mean that "the size of the indivisibility is greater than the size of the market,"[13] there is then no economic case for producing the good or service. If, in a system of individual segments, cost or demand conditions may be taken to differ from segment to segment, then the pure indivisibility of our first type of decreasing costs may merge into the "indivisibility-plus" of the second type.

The second and third variants are long-run decreasing costs with indivisibilities (Figure X-2) and without them (Figure X-3), depending on discontinuities or the possibility of continuous modification in the process of achieving long-run economies of scale.

Figure X-2 illustrates two different kinds of indivisibility: whereas BAC_2 intersects BAC_1 beyond the minimum point of BAC_1, BAC_3 intersects BAC_2 short of the minimum point of BAC_2. As the accompanying short-run marginal cost curves indicate, the transition from

[12] See the essay by R. B. Heflebower, Chapter III, for a definition of these cost concepts. Note that both basic facility and equipment costs are included in the basic facility cost curve. (These curves represent the unit cost per ton-mile for a given quantity of basic facilities.)
[13] A. P. Lerner, *The Economics of Control* (Macmillan, 1944), p. 180.

FIGURE X–1. *Cost and Demand Curves, the Indivisible Minimum Productive Unit*

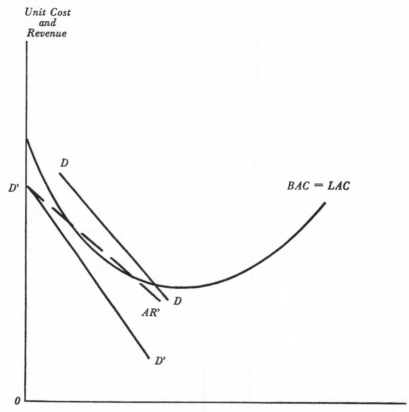

BAC₂ to BAC₃ is a source of discontinuity. But for the very abrupt discontinuity from BAC_1 to BAC_2 the word "transition" is too moderate; something more cataclysmic is required—at the very least, "break."

A prospect of feast-or-famine seems to be held out as we rise along MC_1 with expanding output until MC_1 exceeds BAC_1, with accompanying excess profits, then plunge vertically to MC_2, and thereby convert these profits into substantial losses. Fortunately, we need not despair; in an expanding industry working at different densities (i.e. at different levels of output per unit of *length of facilities* as well as per unit of time), these extreme peaks and valleys are largely the artificial product of applying purely static analysis to a situation in which such analysis provides only a first approximation and not a final basis for price-making.

The important evidence of Figure X-2 is that the average unit cost of incremental output (or the increase in total cost associated with the installation of capacity to produce successive blocks of output) is consistently below the average costs shown by BAC_1, BAC_2, BAC_3, and so on. This would obviously not be true if the minimum points for all of the short-run average cost curves lay along a horizontal line; therefore it is evident that the concept of decreasing costs is not identical with that of indivisibilities.[14]

If growth is slow or if high interest rates increase the cost of building ahead of demand, indivisibility may take on a life of its own as a source of pricing difficulties: a strict marginal cost rule would require prices to soar and swoop, with attendant alternations between profit and loss (or lesser losses and greater ones) that would greatly complicate management, budgeting, and public relations.

If growth is more rapid, the intermediate-run marginal cost loses importance relative to the average incremental cost already described. This, in turn, leads us from the discontinuities of Figure X-2 to the continuities of Figure X-3.

Among the variants, the case illustrated by Figure X-3 is the only one in which long-run marginal cost has a clear and unambiguous meaning for each unit of output. Thus, since long-run marginal cost has a clear meaning for all levels of output, there can be no "fixed" costs, "sunk" costs (i.e. "fixed" costs of factors that are both immortal and completely specific to this use), or "common" costs. All one can say, or needs to say, in this case is that a price which covers marginal cost at a given level of output will not produce revenues adequate to cover total costs at that level.

The second variant, as shown in Figure X-2, is relatively more likely (or less unlikely) in most underdeveloped than in most developed countries. But the hill-and-dale topography of Figure X-2 should not

[14] For elaborate diagrams of the discontinuity problem, see Edward H. Chamberlin, "Proportionality, Divisibility and Economies of Scale," *Quarterly Journal of Economics*, Vol. 62 (February 1948), Figure 2, p. 232, and Figure 3, p. 233. Professor Chamberlin's conclusions are similar to those of this discussion, although he arrives at them by a rather different route (see *ibid.*, pp. 229-262; see also "Comments" by A. N. McLeod and F. H. Hahn, and "Reply" by E. H. Chamberlin in *Quarterly Journal of Economics*, Vol. 63 [February 1949], pp. 128-143).

FIGURE X–2. *Long-Run Decreasing Costs, With Indivisibilities for Plant Capacity Beyond Those of the Minimum Plant*

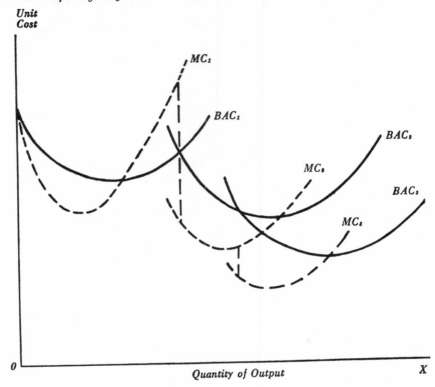

Quantity of Output

be nearly as important in transport costs as in the retailing of the familiar "public utility" services which are delivered direct to the ultimate individual consumer by means of completely specialized capital equipment. In transport, scale and versatility can operate to smooth out irregularities which cannot be eliminated in highly localized utilities. Fortunately, an economy which is in the process of rapid economic development can also shorten the time required for the rise-and-swoop of the marginal costs depicted in Figure X-2 until, as a practical matter, the significant concept may become the *average* cost of *incremental* output.

This smoothing may occur for a number of reasons: heavier densities of use of transport services, faster rates of growth of use, successive increases in alternative routes open to each shipment. Moreover, if

FIGURE X–3. *Long-Run Decreasing Costs, Without Plant Indivisibilities*

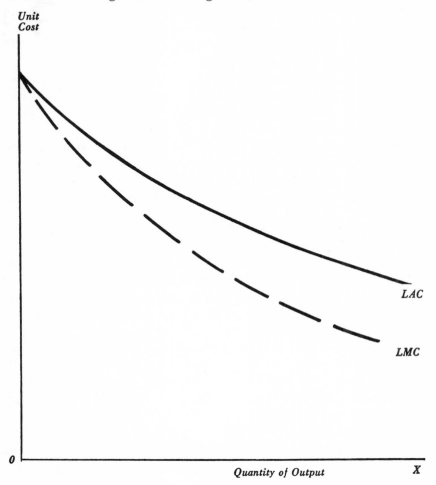

different segments of a connected system exhibit cost behavior appropriate to points chosen more or less at random from BAC_1, BAC_2, BAC_3, etc., in Figure X-2 (as seems probable in transport), it may be legitimate to hypothesize continuous marginal cost functions for representative transport movements. Discontinuities in marginal cost should tend to cancel out for shipments moving from everywhere to everywhere else.

Even if this smoothing process should convert Figure X-2 into Figure X-3, there is nothing in the logic of decreasing costs which

204   PRICING TRANSPORT SERVICES

permits one to associate this condition with "fixed" or "sunk" costs. As Figure X-2 clearly shows, marginal cost pricing produces deficits if marginal costs are consistently below average costs. But a command to disregard "fixed" or "sunk" cost implies a different and economically disastrous policy: it assumes that some or all capital goods become free goods, in perpetuity, once they are installed and ready for use.

This brings us to the basic controversy: if we can sidestep the indivisibility problem by assuming the conditions reflected in Figure X-3, should a single price be charged which is just adequate to cover the marginal cost shown in that figure? Or should a spectrum of prices be charged—the lowest to approach or reach marginal cost, and the higher to provide sufficient extra receipts to bridge the gap between marginal cost times output, on the one hand, and total cost, on the other?

Average cost pricing is less common in transport than in most other industries. It is anathema to most economists. Their choice is either marginal cost pricing or price discrimination subject to constraints: no price below relevant marginal cost (for an expanding industry, presumably long-run marginal cost); average receipts just equal to average cost; or one or both of the preceding plus a condition of maximum output.

In spite of its many devotees in the economics profession, marginal cost pricing is open to two fundamental objections.[15] First, even if all prices throughout the economy should equal marginal costs, there would still be no proof that decreasing-cost industries ought to be permitted to exist at all. That is, the *total* benefit (*AR'* in Figure X-1, on the assumption that every last customer will be charged every last penny he will pay for every last unit he is willing to buy) may be less than, as well as greater than, their total costs. Second, even if total benefit exceeded total cost, there would remain the problem of financing the industry's deficit by tax or other measures without causing economic damage in excess of the total net benefit derived from the decreasing-cost industry.[16] Moreover, the proposal involves interper-

[15] For an inclusive survey of the position at the peak of the marginal cost controversy see Nancy Ruggles, "Recent Developments in the Theory of Marginal Cost Pricing," *Review of Economic Studies*, Vol. 17 (1949-1950), pp. 107-126. For Mrs. Ruggles' own views, which are not those of a devotee of marginal cost pricing, see "The Welfare Basis of the Marginal Cost Pricing Principle," pp. 29-46 in the same volume.

[16] C. J. Oort, *Decreasing Costs As a Problem of Welfare Economics* (Drukkerij, Holland N.V., 1958), p. ix.

sonal comparisons of quite a special sort. By implication, it assumes
that those who have relatively great need for transport services at a
low price, and relatively little need at a high price, should be subsidized at the expense of the general public. There is no a priori reason
to believe that this group has any special merit, or even that it constitutes a group for any other economic purpose or in any other respect.

This argument returns the analysis to roughly the point it had
reached in the hands of Dupuit, more than a hundred years ago. Pro-
ceeding now beyond the partial equilibrium analysis which came nat-
urally to Dupuit into the world of general equilibrium, a question is
raised: should marginal cost pricing be attempted, or enforced, in
one part of the economy if it is not simultaneously attempted, or enforced, in all parts of the economy? For many years after Dupuit, the
question was evaded. It was assumed that all industries were either
competitive, in which case competition took care of the problem of
optimum allocation, or monopolistic, in which case the question of
externally imposed prices had to be faced. There is no doubt that the
competitive analogy greatly affected attitudes toward transport and
utility prices even before anyone ever heard of a Pareto optimum.[17]
But, except for specialized analysis having to do with certain forms of
highly artificial behavior on the part of duopolists, the Pareto optimum
antedated almost all imperfect competition theory. To bring the
argument up to date: if prices tend to exceed marginal costs in much
of the rest of the economy, why should they be forced into equality
in the realm of transport?

This question can, in theory, be puffed up to overpowering dimensions. If the services of transport enterprises were substitutes for the
products of monopolies, then it could be argued that prices for transport might appropriately be raised. Even if, as would appear to be
the case, transport stands in a relationship of complementarity to the
goods (if not the people) to be transported, the appropriate price
policy for the transport service is still questionable. Once the argument is extended to the extreme "almost any old price which is not
ridiculously low or high is as good as any other."[18]

[17] A Pareto optimum is a state in which no person can be made better off without making someone else worse off. For a clear picture of the Pareto optimum in
its various aspects, see Paul A. Samuelson, *Economics*, 5th ed. (McGraw-Hill,
1961), p. 680.
[18] R. G. Lipsey and Kelvin Lancaster, "The General Theory of Second Best,"

Thus an argument which began, mildly enough, with a question as to the applicability of the Pareto optimum conditions appears to end with a call for the destruction of economics. Even without such hammer blows, however, the idea of optimum allocation may not be capable of standing up to the problem of decreasing cost industries. Assume that many other prices are above marginal cost. Then how can it be seriously argued that industries which supposedly most need to be restricted to marginal cost pricing are precisely those industries in which marginal cost pricing produces deficits? In the context of the old model of pure competition vs. pure monopoly, such an argument was perfectly appropriate. Today it is not.

Nevertheless, we can conclude this section on a more positive note by relating the general economic discussion of pricing to the specific attributes of transport costs as exemplified by one or another of Figures X-1, X-2, and X-3 above.

1. *No transport service should be priced at less than marginal cost. If demand for the transport service may be expected to grow, this should be construed to mean long-run marginal cost.*

a. In the extreme "minimum asset" case depicted in Figure X-1, minimum values for long-run marginal cost, at each successive level of output, will be equal to short-run marginal cost. If the minimum asset can be shifted without difficulty to another use or another location, then it may be said that the first unit of output has a marginal cost equal to the entire short-run fixed cost. At this point in the argument, Dupuit's total cost formula may be superimposed upon his marginal cost formula; alternatively, one may speak of a marginal cost for the asset as such. If the minimum asset can be shifted—in function, in space, or in time—but only with difficulty, then the potential loss involved in such a shift will produce an opportunity cost for the asset below its original cost. But any degree of asset mobility will nevertheless create a cost additional to those costs which vary, in the short run, with output.

The essential point may be summed up in the distinction between "fixed" cost and "sunk" cost. The former is invariant with respect to short-run changes in output, but not with respect to the level of receipts after payment of all costs which do vary with short-run

Review of Economic Studies, Vol. 23 (1955-1956), p. 30; also M. McManus, "Comments on the General Theory of Second Best," *Review of Economic Studies*, Vol. 26 (1958-1959), p. 222.

changes in output. Sunk costs, on the other hand, are invariant with respect to all changes of output which are technically possible, given the character and capacity of the sunk asset. They are invariant, moreover, for all future time. If a cost is truly sunk, it need not be recovered, via pricing, even in the long run. This is not to say that it should not be.

b. In the intermediate, "indivisible asset," case depicted in Figure X-2, which represents an extension to higher outputs of the first-stage case shown in Figure X-1, the pricing rule may yield widely varying results. If the demand curve for the transport service intersects BAC_1 between its minimum point and its intersection with BAC_2, marginal cost pricing will produce excess profits. If some demand curves, on some segments of a transport system, are so located, these excess profits would produce some automatic offset to whatever losses might be incurred by covering only short-run marginal costs (or long-run marginal costs to the exclusion of sunk costs) in Figure X-1.

If the whole system has grown beyond the minimum level shown in Figure X-1, and the successive minimum points of BAC_1, BAC_2, etc., lie along a horizontal line, indivisibility in itself probably creates no very great pricing problem. On one hand, "the demand curve" may cut short-run marginal costs at levels ranging from well below the relevant average cost curve to well above it. On the other hand, this dilemma is largely the fictitious product of artificial assumptions: "the demand curve" for transport services is actually a congeries of different demand curves, applicable to individual segments of the system; conversely, for all through shipments, "the demand curve" for any one segment necessarily spills over into other segments. In this context, what is important is not marginal cost by some narrow definition (of a ton, or a ton-mile, or a carload), but the *average unit cost of incremental output*—which will, of course, vary with different geographic configurations of desired movement or different product mix. For an expanding system, the roller-coaster ups and downs of transport prices which would be created by slavish adherence to short-run marginal cost, as segments of plant are first filled to capacity and then enlarged, would serve only the negative economic purpose of manufacturing a new type of uncertainty.

If the successive minimum cost points for the transport system decline steadily as volume grows from BAC_1 to BAC_2, etc., a classic decreasing cost problem still remains, even if indivisibility, as such, has been taken care of. Average unit cost of incremental output will now always fall below average unit cost of total output (see Figure X-2).

c. In the "pure decreasing cost" case depicted in Figure X-3, indivisibilities cease to be a problem. Short-run marginal costs may still be highly erratic, rising steeply as output is expanded in each plant of given capacity and then dropping abruptly to a new short-run marginal cost curve as new capacity is added. But, in view of the infinite divisibility of plant sizes assumed by the smooth curve, the ups and down of short-run costs are not reflected in long-run problems. It is, perhaps, doubtful that a curve of long-run decreasing costs could ever drop continuously. Once such an assumption is made, however, the problem of short-run cost behavior which is independent of long-run costs simply disappears. Here, most clearly, even a price which is equal to long-run marginal cost must fail to cover average cost.

It should be noted that emphasis on density per unit of distance, which is the hidden thread in most transport discussion, may conceal quite different relationships for terminal costs. Transport economics involves not only "between," but "from and to." Costs of service between Paris and other main traffic nodes may be low by any definition, but this could be offset by terminal costs in Paris and other traffic nodes. Therefore, it is inappropriate to rack one's brains for sources of subsidy to bridge the gap between average and marginal cost of the line haul until one has at least investigated the prospects for making up the difference by profits derived from marginal costing at the terminals.

2. *New transport services should be expected to pay their full costs, possibly, but not necessarily, by tolls collected from transport users.*

The distinction between transport costs and the liabilities of transport users will be more fully developed in the last section of this chapter. Here, in brief, it can be said that a new transport service must involve a rearrangement of geographical relationships which may affect site values and incomes derived from any form of comparative advantage in numerous ways—positively and negatively—quite apart from ways that can be measured by ton-miles or passenger-miles. (This familiar proposition is, of course, not restricted to transport.) If the collateral effects are positive, the economist must avoid an asymmetrical argument: the possibly spurious dilemma created by contrasting a cost curve which *includes* costs which are not a function of ton-mile output with a demand curve which *excludes* utilities which are not a function of ton-mile output. In some cases, the problem may be taken care of more neatly and simply than by a vague general reference to "external economies." The secret may be simply to add a further dimension to the problem, reflecting both costs and utilities expressed in some unit other than ton- or passenger-miles.

3. *Decreasing costs may exist which are related to units of transportation service and cannot be charged off against other dimensions of utility.*

So a combination of the first point of our summary (charge at least marginal cost on each unit) with the second point (cover full costs on new services) may require the use of value-of-service pricing, as an auxiliary to marginal-cost pricing, to satisfy the full cost condition without needlessly sacrificing useful output by average-cost pricing. The theoretical case for value-of-service pricing, subject to marginal and total cost constraints, is that it is a means of increasing both total output and net satisfaction from total output. It is simultaneously a method of assuring that total output is worth at least as much as the total cost of providing it. Hence it can fulfill the full cost condition at the expense of modification, rather than elimination, of the marginal cost condition.

This case for value-of-service charging is not, of course, accepted by all economists as a valid guide for policy recommendations. Many economists have at least some sympathy for a pure marginal-cost position, based on the proposition that value-of-service charging (if carried out in the traditional form of one unit price, regardless of volume, for each separate buyer) must lead to misallocation of resources within the transport industries. Moreover, a whole school of economists could probably be found who maintain that the only thing that matters is whether buyers would be willing (even if not required to do so) to pay extra to cover deficits that might be incurred as a result of marginal cost pricing.

But this line of argument is more attractive in theory than in practice. Even in theory, its weakness is that it suppresses important questions of interpersonal comparison. Why, for example, should one person pay for part of another person's consumption of transport services, simply because no one has been ingenious or persuasive enough to introduce a system of pricing related to the value of the service for each individual? The second person may be indigent or possess very limited earning power. Is there any economic justification for supporting a transport service partly through levies on individuals who may have little or no use for the service on any terms?

4. In terms of the "general theory of second best," relationships within the field of transport are likely to be dominated by substitution, while relationships of transport to other parts of the economy are more likely to be complementary.

The "general theory of second best" was obviously not put forward to simplify the determination of optimum allocation, and has, in fact, performed the opposite function in this chapter. But it can be used as a point of departure toward a most important distinction which will be the underlying theme of the rest of this chapter: in developed economies, the central problem of transport arises from the competition between established forms of transport; in underdeveloped countries, the central problem is the allocation of resources within the transport sector on the one hand and the remainder of the economy on the other.

Transport Investment and Pricing in Developed Economies

This section concentrates on the importance of substitution in transport pricing in developed countries. In view of the central emphasis on problems of economic development, however, the discussion intentionally takes a negative tack to indicate why many features of current transport policies of developed countries are not necessarily applicable to developing countries.

The most recent statement on the appropriate role of cost in American transport pricing, prepared by ten leading economists under the auspices of the Association of American Railroads, is addressed both to economic theory and to transport practice.[19] The statement reflects a number of issues in transport economics which are fundamental for American policy but of limited relevance to underdeveloped countries.

One is the emphasis on minimum, rather than actual pricing, with a correlative emphasis on the range of discretion to be allowed private managements by the public regulatory body (the Interstate Commerce

---

[19] William J. Baumol, Burton N. Behling, James C. Bonbright, Yale Brozen, Joel Dean, Ford K. Edwards, Calvin B. Hoover, Dudley F. Pegrum, Merrill J. Roberts, and Ernest W. Williams, Jr., "The Role of Cost in the Minimum Pricing of Railroad Services," *Journal of Business of the University of Chicago,* Vol. 35 (October 1962), pp. 357-366. See also comments by Joseph R. Rose, J. W. Hershey, Romney Robinson, and the original authors, *Journal of Business of the University of Chicago,* Vol. 36 (July 1963), pp. 336-361.

Commission). Since outside of the United States railroads are typically owned by governments, American reactions to the costing problem must include rather atypical interest in the division of pricing responsibility between private owners and public controllers. Moreover, the United States is possibly the only country in the world to encourage competition among railroads. A part of its early national transportation policy, competition continues through the years as a desideratum. When railroad competition is combined with private ownership and extensive recourse to value-of-service pricing, the effects spill over into economic analysis of railroad rates. Not least, these factors produce unusual concentration on rate relationships and on permissible minimum rates.

The AAR statement also makes assumptions that are of limited relevance to any transport industry that is neither mature nor more concerned with loss of present business than with conquering new terrain. Assume specialized resources, which for all practical purposes can scarcely be shifted, economically or legally, to other uses; assume also an industry that is earning more than enough to replace its assets but less than enough to be willing or able to attract new capital from external sources. Then the emphasis of economists must be on *short-run* marginal costs and on the problems of maximum use compatible with minimum economic return on *existing* assets.

From both the historical and the current standpoint, the emphasis is bound to be on price as a mechanism for inducing substitution of one transport service for another, and not on price as a method of regulating the appropriate flow of resources into the transport sector as a whole.

France is the only country in the world which has avowedly introduced marginal cost principles as a matter of deliberate long-term policy into transport (and public utility) rate-making.[20] Even in France,

[20] For an extensive theoretical discussion of the problems involved, by an official of the Société Nationale des Chemins de Fer who was influential in the postwar recasting of the French rail freight rate structure, see Roger Hutter, "La théorie économique et la gestion commerciale des chemins de fer: Qu'est-ce que le coût marginal?" *Revue Générale des Chemins de Fer* (Paris, February 1950), pp. 53-63; "Le problème tarifaire," *ibid.* (July 1950), pp. 318-332; "La coordination des transports," *ibid.* (October 1950), pp. 443-460. C. J. Oort relies heavily on French discussion in his *La Théorie Marginaliste et les Prix de Transport*. A recent paper describing the French experience and the present structure and rationale of French freight rates in English is Dagobert M. Scher, "Cost Analysis and New Rate Structure of the French National Railroads," *Transportation Research Forum, Papers, Fourth Annual Meeting* (Boston, December 1963), pp. 336-341. I am

the institutional structure has not permitted systematic allowance for all substitution possibilities either in transport or in energy supply. The government owns the railways, via the Société Nationale des Chemins de Fer Français, and provides the highways, but the SNCF and the highways have separate administrations, separate budgets, and at least the possibility of separate investment criteria. In the energy sector, application of marginal analysis to the prices of electricity, gas, and coal still leaves a door ajar for the price of crude oil. But, in that part of the transport sector which is completely subject to public control of prices, the nationalized railways, the basic objective of marginal cost pricing well illustrates the theme already stated for developed countries in general:

> . . . we were not looking for a general level of tariffs, which should cover all expenses, but only for a rational variation of rates.

> What can the French National Railroad expect from their rate reform? It is still too soon to say; however, it is expected that sooner or later transfers of traffic between carriers will occur.[21]

The one really major type of new investment in railroad way and structure which is of practical interest to the SNCF is electrification. Major geographical extensions of the rail system are not planned; indeed the trend has been, and will continue to be, the opposite. And the marginal cost analysis appropriate to electrification is quite different from that which would be employed to determine the feasibility of extending the rail net.

Here, then, is the first difference between developed and underdeveloped countries: the former have rail systems which are already as geographically extensive as they are ever likely to be. Much of the marginal analysis in France is cast in terms of what are called "marginal costs of regression," i.e., the reductions in cost which may be expected to accompany a shrinkage in services rendered. These need not be identical with marginal costs of expansion or development (the whole marginal cost curve may, in short, be irreversible) except over a time

---

editor of a volume describing the experience of Electricité de France with the development of marginal cost pricing: *Marginal Cost Pricing in Practice* (Prentice-Hall, 1964); see especially Parts I and II, written mainly by Marcel Boiteux but with contributions also by Pierre Massé and Paul Stasi. See also Marcel Boiteux, "Sur la gestion des monopoles publics astreints a l'équilibre budgétaire," *Econometrica*, Vol. 24 (January 1956), pp. 22-40, especially pp. 38-39.

[21] Scher, *op. cit.*, pp. 339-341.

period so long that some other method of transport might conceivably take over the whole rail function anyway. To base rates on this "long-term marginal cost of regression" would simply hasten the process of regression itself, and probably even belie the marginal cost data originally taken as a parameter in trying to solve the pricing problem. In this situation the Hotelling cost assumptions, based on fixed plant, may be quite realistic.

But many of the underdeveloped countries have rudimentary rail systems, related, in some cases, to a single export product or exporting region. In any event the systems are often neither extensive nor adequately located for the kind of growth of economic activity that is anticipated or desired. Here the road-rail question is not so much how to wring maximum output from the existing rail facilities as whether to invest in new railroads, or in new highways (or new inland waterways, docks and harbors, or in new airports). So the Hotelling marginal, or infinitesimal, cost conditions for optimum pricing may be distinctly secondary to the Dupuit total, or finite, cost conditions.

Just as irreversible elements may be found in rail cost curves, so too they may be found in demand for rail service. The consequences may be illustrated by starting with Oort's application of the rules for optimum price discrimination to a struggling industry:

> [Assume] an enterprise which, even in following the most deliberate policy of monopoly pricing, can only realize a meager profit or struggle to avoid losses. In this case optimum conduct is the same whether it is considered as maximization of profit or as marginal calculation of prices, linked to the requirement of profitability. In this case, the maximization of profit barely achieves coverage of total costs, while any other course would produce losses.[22]

This statement derives from the fundamentals of comparative statics. Within its own terms of reference, it can be challenged only by an economist who wishes to deny the appropriateness of value-of-service charging in any circumstances. But, as a practical matter, the precept "maximize profit!" may conceal the fact that a relatively low price can be justified, within these terms of reference, only as a response to a high demand elasticity. In a developed country this condition is most likely to derive from the ability to attract relatively very large volumes of traffic from other transport media. Since this traffic must normally

---

[22] Oort, *La Théorie Marginaliste* . . . , p. 48. My translation.

have moved by rail before it was captured by other methods of transport, the precept may be the equivalent of saying, "Wait till you lose most of your volume of any given type of business before you cut rates to try to get it back." Furthermore, some part of each quantity of traffic which is potentially recoverable by the railroads, and hence adds to the elasticity of demand, might have been held at a price lower than the old level but higher than the proposed new one. At the same time some additional amount of traffic is probably lost forever because the original loss of traffic was accompanied by some reorganization of the geography of economic activity unfavorable to the railroads.

This same problem of demand irreversibility is also a possibility in an underdeveloped country. In fact, however, it probably would not arise there because parallel first-class rail and highway facilities are much less common than in the developed countries.

Practically every country, developed or underdeveloped, has the common problem of railroads encumbered with services for which prices are less than their marginal costs. This requires stretching "normative" pricing rules to cover not only the hiatus between average and marginal cost but also the additional gap (of indeterminate magnitude) between higher costs and lower prices on a certain portion of the traffic. In nearly every developed country, passenger service is an important source of loss. And, owing to the inherent costliness of shrinkage, the loss may at least temporarily become greater as the importance of the service becomes less. For some, but by no means all, underdeveloped countries passenger service may be less important. Or it may not be subject to such heavy relative loss per unit, or at least not subject to quite such rapid erosion of demand from the competition of highways (and especially passenger automobiles).

In practically every country, too, the main "artificial" constraint on highway competition with rail has been the limitation of the government's highway budget. Here the economic rationale may be quite different in developed and in undeveloped countries.

Rail connections already exist in the developed nations between all major industrial areas, and there is usually little expectation of major future shifts of industrial activity to locations beyond the rail system. However, in the underdeveloped countries, existing or potential centers of economic activity are less likely to have good rail service. Therefore the constraint on highway construction is less likely to be influenced by its impact on the revenues of railroads and more likely to be influenced by its impact on the scramble for governmental finances and for resources generally. A new highway in a developed country generally provides a substitute, not a complement, for rail movement. A new highway in an underdeveloped country may be either substitute or complement.

Applying Marginal Cost Pricing to Transport in Developing Economies

This section will confront the more positive aspect of our problem: what principles of transport pricing should be applied in developing countries?

The search for these principles may be somewhat the easier. Developing countries are not faced as much as developed countries are with the extraordinary problems involved in trying to prescribe optimum pricing rules for two decreasing-cost industries (road and rail). Both services provide similar but not identical services, and their rates of growth vary from rapid expansion for road to practical stagnation for rail. Also, in many developing economies the transportation system will have to be expanded more rapidly (in terms of the creation of new facilities for the support of long-distance transport service) than in the developed nations; this expansion will occur mainly through the construction of new or improved highways.

The economic case for highway construction differs in a fundamental way from that applicable to railroads. Assume, for example, that the total cost of a highway movement is the same as the total cost of moving an identical tonnage over an identical distance by rail. Assume further that the structure of this total cost, in terms of division between roadbed and transportation cost, is likewise the same for both. (Of course, this may be contrary to fact: highways may not involve decreasing costs.) The cost allocable to transportation will still not be identical in each of the two cases, even granting these very artificial assumptions.

This may be illustrated by a simple decreasing-cost function of the following type:

Total Cost $= a + bx$

where $x =$ ton-miles of freight per mile of transport facility.

For highways, much or all of *a* may appropriately be charged off against elements in demand which are not a function of ton-miles:

> . . . even in the absence of any sort of long-distance automobile travel, owners of economically utilizable property would still want access to their sites.[23]

It is even conceivable that this cost function might coexist with increasing costs of ton-mile movement in some environments, due to association of denser traffic with declining (or increasingly negative) marginal access values. For rail, on the other hand, with road crossings at grade, local access values may be negative even for low-density lines. An increase in the number of stations to improve access may affect the general quality of service or the general level of costs even at low densities.

So an economist must exercise care in relating the cost structures of each industry to the demand for their services. It may be reasonable to associate all railroad demand with volume of movement even though this simplification conceals both positive and negative access values, but to use it as the sole demand parameter relevant to highway costs is much less reasonable. If all threshold costs in highway transport could be charged off against access, marginal cost pricing applied to movement could simply be adequate to cover bx in the formula given above, and no decreasing cost problem would arise. Instead there would be an allocation problem of assessing costs against access as well as movement.

Moreover, it is obviously unrealistic to assume that cost structures for road and rail are even similar. The use of trailers produces only a very small part of the special economies that can be provided by using the longer trains that become more feasible with heavier rail traffic density. Conversely, the railroads fought the battle of the gauges early in their history and must now be content with uniform gauges for integrated systems, in view of the heavy costs of transshipment or adaptation of equipment. On the other hand, larger trucks involve wider and more strongly built highways—which in turn may or may not involve decreasing costs per unit of *capacity* and could even produce sharply increasing costs (as well as decreasing costs) per ton-

[23] J. R. Meyer, Merton J. Peck, John Stenason, and Charles Zwick, *The Economics of Competition in the Transportation Industries* (Harvard University Press, 1959), p. 72.

mile actually moved over the highway.[24] The truck does provide a more flexible and very often a quicker service, but at the expense of much higher direct transportation costs per ton-mile. These considerably greater costs tend to reduce the relative importance of the highway itself; hence the lesser relative importance of highway cost structure (whether increasing, constant, or decreasing per unit of traffic or in response to other parameters). The net effect of the pros and cons noted in this paragraph probably operates to reduce the significance of decreasing costs for highways in comparison with railways.

Thus the problem of covering total costs via prices for transport services which approach marginal cost may be less in under-developed countries. Expenditure on fixed transport plant may normally be expected to concentrate on highways. Compared to the practice in developed countries, more expenditure will go into extension of the modern highway network (with attendant creation of new access values) and less into improvement of an existing network. Even the problem of adjusting total costs to current realities by writing off obsolete railroad properties should be less acute than in most developed countries.

A general problem in connection with highway pricing and highway investment arises from the common tendency to confuse costs and expenditures. Since in all countries the provision of highways is a budgetary function of governments, such provision tends to be viewed as a current expenditure only. Because the capital cost of highways must be an estimated or prospective cost, in the sense that the opportunity cost of capital embodied in any one form is the anticipated future cash flow that could have been obtained by committing this capital elsewhere in the economy, a current expenditure may seem a more realistic and more readily calculable measure. But this expenditure may, in turn, be regulated by an inward flow of earmarked taxes and user charges derived from the current services rendered by existing highways. Even if these taxes and user charges had a cost rationale, any resemblance between their annual amount and the outlay on highways warranted by a comparison of estimated future costs and future receipts would be purely coincidental. If these taxes and charges have no such rationale, or if they are unrelated to highway outlays,

[24] For a systematic presentation of the relationship between highway costs and truck dimensions, see Wilfred Owen, *A Study in Highway Economics* (Harvard University Phi Beta Kappa Society, 1934), especially Table V, p. 65.

expenditure on highways becomes simply a brute economic fact without even a spurious logical relationship to costs.

The particular problem for the developing country, in this context, is likely to be the relationship of both costs and expenditures to inflation. The very existence of inflation spoils the usefulness of the prime index of capital costs—"the going rate of interest." This going rate is clearly inadequate to hold the sum of all demands on resources down to the sum of all resources available at constant prices. Conversely, it may be argued that the going rate of interest is in some sense appropriate, but that the government's budget should provide for either more receipts or fewer expenditures. This argument, in turn, would imply possible fluctuations in highway programs and their financing wholly unrelated to cost-benefit analysis. Therefore, in inflationary surroundings, the issue becomes the relevance and practical feasibility of any cost criterion—not just the criterion of marginal cost—to the investment program for highways.

No one can devise a magic formula for correcting a disequilibrium rate of interest so as to make it an equilibrium rate. The only answer lies in trial and error. Nor can anyone arbitrarily determine an optimum admixture of monetary and fiscal policy. But, within these limits, it may be argued that current expectations as to future marginal costs are clearly more relevant to highway investment policy than average past costs or total current receipts from user charges. Current expectations as to future costs may not, of course, be identical with expected marginal costs. Here the familiar problem of indivisibility reappears: an expected (or actual) cost per unit of input cannot be directly and continuously converted into an expected cost per unit of output. But, with or without a struggle with the problem of indivisibility, any unbiased estimate of marginal costs provides at least some localized protection against the real counterpart of galloping inflation: progressive misallocation of resources.

Some of the countries with plans to use highways for all transport extensions may already have a significant railroad mileage. In India, for example, the basic long-haul facilities consist largely of rail. In such cases, as long as highways prove to be the most economical current way to extend transport facilities, "value-of-service" rate-making by rail should be strongly influenced by marginal costs of truck operation over highways, even though no highway movements compete directly on parallel routes with rail movements. Value-of-service rates that produced transport costs by rail higher than those available elsewhere by highway would set up strong economic pressure for parallel highway construction. Rates far below truck rates might overstrain rail capacity, and, by hypothesis, all additional investment would eventually be in roads. Parallel construction, as in the first case, would be wasteful; so would a distribution of economic activity, as in the second case, conditioned by today's average costs and not tomorrow's marginal costs. When two methods of transport compete and only one is expanding, it is uneconomic to attempt value-of-service charging without reference to the marginal cost of the expanding industry.

Marginal cost pricing for the use of highways is very different from marginal cost pricing on the part of the transport services using the highways. An economic advantage that many underdeveloped countries have over practically all developed countries is the tendency of the former to allow competition to set the rates for over-the-road services (passengers as well as freight). Truck regulation in the United States takes the form of raising the costs of common-carrier trucks by route and service restrictions and of permitting trucks to develop their own value-of-service rate structures even in the absence of any significant decreasing costs in operations. In Western Europe, it takes the form of limitation of the numbers of for-hire trucks. Either system may create an economic advantage for large concerns which are not common carriers and can use their own (unregulated) trucks with fewer diseconomies than those suffered by smaller private firms; either may also create an artificial incentive for all firms to operate more trucks in private carriage than would be economic if for-hire rates were at a minimum competitive level.

But decisions as to the role of common carriers and private trucks still do not answer the question of how the highways themselves are to be paid for. Even in an economy which generates very low supplies of or demands for goods and services requiring transportation per unit of land area, an individual motor vehicle is still likely to be a small unit of productive capacity relative to the tonnages and people to be moved. Single ownership of fleets of trucks is also not an obvious source of economies of scale. Therefore, constant costs may provide a reasonable approximation to the long-run economics of motor vehicle movements—in developing countries scarcely less than in developed economies.

It was argued at the beginning of this section that highway costs are not as likely as rail costs to involve a decreasing cost structure attributable to volume of transportation. Two questions remain: how to cover threshold costs, or any other costs not attributable to volume of transportation (e.g., because such costs are attributable to access), and how to cover such transportation costs as may still remain in the accounts after payment has been received for the marginal cost of transportation.

One of the more ingenious forms of payment for costs incurred to satisfy demands other than that for volume of movement was devised by the Congress of the United States to finance the original federal land grant railroads. Half of the public domain within economic distance of the railroad right-of-way was turned over to the railroad to help defray its cost of construction; then the price of the other half of the land still in government hands was doubled. Thus a subsidy to the railroad builder might cost the government nothing.

In its pure form, this device can scarcely be adopted in countries possessing no valuable public domain. It can nevertheless be applied in the form of special property taxes or assessments—to be used for transportation purposes—on property which benefits from the provision of such facilities. This is the economically appropriate way to recover road costs attributable to the provision of access, and has, in fact, been employed in the United States and other English-speaking countries. But application of this benefit theory of taxation becomes less straightforward when it comes to allocating such costs of movement (not access) that are not strictly proportional to ton-miles of haulage.

To the extent that the cost divergence is caused by differences in vehicle *sizes*, the problem is that even a highway being used to its capacity in terms of *number* of vehicles might still have a wide margin of excess capacity for the very largest vehicles whose size determines the outer dimensions of the highway. Moreover, there is no reason to assume that an entire highway network must be expanded, as traffic expands, in an amount just sufficient to maintain the exact previous proportion between highway costs and volume of highway movements. And improved facilities for *movement*, unlike those for *access*, may destroy as well as create site value. Access is essentially local; movement involves passage through as well as origination and termination. As a special case, improvement of transportation facilities could reduce all economic rents: for example, as in von Thünen's theory of differential economic rent in terms of the relative distance of different areas of physically identical land from a central market.[25]

A general solution to this problem may be obtained by first assuming that the larger cities in a country obtain more benefit than that obtained by the towns and villages, per capita and per ton of freight entering and leaving, from the entire transportation network. After constant costs of highways have been recovered from gasoline taxes and possibly also from vehicle license fees, and after access values have been recovered from special assessment, any remaining cost might be recouped by a volume tax, graduated according to the size of the market for which the goods are intended.

The exact form of such a tax is more a matter of administrative feasibility than of economic theory. But it might be a tonnage tax with a ton-mile coefficient to offer some reflection of total benefit received from the existence of a larger transportation network; or even a progressive tax varying with the "home port" of the concerns operating the trucks. The essential idea would be to derive funds from the most "developed" part of the economy—the part which normally would receive the greatest absolute increments in benefits from an expansion of a national highway network. This arrangement should help provide facilities for those areas which would otherwise be caught in a vicious circle if asked to pay the full cost of new facilities: their inability to pay this full cost might actually be a measure of their need for the service rather than of the absence of need.

Conclusions

1. "Price transport services at the marginal cost of providing them" is the classic recipe of economists who employ the approach of comparative statics.

2. Since decreasing costs are involved in practically every form of transport—at least in the provision of infrastructure—the recipe would necessarily produce receipts inadequate to cover costs.

3. Of all the classical writers on marginal cost pricing, Dupuit is the greatest name. And Dupuit combined a belief in *marginal* cost

[25] J. H. von Thünen, *Der isolirte Staat* (Verlag von Wiegandt, Hempel & Parey, 1875), Volume One, Book One, pp. 1-263.

pricing with a belief in levying extra charges to cover *total* costs as well

4. In the history of transport rates, this approach to "value-of-service" charging tended to become submerged beneath a superstructure of pricing customs based rather crudely on charging what the traffic would bear. But marginal costs as a minimum need not be incompatible with some employment of rudimentary value-of-service principles to enable the transport enterprise (whether publicly or privately owned) to carry on without loss.

5. The revival of interest in marginal cost pricing has tended to emphasize the significance of always setting prices equal to marginal cost. This special form of the argument requires deficits for decreasing cost industries, and presumably must assume that they are paid, somehow, by the population in general. Thus the argument ends in a departure from both cost-of-service and value-of-service principles of rate-making, and implicitly assumes interpersonal comparison of utilities as well.

6. The simplest form of the decreasing cost argument involves an indivisible minimum capacity, which is more than adequate for all feasible outputs. Once the argument is extended beyond this special case, "decreasing costs" and "indivisibilities" (in the sense of cost discontinuities, or "lumpiness" tend to part company. Indivisibilities may exist without an overall decreasing cost trend; and conversely. Where both exist together, indivisibilities theoretically complicate the marginal cost argument as it applies to decreasing costs. Marginal cost may even exceed average cost for certain restricted ranges of output; in this case, marginal cost pricing would create an excess profit. But in a rapidly developing economy, these marginal costs must be very temporary and hence of limited interest. Moreover, for a whole transportation network, cost discontinuities tend to cancel out. What matters most is the *average* cost of an increment of new output spread over most or all of the transport system.

7. The basic difference between the pricing problem in developed and in developing countries arises from the fact that *substitution*, in the form of the competition between a mature rail system and a growing industry of highway transport, dominates the transport scene in a developed country, whereas *complementarity*, or the necessity for added transport of some kind to permit the rest of the economy to expand, is the basic attribute of the process of development. In the

former case, *marginal* analysis must dominate. In the latter, the important consideration is the recovery of *total* costs.

8. This emphasis on total costs is reinforced by the additional probability that decreasing costs of transport movement (e.g., of ton-miles) will be less important in a developing country than they were, or are, in a developed country. Developing countries will tend to rely more on extensions of highways; hence they can legitimately charge off much of the excess of average over marginal cost to the creation of additional access values.

9. The emphasis on both total and marginal costs becomes yet more important in a country subject to inflationary pressures, which are a frequent if not logically necessary concomitant of economic development. Although "total costs" must not be confused with "total current expenditure," the case for incurring a present cost in the absence of an assignable future benefit is even weaker in the presence of inflation than in its absence.

10. Due to the governmental character of highway development and the combination of access and movement utilities which highways provide, developing countries may face technical problems of collecting for value of service rendered. Special assessments or other localized fees and taxes should be used to recover access values. Straight-line taxes and fees (as a first approximation, a gasoline tax) are adequate for the portion of highway costs which changes in exact ratio to volume of transport. Special charges against transport entering or leaving the largest cities may be required to recover any residual highway costs, on the rationale that a metropolis typically receives and dispatches shipments for longer average distances and obtains more net benefits, per capita or per ton, from the existence of an integrated transport network.

XI

Financing Transport Investment

A. ROBERT SADOVE* AND GARY FROMM*

In formulating normative prescriptions for establishing project priorities and framing expenditure programs, economists generally have restricted their attention to an incomplete analysis which neglects financial factors. It has often been assumed that if resources are valued at their opportunity costs and project benefits are estimated within a general equilibrium or national income context, conditions for making optimum investment decisions are assured. Unfortunately, such results can be misleading, both from the standpoint of an individual project and in the aggregate. Because resources are not transferred directly from one use to another but indirectly through a monetary mechanism, consideration of the financing of investment leads to additional constraints and criteria for selecting projects—a matter which is explored in this essay.

Four major topics are most relevant to the subject: (1) the scope of the financing problem for national transport investment and individual transport projects; (2) the determination of financial requirements and returns of transport investment projects; and (3) the relationship of economic to financial analysis; and (4) the impact of financial factors on project priorities. Emphasis is given to the role of financial analysis in allocating investment funds rather than its more traditional role of organizing the types of securities to be issued, the sink-

* The World Bank; The Brookings Institution.

This essay is a revision and expansion of the seminar presentation given by Robert Sadove, who had primary responsibility for the materials on economic and financial analysis in practice. Some of the more theoretical, normative aspects of these analyses are the concern of the second author.

ing fund provisions, and other financial arrangements of already selected projects.

Scope of the Financial Problem

The financing of transport is especially important because in many underdeveloped countries transport is the largest component of total investment. Of ten countries where information for a recent year is readily available, investment in transport has ranged from around 2 percent to 5 percent of Gross National Product and from 10 to nearly 50 percent of total fixed investment (See Table XI-1). Often the major burden of transport investment is borne by governments. In several countries transport has accounted for over 25 percent of total public investment (See Table XI-2). Transport investment plus substantial deficits in operating these facilities has placed a significant burden on national budgets. Currently, there are several cases where well over half of large annual deficits in the public budget are directly related to losses in the operation of publicly owned railroads.

In practice, the amount of financing for transport investment can be so large that it may severely restrict a government's freedom to allocate funds to other uses. This forces the analyst, at least in part, to adopt a financial approach in reviewing investment proposals. Consider the case of Nigeria. In the year 1958-59, not only did government investment in transport amount to about half of all public sector investment, but, in addition, private investment expenditures for motor vehicles alone amounted to about one-third of all private investment and 3 percent of GNP. A similar situation exists in a number of other countries.

As of September 30, 1964, the World Bank and its affiliate, the International Development Association, had made loans and credits for transport projects amounting to more than U.S. $3 billion. (See Table XI-3.) The amount of additional domestic investment needed to complete the projects involved is estimated at another U.S. $3-$4 billion.

It is not unusual to find individual projects requiring as much as 10-20 percent of a government's annual investment budget (cf. Table

TABLE XI-1. *Transport Investment in Relation to*
Gross Fixed Investment and Gross National Product[a]

Country	Gross Fixed Investment as a Percentage of GNP	Transport Investment as a Percentage of GNP	Transport Investment as a Percentage of Gross Fixed Investment
Colombia	19.6%	5.3%	26.9%
India	11.5	2.1	18.7
Israel	26.5	4.5[b]	17.3[b]
Japan	42.6	4.9	11.4
Mexico	13.8	2.4	17.2
Nigeria	13.8	4.9	49.0
Pakistan	11.9	1.8	15.4
Sudan	13.3	2.0	15.6
Thailand	16.6	2.8[b]	16.5[b]

Source: Statistical Office of the United Nations. Department of Economic and Social Affairs, *Yearbook of National Accounts Statistics* (New York: United Nations, 1962).
[a] All estimates pertain to one year in the period 1959–62.
[b] Including communications investment.

TABLE XI-2. *Public Transport Investment in Relation to*
Other Investment[a]

Country	Public Sector Investment as Percentage of GNP	Public Transport Investment as Percentage of Public Sector Investment	Public Transport Investment as Percentage of Public Sector Domestic Investment	Public Transport Investment as Percentage of Total Domestic Investment	Public Transport Investment as Percentage of Total Transport Investment
Colombia	5.1%	54.0%	55.0%	26.0%	53.0%
India	—	—	—	27.0	80.0
Japan	9.8	25.6	34.5	—	51.0
Mexico	5.9	18.4	22.5	—	46.0
Nigeria	6.0	30.5	51.5	54.5	36.7
Pakistan	5.7	17.5	27.0	23.0	57.0
Sudan	7.4	20.4	25.2	21.0	74.0
Thailand	6.1	24.1[b]	—	—	54.0[b]

Source: Statistical Office of the United Nations, Department of Economic and Social Affairs, *Yearbook of National Accounts Statistics* (New York: United Nations, 1962).
[a] Estimates pertain to one year in the period 1959–62.
[b] Including communications investment.

TABLE XI-3. *Transport Loans and Credits, World Bank and International Development Association, September 30, 1964*

(In millions of U.S. dollars)

World Bank		
Railroads	$1,189.8	
Roads	1,014.4	
Ports and Waterways	327.2	
Airlines and Airports	56.9	
Pipelines	79.0	
Shipping	12.0	
Total Bank		$2,679.3
IDA		
Railroads	116.5	
Roads	218.7	
Ports and Waterways	27.5	
Total IDA		362.7
Total Transport Loans and Credits		$3,042.0

Source: Statistical Division, International Bank for Reconstruction and Development, *Bank Loans Classified by Purpose and Area as of September, 1964.*

XI-4). This is aside from any related investments that private firms must make for rolling stock or other auxiliary equipment. Given the magnitude of these outlays, it is imperative that project evaluation be properly conceived and that project costs and benefits be measured as accurately as is realistically feasible.

Investment Evaluation Theory

In a world with no increasing returns to scale or external economies, no monopoly elements or financial constraints, no differential social welfare effects, and so forth—and with perfect knowledge—it would be a simple matter to determine investment priorities. Maximizing the discounted value of Gross National Product would be consistent with maximizing "social welfare." It would only be necessary to ascertain the magnitude of GNP with and without any given investment. Projects would then be selected which yield the highest net benefit per dollar invested, and resources would be allocated in such a way that the last dollar's worth of resources in each use yields equal returns.

228   FINANCING TRANSPORT INVESTMENT

TABLE XI-4. *Representative World Bank and IDA Transport Investments in Relation to Annual Government Expenditures and Annual Government Investment, 1958-1962*

(Dollar items in millions of U.S. dollars)

Project	Annual Government Expenditures		Investment in Project			Ratio of Investment in Project to Government Expenditure[a]	Ratio of Investment in Project to Government Investment[a]
	Investment (1)	Total (2)	Domestic (3)	IBRD/IDA (4)	Total (5)	(5)/(2)	(5)/(1)
Roads							
1	$ 450	$2,000	$ 62	$48	$110	5.5%	24.5%
2	390	1,100	44	25	69	6.3	17.7
3	200	940	37	25	62	6.6	31.1
4	210	1,450	62	30	92	6.3	43.5
5	1,680	6,600	121	50	171	2.6	10.2
6	300	700	8	7	15	2.2	5.0
7	40	80	30	25	55	69.5	136.0
8	10	50	6	8	14	28.0	140.0
Ports							
1	210	720	27	28	55	7.5	26.2
2	300	900	12	13	25	2.8	8.3
3	1,680	3,570	30	29	59	1.6	3.5
Railways							
1	90	260	25	14	50[b]	19.2	55.6
2	160	1,300	235	25	277[b]	21.3	173.1
3	780	2,310	339	11	350	15.2	45.0

Source: World Bank Project Reports and United Nations, *Yearbook of Statistics, 1963* (New York: United Nations, 1964).

[a] Since project investment expenditures may take place over a few years' time, some of these percentages are biased upwards. Note, however, that current expenditures by projects initiated in the past will tend to offset this bias.

[b] Components do not add to total because other foreign sources of loans are not shown.

However, an economy is seldom so static or so small that the impact of any potential project on national income can be isolated from other changes that might take place. All that can be done, in practice, is to evaluate the possible direct effects of an investment proposal and describe any indirect and intangible results, under certain simplifying assumptions and adjustments for conditions which depart from the theoretical norm. Occasionally some quantification of indirect effects is also feasible. These evaluations range from predictions of possible outcomes to subjective appraisals of social needs and preferences to the use of hypothetical "real" or "true" economic parameters in the analyses.

For example, attention has often been called to artificially low interest rates, overvalued exchange rates, and wages that are not as low as would be expected in underdeveloped countries which are presumed to have an excess supply of labor. These are all indications that the market prices of inputs and outputs do not reflect the "true" opportunity values of using resources. Therefore, a strong case is made for the use of "accounting prices" (sometimes called "shadow prices") in calculating economic returns in cases where market prices are distorted.[1] On the other hand, no satisfactory method currently exists for determining the proper accounting prices. Furthermore, these theoretical prices are not applied in the market place so distortions in demand, incentives, or resource allocation may still occur.

In addition, even where the market prices of inputs and outputs reasonably reflect their real scarcity value, there is still the difficult problem of trying to determine and measure the direct, and especially the indirect, effects of an investment. Will the improvements made in a port reduce the costs of a country's exports? Will the reduction of costs be reflected in lower export prices? Will lower export prices lead to an expansion of exports and foreign exchange earnings? If so, by how much will foreign exchange earnings increase? Is the situation further complicated by the fact that the increased foreign exchange proceeds accrue to foreign-owned firms? This is only a very small sample of the kinds of questions to which answers are required in an economic analysis.

Economic Analysis in Practice

Nevertheless, in spite of the fact that there are overwhelming obstacles to the complete quantification of all costs and benefits, economic calculations must play a leading role in the selection of investment projects. In practice, project appraisal is frequently carried out along

[1] Strictly speaking, in a general equilibrium, linear programming context, a "shadow price" is the unit marginal value of a resource under perfectly competitive conditions. Thus, a shadow price is somewhat narrower in scope than an accounting price; the latter includes adjustments to reflect monopoly elements and market imperfections.

the following lines. A general review of the economy and a detailed examination of the investment program of the country is undertaken. Then a judgment is often made as to whether the particular economic sector containing the project to be appraised is a "priority" sector—one in which investment is essential if development is to be stimulated. Following these steps, a preliminary calculation should indicate whether there is a prima facie case that the economic return from a particular project would be higher than the return from alternative uses of this capital. If the result is positive, a detailed economic analysis would then be carried out to determine whether the project in fact is a more beneficial investment than other projects which might be undertaken with the capital involved. Obviously, the determination of this opportunity cost of capital—sometimes called a target rate of return—is a critical matter.

Of course, the obstacles encountered in the calculation of economic returns mean that those returns will be emphasized which are relatively easy to measure. In the case of road projects, it will be savings in user costs; in the case of congested ports, ship waiting days saved; and in the case of railroads, reductions in transport costs. In addition, attempts are made to estimate more or less precisely such indirect returns as the development that will be induced by the project. Agricultural development along a road, or expansion of exports, or reduction in the cost of imports resulting from a port improvement are examples.

On the other side of the ledger, estimates of investment costs require a substantial amount of very detailed and time consuming engineering and financial work. In a number of large projects recently examined, detailed re-examinations of the cost estimates at a late stage in the appraisal were necessary. In some cases, these late stage reviews resulted in an increase in the estimates by at least 10 percent, despite the advanced stages of the engineering and the fact that the original analyses had been made by engineers who were experienced in preparing such cost estimates. In part, such discrepancies arise because the exact location of a transport route, the variability of design standards, and the use of alternative construction materials and methods usually introduce factors which are difficult to evaluate.

Since the margin of error in the estimates may be substantial, a generous allowance for contingencies is usually necessary. The unanticipated factors that may arise vary from case to case. These may be technical problems. For example, the quantity or quality of the earth to be moved may differ greatly from one road to another, and little may be known of the local geological conditions. This kind of uncertainty often occurs in less developed countries when the engineering of projects has often only reached the preliminary stage.

To estimate financial requirements accurately, it is also important that contingency funds be provided to cover possible increases in costs resulting from a rise in the general price level or changes in specific conditions of supply and demand. For instance, wages and prices often increase when large projects create an unusually great demand for labor in the more underdeveloped parts of countries. Although the relationship between the prices of different goods and services may not change, there may be increases in the absolute price level. These increases are not usually important to the economic analysis, but the financial effects of this kind of inflation cannot be ignored.

The serious consequences of underestimating project costs frequently dictate allowances for contingencies ranging around 20 percent, or even higher. Yet, despite these precautions, there continue to be risks of over-runs in costs. Such over-runs have sometimes led to a slowing down in construction and the danger that the project would come to a halt because of a shortage of funds. In turn, long construction periods increase the chance of a difference between the actual and the estimated costs. Obviously, an estimate that is too low has more serious negative consequences than one that is too high. For this reason, the cost estimates that are finally accepted may have to be on the high side. Experience shows that generous estimates tend to be more correct in the long run.[2]

To complete the economic analysis, account must be taken of various indirect costs engendered by a project. For example, in order to take advantage of new transportation facilities, much present commercial activity might have to be relocated or reoriented.

The Role of Financial Analysis

Prudent decision-making requires ways of supplementing and checking the results of the calculations of economic returns and costs.

[2] Cf. the discussion regarding cost estimates in the Brookings transport cases— e.g. the Atlantic Highway in Guatemala—soon to be published.

This is where financial analysis can be particularly useful to the economist. Economic analysis takes a wide view. It does not limit itself to the organization carrying out a project but extends its purview to include the country or region as a whole. It also takes into account benefits and costs which may not involve cash expenditures or receipts by the entity responsible for a venture. Financial analysis, on the other hand, is generally restricted to the outlays and revenues accruing to a project.

Financial analysis is both a supplement to the economic evaluation and a basic source of data for the calculation of the economic rate of return. However, financial analysis uses its information to examine matters which economic analysis frequently neglects, or at the least, tends to minimize.

In financial analyses particular emphasis is placed on the ability of projects to meet all operating costs continuously (that is, satisfy their liquidity requirements) and, also, to earn an adequate return on the funds invested. This return, although not always defined in precise terms, is usually interpreted to mean a return which covers at least depreciation charges and the actual cost of capital to the enterprise concerned. Where a significant amount of private equity is involved, the cost of capital should include an allowance for a minimum return on these funds. When financing an economically desirable future expansion of a project is extremely difficult, the return may also include an element for partial internal funding of such investment from the project's revenues. The insistence that examination of the financial self-sufficiency of projects (financial "health" or "soundness" are synonyms commonly employed in financial circles) be part of the project appraisal stems from the difficulties that governments in less developed countries experience in raising revenues for investment and other expenditure needs.

Because of the literacy and administrative requirements of income taxation, less developed countries rely mainly on indirect taxes—such as customs, excise, sales, and property taxes—to obtain revenues. However, the income which can be raised by indirect taxes is limited. First, excise and sales taxes increase prices and lower demand, therefore raising the elasticity of demand. When the elasticity exceeds unity, further tax rate increases result in decreasing returns, i.e. absolute declines in tax revenues. Second, indirect taxes tend to distort prices and resource allocation. Third, high levels of indirect taxation foster evasion. And when there is no apparent relationship between the taxes collected and direct benefits received, public pressures to reduce taxation develop.

In advanced countries it has long been a tenet of taxation (for reasons of both equity and resource allocation) that the beneficiaries should, in theory, pay for the costs of government-provided, nonwelfare goods or services. The principle is also relevant for the less developed nations. Its application also relieves some of the pressure on national budgets.

This does not imply that transport services produced under conditions in which average cost is greater than marginal cost (i.e. there are economies of scale) should be priced at average rather than marginal cost. Nor does it preclude the use of multipart tariffs, specific indirect taxation (e.g. reassessment of property values in the areas affected by the transport investment), or "land sale techniques."[3] It does mean that transport projects which are not expected to be financially self-sufficient should clearly meet or surpass the economic opportunity rate of return criteria. Financially self-sufficient projects, of course, should also meet the criteria. But because users and beneficiaries will be confronted and are expected to pay the costs of providing the service, somewhat less stringent standards might be employed. This matter is discussed further at a later point.

Whether a revenue-producing project is self-sufficient or largely supported by general government revenues, financial analysis is still desirable. The possibility that financial difficulties will cause delays in the execution of a project or curtailment of its operations can seldom ever be ruled out, especially in its initial years. For example, the burden of debt is often heavy and for this reason much attention must be paid to the margin by which available earnings are likely to exceed fixed charges.

Short-term financial liquidity may also be significant for a project; for example, the unavailability of funds to meet payrolls may retard construction or vital maintenance. Therefore, studies are usually under-

---

[3] For a discussion of normative prescriptions for transport pricing, see the essay by James R. Nelson in this volume (Chapter X) and Alan A. Walters and Samuel Weiner, *The Finance of Railroad and Highway Facilities in Underdeveloped Countries* (The Brookings Institution, multilithed, 1965).

taken in which earnings during a period are related to the costs of operations. In addition, cash flow statements are prepared which show the money available during a particular period as related to the amount of payments required. This analysis includes various capital items which do not figure in the income account, such as receipts and payments on fixed capital account, receipts from the sale of securities, payments for capital goods and the associated services, or repayments of loans. In other words, all items needed to determine whether the funds available will be adequate to meet all the payments due during a given period should be considered.

Distinctions Between Revenue Producing and Other Projects

The kind of financial analysis outlined above is most easily applied to revenue-producing projects, that is, those ventures where revenues accrue directly to the entity carrying out the project. This includes a large part of the World Bank's operations in the transport field. Of the roughly U.S. $3 billion of loans and credits made in this area through September 1964, approximately 70 percent was for facilities such as railways, ports, toll roads, airlines and pipelines which earn revenues. They can thus provide for repayments of debt incurred and other capital advances out of receipts accruing directly to the project or entity concerned.

There are, however, a large number of other ventures such as toll-free highways, in which revenue is not earned directly. In most of these cases, the question of whether sufficient funds will become available to complete projects depends on the government's willingness to allocate funds, and its ability to raise additional general revenue or reduce other expenditures.

For nonrevenue producing projects, financial analysis takes several forms. However, it is usually related to the revenue position of a particular government department (such as a highway department) and the ability of a government to raise revenues over time from those who benefit from transport (e.g. by means of user or other taxes) which could be earmarked for transport development. Thus, there may have to be an analysis of all government revenues obtained from activities related to the project or earmarked for the same purpose, e.g. road transport. On the other hand, the analysis may have to be limited to the government's overall fiscal position.

Whatever its form, some kind of financial analysis is vital because most underdeveloped countries face serious difficulties in their efforts to finance development. These efforts include increasing government revenue by passing burdensome tax measures—which often cannot be enforced. They also encompass controlling the increase of recurrent expenditures arising from development and coping with the tremendous financial pressures resulting from the need to expand basic services. Finally, restraining inflation (resulting in part from government deficits) is often one of the most difficult tasks. The lack of savings in general and public savings in particular, too, is one of the most imperative reasons why financial requirements should be emphasized in project appraisals.

Shortcomings of Financial Data

Calculating and interpreting financial projections is difficult at times because of shortcomings in data. This situation in turn casts some doubt on the validity of the financial appraisal and the more comprehensive economic analysis. For revenue-producing projects, the data generally depend upon some form of conventional commercial accounting of the operations of the entity carrying out the project. Unfortunately, experience in the field of transport indicates that unsatisfactory accounting systems are a widespread phenomenon.

Financial projections should be assembled in such a way that they ascertain whether the amount of money required to bring a project to completion and to continue it in operation will be available. Frequently, however, financial statements have been examined which fail to reflect the actual situation and the cost of operations. For example, where serious inflation has existed, financial results are only meaningful if adjustments have been made over the years to adjust for the inadequacy of historical cost depreciation to meet current and future replacement costs. In the absence of adjustments, the record of past financial returns may tend to be misleading, too. This is particularly true for railroads since many projects consist of rehabilitating long-established systems with extensive existing facilities.[4]

[4] Robert T. Brown's case study of the Chilean railroad decision (Chapter XII) amply demonstrates the need for such adjustments.

Because of the need to remedy poor accounting practices, much technical assistance is now underway to finance accounting advisers. Regular independent auditing of accounts is becoming commonplace. Bringing about improvements in the quality of financial reporting for revenue-producing projects has been one of the more significant contributions of the emphasis placed on financial analysis. In spite of the shortcomings of presently available financial data, the lack of comparable statistical information has been one of the most difficult problems encountered in evaluating projects which produce no direct revenues.

Government Intervention and Project Evaluation

There are many other factors which make it necessary to exercise care in drawing conclusions from financial and economic analyses of transport projects. Government subsidies which favor one mode rather than others are said to be widespread in the transport field. (Note that these subsidies need not take the form of direct grants or payments; they can simply be a failure to charge the transport user or beneficiary enough to cover the cost of facilities or services.) If not properly taken into account, this practice distorts the financial results and economic evaluation. At present, the effects of not imposing full costs on the users of the various transport facilities are difficult to measure. Yet, it is possible that with more knowledge it could be established that the demand for roads of high standard would be substantially reduced if users were required to pay the construction and maintenance costs involved.

The desirability of subsidizing alternative facilities is only now receiving serious attention in transport surveys in several developing countries. It is too early to generalize about the findings, but in a number of cases it appears that road transport operators pay only a small part of the cost of providing the facilities used. So many different factors enter into the determination of traffic that it is nearly impossible to separate the influence of subsidies. It cannot be stated with certainty that substantial distortion of traffic has taken place, or that there would be a decrease in traffic if transport were charged its true economic cost. However, these are important questions for further research.

The most difficult distorting factor to isolate and evaluate is the impact of governments' transport regulatory activities, or the lack of them. These, of course, are designed to further social and economic objectives, but they may also incur substantial financial and economic costs. For example, railways, government-owned as well as private, are regulated, and concurrently they operate in competition with other forms of transport, especially highways. Where highways are subsidized and trucking rates are not regulated, competition puts a ceiling on the rates which railways can charge. At the same time, regulatory authorities often determine railway rates, thus limiting the railroad's ability to raise revenues. This can lead to situations in which railway operations present a state of chronic deficit and appear administratively, financially, and economically inefficient. Actually, the deficits may have arisen primarily from artificial regulatory constraints.

A case was studied recently where deficits were definitely the result of a particular pattern of rates and charges imposed on the railways by regulatory agencies. Revenues per unit of output lagged badly behind costs, even though productivity was high and costs were low. Passenger fares as well as rates for particular categories of freight, were also kept at artificially low levels by the government. Furthermore, the railroads were required to bear the heavy costs of social service facilities for their staff. A careful analysis concluded that the poor financial results were misleading and that the railroads were actually an economic carrier of freight.

Also, occasionally, railways are obliged by regulatory authorities to maintain service on branch lines which have been rendered unprofitable by the construction of highways or the disappearance of traffic which they were built to carry. In addition, some railways have had to build and maintain service on lines with strategic military importance but no economic justification.

Even where some of the factors responsible for a low rate of return appear to be under the control of a railroad, its freedom of action may be limited. For example, recent transport surveys have revealed a large number of cases where railway employment appears excessively high. In most of these instances it is said that it would be politically difficult or impossible to lay off all the excess staff.

How Financial and Economic Analyses
Supplement Each Other

Despite the difficulties with economic analysis and the limitations of financial analysis, the two can supplement each other in making investment decisions. The emphasis in economic analysis is on the best alternative use of resources, especially as it relates to current investment programs. The emphasis of financial analysis is on the cash-flow of private and public sector funds related to a project and its effect on resource use, especially on investment in future periods. The interactions of the two analyses are best illustrated by a consideration of some of the types of cases which are encountered in practice:

1. *Cases where both the economic and the financial analyses indicate an adequate return for a project.* This is the simplest case from the practical point of view. For example, an appraisal of a proposed railroad link which will carry high density and relatively bulky traffic indicates that large benefits will result from a properly functioning railroad in the area. The high financial return provides assurance that the project will not be a burden on the government budget. This is obviously a high priority investment.

2. *Cases where both the economic and financial analyses indicate low returns from the project.* This again is a simple case, indicating that it would be a waste to allocate resources to this project.

3. *Cases where economic return is high and the financial return low.* This is a not uncommon case which best illustrates the interactions between financial and economic analyses. There may be several possible explanations of the difference in returns. Basically, however, all such cases fall into two categories: (a) those in which the economic returns are calculated according to accounting prices but the revenues and costs of a project are determined by market prices; and (b) those in which a significant proportion of the benefits of an investment cannot be captured by its operators.

To illustrate (a), there are cases in which facilities are constructed with market wage rates above accounting price wage rates. On the revenue side, subsidies, regulation and competition may so constrain user charge rate schedules that low receipts result. In both situations, the financial return is depressed even though the economic return may be high.

To illustrate (b), it is often true of urban transport that the users of a new facility are not the main beneficiaries. The study of the Victoria subway line in London shows that more than half of the benefits will not go to those who use the line but to those who continue to use existing facilities, where, because of the Victoria line, congestion will be less. Might the latter beneficiaries not also be charged even though they are not users of the new facilities? In practice, such charges are rarely levied. Furthermore, rates of existing facilities impose constraints on the new, and financial deficits may result.

There are many other projects with external economies where it is not administratively, economically, or politically feasible to impose charges on the indirect beneficiaries. Depending on the magnitude of the direct and indirect effects and the cost of the project, deficits or low financial returns may result. There are also instances when it is economically or politically desirable to set user charges below those which might be obtained.

Nevertheless, the impact of budgetary deficits which arise from subsidizing potentially self-sufficient projects or of selecting projects irrespective of their net financial returns should not be passed over lightly. If a public enterprise operates at a financial loss, the deficit must be made up from the government's existing general revenues, or from additional taxation and borrowing, or, in extreme cases, by printing currency. If the funds are drawn from general revenues, other vital projects may have to be foregone. On the other hand, an increase in government debt or outstanding currency might be inflationary.

There may also be an effect on total investment. The government's deficits are, of course, implicit subsidies to the users, who may employ them for consumption purposes or for investment which is not highly productive. Conversely, it is also conceivable that the project's beneficiaries might use the funds more productively than the government. Furthermore, the low subsidized transport rates may offer an incentive to additional productive private investment.

Notwithstanding the latter possibilities, the consequences of undue government deficits are generally undesirable. Furthermore, there is no method at present for truly identifying and measuring the costs and benefits of subsidies. Therefore, it would seem best, other things being equal, to assign lower priorities to projects requiring subsidies. In other words, if two projects have similar economic returns, the one that is not a drain on the budget would be preferable. This places considerable emphasis on the "if," yet it does not seem unreasonable to require projects needing subsidy aid to show a clear economic and social advantage over alternatives that are financially self-sufficient. Another conclusion is that, before deciding to subsidize a transport project, all possibilities of having the users pay for it be considered.

4. *Cases where the economic analysis assigns low priority to a project whose financial return is high.* In this case the economic return is the determining test. The low economic return is sufficient reason for rejecting the project, and the high financial return is misleading.

This case can be illustrated by a project which duplicates an existing facility. For example, assume a railroad line of 500 miles between two cities with heavy traffic making it a success from both the country's and the company's viewpoints. Assume a new project, perhaps even of an alternative mode, which essentially duplicates the functions of the existing facility. Given more modern equipment or a significantly improved technology, the new facility may have lower total operating costs and be able to charge lower rates. The old facility may not be able to compete even though it regards its capital as sunk and charges rates equal to its short-run marginal costs. Much of the traffic would be diverted to the new line, making it very successful financially. The saving in overall transport costs, however, may not be sufficient to justify the country's constructing the new line.

Although such project proposals are not uncommon or unrealistic, the economic rationale for them is generally so weak that they rarely should be considered acceptable in practice.

Conclusions

The chief lesson of this essay is that the conclusions of economic and financial analyses can conflict. Conclusions based solely on either economic rates of return or financial analysis should not determine investment priorities. A combined approach should be utilized.

In project appraisal the basic data being used in the calculation of returns frequently are subject to unusual error or regulatory distortion. Experience in a number of cases indicates that these calculations may not only be based on faulty data or subject to wide margins of error, but they may not always encompass the largest developmental effects associated with a project. Furthermore, there is rarely complete agreement in any particular case regarding either the opportunity rates of return throughout the economy or the minimum rate of return acceptable for the particular project being appraised. The rates for different sectors may not be identical because resources, including capital, are not equally available to, or fully transferable between, sectors. That is, different resource constraints may cause different opportunity rates of return. In practice, the rate usually has to be chosen under the stress of operational time pressures and often with insufficient knowledge of the returns from alternative investments.

The role played by each of the calculations in project appraisal has, in some cases, resulted in confusion. Where both the economic return and the financial return indicate similar directions and orders of magnitude, there is obviously no problem. Furthermore, it can usually be said that if the economic return is unsatisfactory, a project should be rejected regardless of its financial return. The critical point, however, is that projects with adequate economic returns should not be selected without considering their financial returns. The indirect economic effects of undue financial pressures on government budgets can be grave. Therefore, projects which are economically justified but require subsidy should be scrutinized especially carefully, with the deficits being evaluated at the opportunity cost of the funds. Where the social returns of a subsidized and a financially self-sufficient project are equivalent, the latter may well be preferred.

XII

The "Railroad Decision" in Chile

ROBERT T. BROWN*

Chile's transportation problems are not typical of those of most underdeveloped countries because Chile already has most of the elements of a truly integrated national transport network. A long, narrow strip of a country, 2,600 miles in length with an average width of only 110 miles, Chile has a railway which extends from Iquique in the North to Puerto Montt in the South, a distance of some 1,500 miles. A section of the Pan-American Highway from the frontier with Peru to Puerto Montt, a distance of some 1,600 miles, will be completely paved by 1966. Even the southern one-third of the country, mountainous and sparsely inhabited, is tied to the rest of the nation by coastwise shipping and air transport.

Chile's key transportation problems, in fact, are more similar to those in the United States, where the rapid increase in highway transport has eroded the revenues of the long-dominant railways and occasioned losses for many. Chile's state-owned railways broke even, on the whole, until the end of the Second World War, but the competition from trucking since then has so decreased operating revenues that by 1962 they barely covered 49 percent of costs, the difference being met by a global subsidy from the national budget.

* Institute of Economic Research, University of Chile, and the Brookings Institution.

PERU

La Paz

BOLIVIA

Arica

Iquique

BRAZIL

Tocopilla

PARAGUAY

Antofagasta

Taltal

Chanaral
Caldera

Pueblo Hundido

La Serena

ARGENTINA

Calera

Valparaiso

Mendoza

Santiago

South
Pacific
Ocean

Concepcion

RAILROADS

Scale 1:8,000,000; 1" = 250 Mi.

50 0   100 200
Kilom.

Northern System: Pueblo Hundido to Calera
Southern System: Valparaiso to Puerto Montt

Valdivia

Puerto Montt

RAILWAYS OF CHILE

Project and Structural Investments in Transport

Chile's transportation planning decisions, on the other hand, are similar to those in countries where the role of the government in transport investments is preponderant. So the question in Chile is: what transportation structure should the government develop? More specifically, what should be the position of railway transport within an integrated transportation structure which is consistent with the nation's development program?

Although Chile already has a developed railroad network, the criteria appropriate for deciding upon the construction of a new national railroad are also those which should be used when it is decided to maintain an existing railroad through massive new investments for renovation.[1] In this sense, Chile's planning decision is not essentially different from that in Venezuela or Brazil, where no integrated nationwide transport network yet exists. In all three countries the planners must come to grips with the question of the place of railway transport within a national transport structure. On the basis of the answer to this question, decisions with regard to investments in both highways and ports will fall into place.

It is, perhaps, desirable to explain the reasoning behind the thesis that the railroad decision, rather than a decision regarding other means of transport, is the critical one. Eventually all countries (leaving aside those countries with rigidly centrally planned economies) will have complete highway networks: trunk highways will unite all the major production and consumption centers and secondary feeder roads will reach every town and farm, tying them to the trunk routes. It may take decades to complete the basic network, but eventually it will come.

Highways

Even in Chile the political clamor for ever-increasing expenditures on highway construction and improvement (which usually parallel

---

[1] Even though the existence of present railway facilities is relevant to the analysis of new investments in Chile's railroads, the "sunk costs" that these physical facilities represent are not relevant. Investment planning need compare only the relation between possible additional new capital outlays and the expected benefits from them in railways with alternative investments in other sectors of the economy.

existing railway lines) cannot be staunched, in spite of its developed railroad network and considerable excess railroad capacity, its shortage of capital for new productive investments in the economy, its balance of payments problems, and the lack of a national automotive industry. Present and potential entrepreneurs believe (rightly or wrongly) that trucking is a good business and exert political pressure to extend the highways. Producers also favor new highway investments, because they see in highway transport a way to reduce their transport costs, either through shifting their goods from the railroads to trucks or merely by threatening to do so in order to obtain railway rate reductions. Politicians see in highway construction a source of employment to absorb unskilled and redundant agricultural laborers from their districts. Thousands of people have an income which permits them to purchase an automobile even at prices three and four times higher than those in the United States, and their political power assures that the highway network will continue to expand.

All these factors (which are either currently operating in other countries or will as the level of development rises) ensure that sooner or later Chile's highway network will be complete. Obviously, the factors enumerated do not prove that the investments in highways are economically justified. They do prove, however, that the highways will be built, justified or not. A transport planner who does not take this fact into account in the preparation of his plans is tilting against windmills; his plans will be filed and forgotten.

The present decisions about highways are, therefore, concerned with the relative priorities of different roads, the rhythm with which investments are to be made, and the technical characteristics of the highway to be built—maximum grades, minimum curve radii, types of paving, etc. These decisions are important: high standards signify that less mileage can be constructed in a given year; erroneous decisions with respect to types of paving can mean the loss of resources because roads break up under unforeseen traffic increases, etc. But no *single* decision of this kind is likely to carry the risk of an economic "disaster" for the country. If a low priority highway is constructed because of political pressure or poor project analysis, there is obviously a loss for the economy. The resources would have been better applied elsewhere, but the highway can still be used. And what is more important: it is unlikely that any permanent damage has been done to the transport *structure* of the country. Sooner or later that same (presently) low priority road would have been built.

Ports

A similar situation exists with regard to investments in ports. The tonnage moved through ports in many countries, either in coastwise trade or in international commerce, is concentrated in a few bulk items which are handled with special port facilities installed specifically for their use. In Chile in 1960, for example, 16 million tons of cargo passed through Chilean ports: 7 million tons of exports, 3 million tons of imports, and 6 million tons of internal freight (double counted as it is handled twice). Of this total, 12.5 million tons (78 percent) consisted of iron ore, petroleum, nitrates, and coal, which almost never use general port facilities. Only 3.5 million tons consisted of other freight, and of this, only 1.9 million tons was coastwise trade.[2]

With this type of maritime transport structure most port decisions can be easily handled on a project-by-project basis. A large share of the remaining decisions can be based on foreign trade with no danger of distorting the nation's internal transport structure. The possibilities of gross errors are limited, and even though errors are committed, they are not likely to be an overwhelming burden on the economy for any great length of time. All projects must, of course, be analyzed carefully, especially when their cost represents a significant portion of the investment resources of the economy. The point here is only that errors in ports, whatever the specific loss to the economy in terms of opportunity costs, are not likely to burden the economy with an inappropriate transport *structure*.

Railroads

Railway decisions, on the other hand, are often of a completely different nature, and this is true whether the decision is one to construct a railway where none of importance existed before (as could be the case in Venezuela), to change the structure of an existing railway network (as could be the case in Argentina), or to completely renovate and modernize an existing railway network without basically changing its structure (as in the case of Chile). These decisions are not "project"

[2] Dirección de Estadística y Censos, *Estadística Chilena, Sinopsis 1960*, pp. 648-49; 672-73.

decisions but rather "structural" decisions. They are basic, fundamental decisions, and if they are in error there is no turning back: the implications of the decision are far-reaching both in space and in time. They are decisions which involve not five or ten or twenty million dollars but rather hundreds of millions. An erroneous decision of this nature can be classed as a "disaster" for the economy.

In many underdeveloped countries a major part of railway investments is composed of imported capital goods which the country is not able to produce economically for itself. Even in Chile, which constructs all its own rolling stock and rail accessories, the imported component of the 1961 railway modernization program of $312.7 million amounted to 37 percent.[3] Not only does this represent an enormous burden on the balance of payments, but also signifies that railway investments can be carried out with frightening rapidity: locomotives and rails can be obtained within a year of reaching a decision and placing the order.

Furthermore, the fact that railways in underdeveloped countries (at least in South America) are today largely state railways signifies that errors regarding railway decisions are reflected directly in a nation's budget. No longer do British investors bear the burden of overseas railway bankruptcies; this burden now signifies increased inflation and lost development opportunities in other sectors of the economy. Last, the fact that these state railways are among a nation's largest employers signifies that even when an error is recognized, it is extremely difficult to turn back, because the resulting labor problems spill over dangerously into the political sphere.

These are among the reasons why the investment decision regarding railways should be considered the key decision. Once it has been rationally decided what is to be the role of railways within a nation's transport structure, the other important decisions will fall into line.

The railway decision must be made at two levels: first, does the country require a railway network (either a new railway or the renovation and continuance of an existing system); and second, if the country does need a railway, what is its proper place within an integrated and coordinated national transportation structure. The decision on the first level is the critical one and must be made centrally. That on the second level is a continuing process, as the role of railroad transport can-

[3] Supremo Gobierno de Chile, *Programa de Transportes para Chile, 1961-1970* (1961), Table 83.

not be frozen over time but must be affected by changes in traffic flows, relative factor costs, changing technology, etc. The second-level decision is likely to fall into error if made centrally (especially as the tendency is likely to be one to attempt to freeze the present pattern) and should be left as much as possible to the market place.

The key first-level decision cannot be made in a vacuum, obviously, but must be based on the relative costs of a transportation structure which incorporates a railroad compared with the costs of one without a railroad—based either on highway trucking alone or highway trucking combined with pipelines, coastwise shipping, etc. In a country which has no railway at present, and where the future development of the country can only be projected imperfectly, the decision is agonizingly difficult. Not only lack of knowledge about the country's future development and accompanying future traffic flows is responsible. The lack of knowledge about physical production functions of railroads which permit the estimation of future operating costs is also a key factor.

In this paper no attempt will be made to examine the elements which enter into the decision to build a railway where none existed before. Somewhat less difficult is the decision to maintain and to renew existing railway capacity, because operating costs are (or can be) known, traffic flows can be studied; and this information can be complemented by costs, revenues, and traffic of the other transport media. Chile in 1959 made a critical decision to modernize completely its State Railways, including renovation of the way, dieselization, installation of centralized traffic control, renovation of rolling stock, and continuation of the electrification of a part of the Southern System initiated several years earlier. This decision was made on the basis of partial and inadequate studies, despite the fact that the original program involved more than $200 million of investment and a commitment to continue railroad transport within the existing transport structure for several decades more.

Most of the remainder of this paper will be devoted to analyzing this decision to determine whether, on the basis of a more careful study (and using the benefit of some hindsight), the decision in Chile was justified.

Renovation of the Chilean State Railways

The basic justification for the 1959 decision to undertake a massive renovation of the Chilean State Railroads was that because of decades of continuing decapitalization, costs had risen to a point where, considering the competition from the highways, no rate structure would permit the railways to cover their costs. It was believed that by new investments these costs could be decreased to a point where the railways could compete effectively with trucks and buses without the need for government subsidies.

Costs and Revenues, 1940-1962

Table XII-1 traces the development of the expenditures and revenue published in the Annual Reports of the State Railways from 1940 to 1962. In order to present figures of comparable value over the period (prices in 1962 were 135 times those in 1940), the original figures have been deflated by the cost-of-living index.[4] Figure XII-1 presents the revenue, operating costs and total costs during the same period for the Northern and Southern Systems,[5] and Figure XII-2 shows the total profit or loss for these systems.

As can be seen in Table XII-1 and Figure XII-1, while total revenue of the Northern and Southern Systems fell from 63.2 million escudos[6] in 1940 to 50.6 million in 1962, total costs rose in the same period from 61.8 million escudos to 120.4 million, thus turning the initial profit of 1.4 million into a loss at the end of the period of 69.8 million. While total revenue in 1940 was 102 percent of total costs, in 1962 it covered

[4] The cost-of-living index is no better or worse than several alternatives, such as an index of railway costs or the wholesale price index. The cost-of-living index is used because the data are reasonably reliable and because primary interest is centered on the relation between costs and revenue rather than on the absolute level of one of them.

[5] The analysis in this paper will be restricted to the Northern System, which extends from Pueblo Hundido to Calera, and the Southern System, which extends from Valparaíso to Puerto Montt. It is obvious without further analysis that the subsidiary line from Iquique to Pueblo Hundido should be abandoned and that the line from Chile to Mendoza, Argentina, should be maintained. The line from Arica to La Paz, Bolivia, must be maintained because of international treaty obligations.

[6] Escudos of 1961, as are all the monetary figures presented. In 1961 the exchange rate was 1.05 escudos to the U.S. dollar, but the escudo was considerably overvalued. A more realistic rate would have been 1.50 escudos to the dollar.

TABLE XII-1. *Chilean State Railways: Revenue and Costs*
(Yearly figures or annual averages in thousands of escudos of 1961)

	1940	1941–44	1945	1946–49
A. Northern and Southern Systems				
Revenue:				
Passengers	18,865.9	19,326.8	21,689.4	17,888.1
Baggage	2,899.3	3,120.6	3,521.3	3,046.2
Freight	40,583.4	47,534.6	54,893.7	45,295.3
Sub-Total Traffic	62,348.6	69,982.0	80,104.4	66,229.6
Other Revenue	854.7	1,482.6	1,139.1	1,345.8
Total Revenue	63,203.3	71,464.6	81,243.5	67,575.4
Operating Costs	46,117.1	53,332.2	61,070.0	55,293.7
Operating Profit or Loss	17,086.2	18,132.4	20,173.5	12,281.7
Other Costs:				
Depreciation	6,742.4	9,904.4	8,994.1	8,341.5
Financial Costs	2,181.3	1,243.0	1,027.7	1,275.2
Pensions	6,316.2	5,009.9	6,657.6	7,364.9
Severance Pay	121.0	166.6	1,068.0	1,569.4
Other Costs	291.2	16.0	18.6	275.8
Total Operating and Other Costs	61,769.2	69,672.1	78,836.0	74,120.5
Profit or Loss Northern and Southern Systems	1,434.1	1,792.5	2,407.5	−6,545.1
B. Loss Subsidiary Railroads	—	619.2	2,486.4	2,214.2
Loss Maritime Service	1,889.3	629.6	1,299.9	1,075.4
Total Profit or Loss	−455.2	543.7	−1,378.8	−9,834.7
C. Payments to Government	4,424.2	1,501.5	1,625.8	1,345.5
Transfers from Government:				
National Budget	—	—	—	4,266.8
Turnover Tax	—	—	—	1,470.0
Import Duties	—	—	—	—
Debt Write-Off	—	1,848.0	—	—
Net Transfer from Government	−4,424.2	346.5	−1,625.8	4,391.3
D. Profit or Loss Balance Statement	−4,879.4	890.2	−3,004.6	−5,443.4
Cost-of-Living Index	0.8427	1.2983	1.724	2.889

Source: Annual Reports of Chilean State Railways.

only 42 percent of total costs.[7] The consistent trend toward increasing losses is clear in Figure XII-2.

Table XII-2 shows the composition of what are defined in this paper as the operating costs of the Northern and Southern Systems. As can be seen from this table and in Figure XII-1, these costs have fluctuated

[7] The revenue in 1962 includes some four million escudos of subsidies from the government for the transport of specific products whose freight rate was reduced at the request of the government. On the other hand, the costs in 1962 include import duties, which the State Railways did not have to pay until 1960.

TABLE XII-1. *Continued*

1950–51	1952–55	1956–58	1959	1960	1961	1962
15,870.1	15,413.5	14,520.0	14,496.5	15,103.4	14,031.8	14,053.0
2,539.1	2,369.6	2,038.0	2,142.9	2,034.6	1,828.3	1,748.4
36,039.7	43,940.9	45,074.9	45,530.5	43,137.7	37,075.1	31,976.0
54,448.9	61,724.0	61,632.9	62,169.9	60,275.7	52,935.2	47,777.4
1,466.9	1,624.5	2,345.9	1,088.0	2,260.5	1,933.1	2,850.5
55,915.8	63,348.5	63,978.8	63,257.9	62,536.2	54,868.3	50,627.9
57,726.2	70,301.2	62,478.8	63,659.4	70,344.9	74,098.1	76,221.1
− 1,810.4	− 6,952.7	1,500.0	− 401.5	− 7,808.7	−19,229.8	−25,593.2
7,077.0	8,978.6	16,095.2	17,974.5	19,112.3	17,817.1	15,639.1
893.1	986.5	6,067.7	1,243.8	649.3	2,770.4	16,372.8
8,734.9	9,241.0	8,959.1	9,509.9	9,611.6	11,312.0	11,551.7
1,147.2	999.0	726.2	1,086.7	1,338.7	2,779.6	610.7
30.3	1,353.9	1,404.1	256.6	3,089.6	—	56.8
75,608.7	91,860.2	95,731.1	93,730.9	104,146.4	108,777.2	120,452.2
−19,692.9	−28,511.7	−31,752.3	−30,473.0	−41,610.2	−53,908.0	−69,824.3
2,264.4	3,769.1	2,335.1	3,647.4	5,019.3	4,628.2	5,340.1
1,038.1	438.7	—	—	—	—	—
−22,995.4	−32,719.5	−34,087.4	−34,120.4	−46,629.5	−58,537.1	−75,164.4
1,101.2	310.8	—	—	—	—	—
26,881.9	32,107.2	18,006.4	32,829.4	50,210.8	57,989.6	65,819.6
5,373.4	6,544.7	7,760.3	9,347.0	2,627.9	—	—
—	—	—	1,826.9	5,876.1	6,300.6	13,831.2
—	—	—	—	—	—	—
31,154.1	38,341.1	25,766.7	44,003.3	58,714.8	64,290.2	79,650.8
8,158.7	5,621.6	− 8,320.7	9,882.9	12,085.3	5,753.1	4,486.4
4.790	12.379	48.24	83.19	92.86	100.00	113.87

widely over the period. Although revenue in general followed the tendency of the operating costs, in 11 of the 23 years studied it was inadequate to cover them. In the last three years of the period total revenue was less than 75 percent of operating costs (including wages and salaries, fuel, materials, but not depreciation, financial costs, pensions and severance pay).[8]

[8] It should be indicated, however, that two of these years were exceptional: in May of 1960 the railroad was severely damaged by earthquakes and in 1961 a railway strike of 28 days reduced traffic.

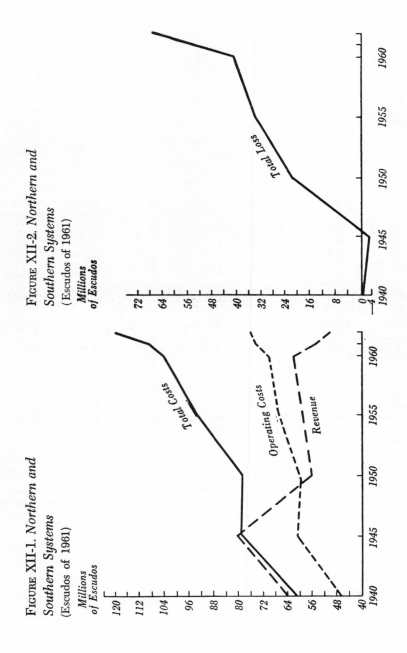

Figure XII-1. Northern and Southern Systems

(Escudos of 1961)

Millions of Escudos

Figure XII-2. Northern and Southern Systems

(Escudos of 1961)

Millions of Escudos

252

TABLE XII-2. *Chilean State Railways: Operating Costs*[a]
(Yearly figures or annual averages in thousands of escudos of 1961)

Year	Administration	Ways and Structures	Transport	Traction	Repair Shops	Welfare	Gratification	Insurance	Total
1940	2,385.6	6,442.6	8,293.5	15,348.9	7,821.9	5,797.5	27.1	—	46,117.1
1941–44	2,980.6	7,817.7	9,470.9	15,247.2	9,447.7	6,102.0	2,266.1	—	53,332.2
1945	3,997.4	9,099.1	10,978.5	16,013.9	10,099.4	7,729.1	3,152.6	—	61,070.0
1946–49	3,466.3	7,523.0	10,730.7	14,614.4	9,442.9	6,313.1	3,052.2	151.1	55,293.7
1950–51	2,943.3	8,331.9	11,910.4	17,331.9	10,389.6	2,585.4	3,689.1	544.6	57,726.2
1952–55	5,885.2	10,180.0	14,360.6	20,509.6	13,079.9	2,515.0	3,112.2	658.7	70,301.2
1956–58	4,262.6	9,176.9	13,070.7	20,798.9	11,858.5	2,163.9	493.3	654.0	62,478.8
1959	4,793.7	8,930.8	11,920.7	22,914.5	11,080.7	1,866.7	1,490.1	662.2	63,659.4
1960	3,868.0	10,467.3	12,670.4	24,751.7	12,844.2	3,284.1	1,881.4	577.8	70,344.9
1961	4,729.7	11,703.3	14,811.9	23,658.0	13,672.6	3,333.0	1,695.8	493.8	74,098.1
1962	5,456.0	11,895.4	14,814.5	21,961.9	16,881.3	3,448.8	1,321.3	441.9	76,221.1

Source: Annual Reports of the Chilean State Railways.
[a] Northern and Southern Systems.

253

It is not difficult to understand why the government which took office in November 1958, was anxious to reverse the ever-increasing deficit of the State Railways. This deficit was a heavy burden on the national budget and an important contribution to the inflation which the government was pledged to halt. The question to be analyzed, however, is whether the factors which had turned the profit on the Northern and Southern Systems in 1945 (the last year in which a profit was made) into an increasing loss thereafter could be best attacked by the investment program which was initiated in 1959–60. To answer this question it is desirable to compare in more detail the costs and revenues of 1945 with those of the period 1956–58, the latest years for which the government had information when it made its decision to embark on the modernization program.

The average annual loss in the years 1956–58 for the Northern and Southern Systems, as shown in Table XII-1, was 31.7 million escudos. Adding this amount to the profit of 2.4 million in 1945 indicates that a total deterioration of 34.1 million escudos in the profit position must be explained by an analysis of the costs and revenue. Total revenue fell from 81.2 million escudos in 1945 to an average of 64.0 million in the triennium 1956–58, a difference of 17.2 million, 50 percent of the amount to be explained. Total costs increased from 78.8 million escudos in 1945 to an average of 95.7 million, an increase of 16.9 million, which explains the remaining 50 percent.

The increase of 1.4 million escudos over the period in the Operating Costs is of little importance. The appreciable increase in the costs of Transport and Traction within Operating Costs is explained primarily by a reclassification of the costs of the family allowance, which in 1945 were grouped under Welfare and in 1956–58 were assigned directly to each department. To explain the increase in Total Costs it is necessary to examine Depreciation, Financial Costs, and Pensions.

A review of annual depreciation statistics reveals that the figures used by the State Railways in their annual balance statements, at least until perhaps 1958, are of little value. Sharp jumps in amortization charges in 1948, 1954, and 1958 were due not to the incorporation of new assets but to a revision of depreciation estimates after physical inventories. Although definitive conclusions are impossible without a detailed study of the real assets in each year, it appears quite clear that either depreciation is overestimated at the end of the period or that it was sharply underestimated at the beginning. Most likely the latter is correct, as the period 1945–58 is usually considered to be a period of decapitalization for the Railways.[9] More support is given this conclusion by the increase in the item "Other Costs," which in 1956–58 represents solely the book loss on eliminated assets. Pending further study, the increase in depreciation should be considered an accounting increase rather than a real increase in costs.

Financial Costs is a heterogeneous cost category subject to sharp fluctuation from year to year. Included in this item are interest payments and commissions to banks, both obviously legitimate cost items, as well as charges made because of adjustments in the balance sheet, which occasionally are not only inappropriate but even duplicate legitimate cost charges made in other categories. For example, in the years 1956–58 the Financial Costs were the highest during the entire period until 1962. The great jump between 1955 and 1956 is due to an adjustment made in the outstanding debt of the State Railways because of the devaluation of the escudo. This was apparently due to instructions from Chile's general accounting office. In effect, during the years up to 1956 the Railways purchased equipment from abroad on credit, and the resulting debt was expressed in escudos in the balance sheet. When the escudo was devalued, this debt in national currency increased sharply. In the years 1956–58 (as well as in other years) this increase was treated as a cost, even though the goods bought were capital goods. Because the assets of the Railways were also revalued due to the continuing inflation, depreciation charges against these assets were also increased, and in effect the same cost was included twice. For this reason it is obvious that the fluctuations in Financial Costs are of little interest in an analysis of the financial situation of the Railways and clearly new investments will not reduce these "costs."

The increase in pensions of 2.3 million escudos between the two periods represents a real increase in costs. The cost even in the period 1956–58 is not out of line, however, with what the State Railways would have to pay even if it were a private company.[10] In this case

---

[9] The sum of the net profit or loss during the period of 1945-58, including subsidiary railroads and government transfers, is a loss of 10.9 million escudos. In other words, the government subsidy during that period was inadequate to cover the losses of the State Railways.

[10] The cost to the State Railways in 1959 for pensions, separation pay, medical benefits, etc. was 14.8 million escudos (of 1961). Had the State Railways been a private corporation and subject to the same employer's contributions for these purposes as other private enterprises, the cost would have been 14.2 million escudos. Manuel Metz Arndt, *Evaluación Económica del Subsidio Fiscal a la Empresa de Ferrocarriles del Estado de Chile* (Santiago: Dirección de Presupuestos del Ministerio de Hacienda and Instituto de Economía de la Universidad de Chile, 1964), p. 79.

TABLE XII-3. *Chilean State Railways: Revenue Traffic*[a]

(Yearly figures or annual averages; millions of passenger-kilometers or ton-kilometers)

Periods	Southern System				Northern System				Total Traffic Units
	Freight	Passengers	Baggage	Traffic Units[b]	Freight	Passengers	Baggage	Traffic Units	
1928–1930	938	815	13	1,440	43	39	1	67	1,507
1931–1933	731	706	11	1,166	42	37	1	65	1,231
1934–1935	998	921	14	1,565	66	55	1	100	1,665
1936–1940	1,266	1,092	18	1,939	78	66	1	119	2,058
1941–1945	1,620	1,541	22	2,567	84	89	1	138	2,705
1946–1950	1,602	1,382	18	2,449	87	76	1	134	2,583
1951–1955	1,781	1,673	26	2,811	104	98	2	165	2,976
1956	1,735	2,168	25	3,061	184	136	2	268	3,329
1957	1,470	2,011	25	2,702	197	137	2	281	2,983
1958	1,500	2,055	24	2,757	172	182	2	283	3,040
1959	1,518	2,062	26	2,781	237	171	2	342	3,123
1960	1,234	1,644	21	2,241	305	141	2	392	2,633
1961	1,157	1,545	18	2,102	270	128	2	349	2,451

Source: Annual Report for 1961, Chilean State Railways.
[a] Northern and Southern Systems.
[b] Ton-kilometers of revenue freight and baggage plus 60 percent of passenger-kilometers.

the problem is a national one and not occasioned by the role of the Railways as a state enterprise. Nevertheless, new investments which would permit a reduction in the number of railway workers will, in the long run, permit a reduction in this cost item, so that this potential benefit should be considered in the evaluation of the Railways' modernization program.

Traffic and Average Revenue

An analysis of the behavior of the costs of the State Railways over the 14-year interval is of little value unless traffic changes are considered. Table XII-3 presents the general development of traffic in the Northern and Southern Systems from 1928 to 1961 and combines metric ton-kilometers and passenger-kilometers into "Traffic Units," defined as metric ton-kilometers of revenue freight and baggage plus 60 percent of passenger-kilometers.[11] It can be seen that the traffic in the triennium 1956–58 was high when compared with the 33 years presented in the table.

Table XII-4 compares specifically the traffic in 1945 with that in 1956–58, in tons and number of passengers, in ton-kilometers and passenger-kilometers, and in traffic units.[12] If it is assumed that the "Traffic Unit" as defined above represents a reasonable relationship

[11] This relationship, obviously arbitrary, between freight and passenger traffic is used by the Chilean State Railways. The justification given in the Annual Report for 1958 (page 9) for this particular weighting is as follows: "In place of the traditional traffic units, which were obtained by summing the ton-kilometers and the passenger-kilometers, these new weighted units are used which, according to international statistical averages, represent, with the weights indicated for passenger-kilometers, a more realistic proportionality in relation to the gross ton-kilometers of freight, baggage, and passengers."

It is of course clear that the weights used should reflect the objective of the analysis, as no single set of weights will be useful for all purposes. For the analysis being carried out here, of the tendency of unit costs over time, the weights should reflect the relative cost to the Railways of transporting one passenger one kilometer compared with that of transporting one ton of freight one kilometer. It is likely that for this purpose a higher weight should be given to passengers.

[12] In Table XII-4 the traffic figures for livestock in 1945 have been adjusted by the author to make them more consistent with the statistics for 1956 and the following years. The original 1945 traffic figures for livestock in the Southern System were 287,216 metric tons and 96,962,634 ton-kilometers. The adjusted figures represent rate ton-kilometers and rate tons. No adjustment was made for the Northern System because of the slight incidence of livestock traffic. No adjustment in either system was made in Table XII-3.

TABLE XII-4. *Chilean State Railways: Traffic and Average Rates, 1945 and 1956-58*

	1945			1956–58 (Annual Average)		
	Tons or Passengers (000)	Ton-Kms. or Passenger-Kms. (000,000)	Average Rate or Fare[a]	Tons or Passengers (000)	Ton-Kms. or Passenger-Kms. (000,000)	Average Rate or Fare[a]
Freight:						
Southern System						
Agricultural Products	1,556	484	25.2	1,078	309	17.2
Forestry Products	877	358	21.8	589	261	22.3
Livestock[b]	463	157	21.2	313	161	27.2
Mineral Products	1,787	415	25.6	1,938	440	26.3
Manufactured Products	1,120	310	42.3	1,160	398	25.1
Miscellaneous	386	104	47.7	—	—	—
Total Revenue Traffic	6,189	1,828	28.5	5,078	1,568	23.7
Own Traffic	586	154	—	817	211	—
Total Southern System	6,775	1,982	—	5,895	1,779	—
Northern System						
Mineral Products	717	38	30.3	2,060	161	27.8
Other Products	219	44	41.8	86	24	26.5
Total Revenue Traffic	936	82	36.5	2,146	184	27.6
Own Traffic	58	10	—	28	8	—
Total Northern System	994	92	—	2,174	192	—
Baggage (Revenue Traffic):						
Southern System	65	23	120.1	70	25	82.9
Northern System	5	1	181.6	5	2	119.3
Total Baggage	70	24	123.6	75	27	85.6
Passengers:						
Southern System	22,479	1,428	13.3	24,851	2,078	6.5
Northern System	1,046	85	16.6	967	152	6.3
Total Passengers	23,525	1,513	13.5	25,818	2,230	6.5
Traffic Units:[c]						
Southern System		2,708			2,840	
Northern System		134			277	
Total Traffic Units		2,842			3,117	

Source: Annual Reports of the Chilean State Railways.
[a] Thousands of escudos of 1961 per ton-kilometer or per passenger-kilometer.
[b] Adjusted by the author for 1945.
[c] Ton-kilometers of revenue freight and baggage plus 60 percent of passenger-kilometers.

between freight and passenger traffic from the point of view of costs incurred, then the average operating cost per traffic unit fell from 0.0215 escudos in 1945 to 0.0200 escudos in 1956–58. If it is believed that passenger traffic should be weighted more heavily than is done in the definition of traffic units used by the Chilean State Railways, then the fall in the average unit cost would be even greater, as passenger traffic increased relatively more rapidly than freight traffic. It is thus difficult to justify the necessity for a crash investment program in 1959 on the basis of increasing operating costs, at least comparing average operating costs of 1945 with those for 1956–58. Although it may well be true that costs were high in 1945, in that year the Railways showed a considerable "operating" profit.

A detailed analysis of traffic is also essential to explain the deterioration of revenue between 1945 and the triennium 1956–58. It can be seen in Table XII-5 that the loss in revenue between the two periods is concentrated in the transport of Agricultural Products and Manufactured Products (including the products not classified in 1945) in the Southern System and in the transport of passengers in both systems. The revenue loss from these traffics totals 21.1 million escudos, which is more than the fall in total revenue of 19.8 million. Even adding the specific government subsidy of some 2.6 million escudos for agricultural products and perhaps one million for specifically subsidized passenger fares, the fall is of great importance in explaining the worsened financial position of the State Railways.

A brief glance back at Table XII-4, in which a comparison is made of traffic and average rates between the two periods, is sufficient to see that the revenue deterioration can be explained but little by an actual loss of traffic. Although ton-kilometers of Agricultural Products in the Southern System fell 36 percent, Manufactured and Miscellaneous Products fell only 4 percent and passenger-kilometers in both systems actually increased 47 percent. Total traffic, measured in traffic units (as defined previously), increased in both the Northern and Southern Systems: from 134 million to 277 million in the first and from 2.7 billion to 2.8 billion in the second.

The real key to the deterioration of total revenue is found in the fall of average rates and fares. According to Table XII-4, the average freight rate per ton-kilometer paid by the public for the transport of Agricultural Products in the Southern System fell 32 percent over the period, while that for Manufactured Products fell 41 percent. The

TABLE XII-5. *Chilean State Railways: Total Revenue, 1945 and 1956-58*[a]

(Thousands of escudos of 1961)

	1945	1956–58 (Annual average)
Freight:		
Southern System		
Agricultural Products	12,209	5,304
Forestry Products	7,775	5,809
Livestock	3,330	4,366
Mineral Products	10,602	11,535
Manufactured Products	13,114	9,915
Miscellaneous	4,969	—
Total Southern System	51,999	36,929
Northern System		
Mineral Products	1,142	4,478
Other Products	1,848	614
Total Northern System	2,990	5,092
Total Freight	54,989	42,021
Baggage:		
Southern System	2,806	2,045
Northern System	244	223
Total Baggage	3,050	2,268
Passengers:		
Southern System	18,961	13,411
Northern System	1,419	952
Total Passengers	20,380	14,363
Total Revenue	78,419	58,652

Source: Traffic Statistics, Annual Reports of the State Railways.

[a] The revenue figures presented in this table differ from those presented in Table XII-1 principally because Table XII-1 includes within the traffic revenue in 1956–58 the revenue from a subsidiary bus line between Coquimbo and La Serena (E° 112 thousand) and the specific subsidies paid by the government for the transport of certain commodities and subsidized fares for students and teachers (E° 4,388 thousand).

average fare per passenger-kilometer in both systems fell 52 percent. Although the average freight rate for some products actually increased over the period in the Southern System, namely Forestry Products, Livestock, and Mineral Products, these increases were insufficient to maintain the average rate for all revenue traffic, which fell 17 percent.

In order to obtain a better impression of the importance of the fall in average rates (which, incidentally, cannot be explained by an increase in the distance the average load is transported), the annual traffic over the period 1956–58 was re-evaluated by applying to it the average freight rates and passenger fares of 1945. Had it been possible to maintain those rates and fares, average total revenue in 1956–58 would have been 84.4 million escudos instead of 58.65 million.

If the deterioration of average rates and fares is the key to the present financial problems of the State Railways, it is extremely important to determine whether present rates are low because of government policy (to hold down increases in the cost of living or for other reasons) or because the Railways themselves have been forced to reduce rates in order to compete with other transport media, especially trucks and buses. Although it is true that for periods of time the government has frozen rates and fares (from 1959 to 1962, for example), it is unlikely that this has been a "prime cause" over a long period of time. Even during the period 1959–62, when theoretically rates and fares were unchanged, average rates were reduced by the State Railways through the reclassification of the category of many products.

Competition from Highways

It would not be surprising if the Chilean Railways have been subjected to increasing highway competition since the end of the Second World War, as this, after all, has been a worldwide phenomenon. Chile's vehicle stock has increased greatly in the postwar era: between 1945 and 1958 the number of automobiles increased 89 percent; buses,[13] 100 percent; and trucks of all types, 183 percent. In the same period, the production of goods increased 44 percent.[14] Because the State Railways transport a relatively small quantity of goods and passengers, the impact of the increase of motor vehicles on the railways has been of overwhelming importance. According to a recent estimate by the Undersecretariat of Transport, 33 ten-ton trucks could have transported all the nonmineral freight in the Northern System in 1961 and 64 buses all the passengers in the same system. The continued improvement in the country's highway network has added to this competitive pressure.

[13] Including both urban and interurban as no breakdown is available.
[14] Production of the agriculture, forestry, mining, industry, and construction sectors. Corporación de Fomento de la Producción, *Cuentas Nacionales 1940-49* and *Cuentas Nacionales 1950-1960*.

It appears to be undeniably clear that the deficit financial situation of the State Railways in 1958 was due to attempts to maintain historical traffic through rate and fare reductions in the face of a worldwide revolution in highway transport. They did not accept the revolution and adjust to it by sloughing off unremunerative traffic (such as passengers and less-than-carload freight) to the highways and abandoning low density branch lines in both systems and large stretches of the main line in the Northern System. Instead the Railways, abetted and even pushed by the government, fought to maintain a railroad structure appropriate for the times when they had a near-monopoly on Chile's transport.

Under these circumstances, a massive investment program to renovate and modernize the Railways is likely to be disastrous. Unless a clear idea has been formed of the proper role of the Railways within an integrated transportation structure, which inevitably would signify a substantial loss of traffic and the abandonment of way, the investment program is likely to freeze the existing railroad structure and to impede this essential adaptation to the modern world. At best the program, if carried through as originally planned by the government (against the desires of the Railways in some instances, it must be added), would result in substantial excess capacity in the Railways[15] and would necessitate sharp restrictions on highway transport, especially through tight controls on truck and bus imports.

This policy, of course, is not unheard of in other parts of the world, even in countries which produce motor vehicles, such as England, Germany and the United States. Whether it is the policy to recommend to an emerging country, even though motor vehicle, fuel, tire, and spare parts imports are an important component in Chile's uneasy balance of payments, is extremely doubtful. In order to recommend a policy of restricting highway transport to maintain a higher utilization of railroad capacity (as opposed to reducing railroad capacity), one would have to be convinced that: (1) the total cost of transporting by highway (alone or in combination with other media) all goods and passengers presently transported by railroad (or to be transported in the future) is higher than the cost by railroad after realizing the railroad investments;[16] and that (2) the long-run marginal cost of transporting additional goods by railroad is lower than that by highway.[17]

---

[15] The Railways estimated that the investment program would increase total capacity by 42 percent.

[16] The problem is somewhat more complicated because consideration would also

Justification of Railroad Renovation

Neither of these two questions was raised when the Chilean government made its decision to embark on a modernization program. Apparently the only memorandum considered by the government in which the costs and benefits of the proposed investments were studied is dated September 1959, when the original railroad renovation program was announced officially.[18] At that time the program was expected to be completed within five years, over the period 1960–64, and contemplated a total investment of $112.5 million and 90.5 million escudos of 1959.[19] Converting the national currency to dollars at the then official rate of 1.05 escudos to the dollar, the total program amounted to $198.7 million. The September memorandum states that the dollar value of assets of the State Railways in 1957 was only $400 million, so that the significance of the proposed program is obvious.

In order to quantify the cost reductions which these investments would make possible, the authors of the September memorandum analyzed the 1959 Railways budget item by item, asking the following question: "Had the proposed program already been carried out, so that in 1959 the Railways would operate with a new way, new locomotives, new rolling stock, etc., what would have been the budget in that year?" The authors' conclusion was that the saving would amount

---

have to be given to the possible impact on the costs of highway transport were the projected railroad investments to be applied there.

[17] It may well be that the marginal cost of carrying some types of additional cargo by railroad is lower than the cost by highway, but at the same time the railroad marginal cost for some goods it is already carrying is higher than the cost by highway. In this case an affirmative answer to both questions is still consistent with the diminution of railroad capacity.

[18] The transportation section of the Ten-Year Development Plan, prepared by the Chilean Development Corporation, was not completed until June 1961, when the Railways investment program was already well underway.

[19] The main components of the September 1959 program, in millions of dollars and millions of escudos of 1961, follow: electrification of the main line from Santiago to Chillán, including substations and locomotives (already contracted for in 1959), $25.6 and E° 5.1; complete renovation of 1,008 kilometers of way, $21.1 and E° 34.3; centralized traffic control from Talca to Puerto Montt, $8.1 and E° 6.4; communications network, $0.9 and E° 0.4; replacement of 5,000 freight cars and 500 coaches and baggage cars, $9.0 and E° 62.0; 82 diesel locomotives for switchyards and branch lines, $13.2; 195 diesel locomotives for the Southern System, with repair shops, $32.3; machinery, tools, etc., $2.3 and E° 0.6. Total program, $112.5 million and E° 108.8 million of 1961.

to 19 million escudos of 1959 (23 million in escudos of 1961), including the saving through reduction in personnel of 3,210 persons and would represent 27 percent of the 1959 budget.

In the quantification of the impact of the investments on the financial situation of the Railways, the memorandum assumed an alternative increase in revenue of from 5 to 8 percent a year, although a 3 percent increase would have been optimistic and a reconsideration of the proper structure of the Railways might well have led to a net decrease. On the basis of the assumptions regarding revenue and possible cost reductions, the memorandum reached the conclusion that by 1965 the Railways could produce a surplus of between 2.5 and 6.2 millions of escudos (of 1961), if the investment program were to be carried out.

It has not been the purpose of this description to criticize the oversimplified analysis of a complex problem but to point out that, apparently, at no time were fundamental questions, such as the proper role of railroads within an integrated national transport structure, seriously considered. The approach used in the September memorandum is that of traditional project analysis and is inadequate for a basic structural decision. No comparative cost analysis was carried out to determine the relative advantages of road versus rail. No historical analysis was included of the development of the Railways' own costs and revenues to determine if massive investments were really the cure for the continuing and increasing deficits. Under these circumstances the decision to invest was a dangerous one, filled with far-reaching implications which could plague the Chilean economy for decades in the future.

Cost of Highways as Alternative to Railroads

Although cost information which would permit an analysis of the kinds of traffic appropriate for the State Railways is not as yet available, it is possible to consider one of the basic questions raised previously: would it be more economical for the economy to transfer all the freight and passenger traffic presently transported by rail to alternative transport media? Using the year 1961 as a basis, an attempt will be made to answer this question.[20]

[20] The estimates which follow were prepared with Carlos Hurtado and are published with more detail in Carlos Hurtado and Arturo Israel, *Tres Ensayos sobre el Transporte en Chile* (Santiago, Chile: Instituto de Economía, 1964), pp. 1-27. For more analysis of the comparative cost of transporting passengers by road and by rail, see Robert T. Brown and Carlos Hurtado, *Una Política de Transportes para Chile* (Santiago, Chile: Instituto de Economía, 1963), pp. 20-22.

The analysis is restricted to the Southern System and only comparative highway and railway costs will be examined. Separate estimates are made for carload freight, less-than-carload freight, passengers, and baggage. An estimate is also made of the share of highway construction and maintenance costs assignable to trucks and buses on the basis of gross ton-kilometers of vehicles using the intercity highways. Using alternative assumptions regarding the utilization of truck capacity for the transport of carload freight and allowing for unanticipated costs in the case of passenger transportation, high, "realistic," and low estimates of total alternative highway costs were calculated. The results are presented in Table XII-6, and the detailed derivation of the figures is presented in the appendix.

TABLE XII-6. *Hypothetical Cost of Transporting by Highway all Railway Traffic of the Southern System in 1961*

(Millions of escudos of 1961)

	Low Estimate	"Realistic" Estimate	High Estimate
Carload Freight	36.80	40.90	45.76
Less-than-Carload Freight	4.55	4.55	4.55
Baggage	0.67	0.67	0.67
Passengers	14.35	17.20	17.20
Net User Cost of Highways	7.31	7.31	7.31
Total	63.68	70.63	75.49

Note: For derivation of these figures see the Appendix.

The table shows that the estimates of the cost of transporting by highway all the traffic of the Southern System of the State Railways in 1961 range from 63.68 million escudos to 75.49 million.

In the annual profit and loss statement, the State Railways separate the costs of the Northern and Southern Systems. The following table presents both costs from the 1961 statement and adjusted cost figures. The adjusted costs reflect the impact of a hypothetical increase of 50 percent in the exchange rate and a reduction of more than 40 percent in the cost of the coal consumed. These costs were adjusted to account partially for the difference between private and social costs.

The result of the comparison of the costs of railway transport with the hypothetical costs of highway transport is so dramatic[21] that it is necessary to remember the purpose of the comparison before continuing the analysis. The comparison is of no value for determining whether or not Chile should have a railroad. For that decision it would be necessary to determine the cost of transporting by railway that traffic for which it has a relative advantage and under conditions of operating efficiency. The comparison *does* show the danger of launching a massive investment program which would freeze the present structure

Costs	Accounting Costs Published by the State Railways (millions of E°)	Hypothetical Social Costs (millions of E°)
Operating Costs	64.29	65.01
Pensions	9.71	9.71
Severance Pay	3.28	3.28
Financial Costs	2.40	2.40
Depreciation	14.78	16.99
Difference with Book Value of Eliminated Assets	0.09	—
Insurance on Freight	0.43	—
Total	94.98	97.39

of railroad transport without carrying out the type of analysis which has been presented here. If it is true that trucks and buses could have transported at a cost of between 64 and 76 million escudos the traffic transported by railway at an adjusted cost of 97 million escudos, it is obvious that the basic structure of the nation's transport should have been subjected to a searching criticism before investment decisions were made.

Referring now to the railroad cost figures just presented, it is clear that despite the adjustments made for the undervalued exchange rate, the overvalued coal, and the elimination of the last two items,[22] they are still not directly comparable to the cost estimates presented for highway transport. Not all the differences between social and

[21] A somewhat similar study of Class I Railroads in the United States in 1950 concludes that for the same cost for which the railroads could transport 567 billion revenue ton miles, trucks could transport only 414 billion revenue ton miles. See John R. Meyer et alia, *The Economics of Competition in the Transportation Industries* (Harvard University Press, 1959), pp. 159-165.

[22] Insurance on Freight was eliminated because it was not included in the highway transportation costs. It does represent a social cost.

private costs have been considered, and social costs, rather than private costs, are of primary interest in making investment decisions.

In the determination of the highway transport costs two adjustments were made to increase private costs so as to approach the social costs: the cost of imported inputs was increased by 50 percent to take into account the undervaluation of the dollar in that year and an estimate was made of the uncovered "user cost" of the highways. Other possible adjustments were not made. The social cost of the construction of highways, which involves considerable unskilled labor, was undoubtedly less than the private cost of 50 million escudos. Tires, an important input in highway transport, are subject to heavy import duties to protect the domestic tire manufacturer. The "normal" taxes paid by the truck and bus companies were included in their costs; only the "extra" taxes were subtracted from the total cost of construction and maintenance of highways.

Similar qualifications should be considered in regard to the railroad costs. In addition to an obvious excess of personnel in 1961, the average wages paid to the unskilled railroad laborers exceed the general average in the economy. The costs of depreciation may also be exaggerated, as insufficient depreciation was charged in the past and present book value is high. It is also possible that included in the financial costs are items which do not correspond to social costs.

In addition, railway traffic in 1961 was considerably below that in previous years; had it been higher, the cost by highway would have been nearly proportionally higher whereas the cost by railroad would have changed much less than proportionally. On the other hand, the transfer of all traffic to the highways would permit door-to-door service, and shippers could avoid the cost they now incur for transporting goods to the railroad station and transferring them to freight cars. Besides avoiding this direct cost, shippers would benefit by faster service.

Renovation and Railroad Costs

The final question to be considered is the impact of the proposed investment program on the costs of the railways. If the State Railways had carried out the modernization plan as originally conceived, would it have reduced the annual costs to a level below the alternative cost of transferring all traffic to the highways?

It was noted above that the 1959 memorandum which analyzed the economic benefits of the proposed program predicted annual savings of 27 percent of the 1959 costs. Applying this percentage to the 1961 total of Operating Costs, Pensions, Severance Pay, and Financial Costs, as adjusted according to the preceding discussion, a total saving of 21.71 million escudos is obtained. Without considering any increase in Depreciation or interest payments as a result of the massive investments, total cost (as adjusted) would have fallen from 97.39 million escudos to 75.68 million, as compared with the high estimate of 75.49 million escudos as the cost of realizing the same transport by highway.

The cost reduction of 27 percent in the 1959 memorandum, furthermore, is concentrated in four principal items: electrification of the main line from Santiago to Chillán (3%), replacement of steam locomotives from Chillán to Puerto Montt by diesel locomotives (7%), installation of centralized traffic control (2%), and "elimination of stations on branch lines and modification of services" (10%). The principal saving associated with the first two items is the saving on the cost of coal by using either electric or diesel locomotives. As has already been noted, the social cost of coal is far less than the price paid by the railroads. The fourth item is apparently quite unrelated to the investment plan, as it is possible to close stations on branch lines and make other "structural" changes without the kind of investments proposed in 1959. For these reasons, it does not seem appropriate to apply the cost saving of 27 percent to the 1961 costs.

The modernization program should result in reductions in operating costs, however, and perhaps a significant part of the proposed program could be justified in terms of these reductions. Furthermore, the Railways had been decapitalized over a considerable number of years, and some investments (especially in the way) were necessary if the Railways were to continue operating. It should be noted, however, that most railroad modernization investments do not in themselves reduce costs, but they make cost reductions possible. Only when the payrolls are cut, trains eliminated and stations closed are these reductions realized. Surely little is gained by replacing aged freight cars if the maintenance shops keep on all the mechanics. (It is for this reason that the author has a personal bias toward investments which increase the productive capacity of an underdeveloped economy in preference to those which might reduce costs.)

Conclusions

In summary, the thesis of this paper is that a decision to construct a national railroad is fundamentally different from a decision to construct either a highway or a port. A port or a highway investment decision is similar to a decision to build a branch line on an existing railroad or to replace locomotives or rolling stock. These are marginal investments and can be evaluated using traditional project evaluation techniques. If the decision is erroneous, the economy suffers a loss, and if the erroneous port or highway investment decision involves a substantial part of the total investment budget, the loss will be important. For the reasons outlined at the beginning of the paper, however, erroneous decisions in these transport media are not likely to distort the basic transportation structure of a nation for any great length of time.

The same cannot be said for an erroneous decision to build a railroad, unless the railroad should be a short line dedicated to a specific traffic, such as transporting ore from a mine to a port, in which case it is not essentially different from a port or a highway project. A decision to construct a national railroad fixes the structure of a nation's transportation for a long period of time. This is especially true when the railway is state-owned and where political considerations shape the economic decisions. If the railroad decision is erroneous, the entire economy pays a heavy price for many years.

Chile in 1959 decided to renovate and modernize a large part of the existing lines of the State Railways. Because of the magnitude of the investments involved, this decision was not basically different from that in another country to construct a railway. It has been the contention of this paper that the justification which was made in 1959 and confined narrowly to the cost saving which the investments would permit was inadequate. Chile, in effect, was making a "structural" decision, and a "structural" analysis was essential to justify the decision.

Two studies of the type which should be carried out when a "structural" decision is made are presented in the paper. According to the conclusions of the first study, the basic cause of the financial difficulties of the State Railways has been the attempt to maintain historical traffic levels by cutting rates and fares to meet increasing highway competition. There are obvious dangers in a massive investment program which freezes the railroad structure without coming to grips with the competitive problem.

The second study estimates the probable social cost of transporting by highway all the traffic of the Southern System of the State Railways in 1961. Although the costs by highway were systematically overestimated and those by railway underestimated, the results clearly indicated that the cost of transporting all railway traffic by highway would have been no greater and probably significantly lower. Again a basic structural defect in the nation's transportation network is obvious.

A third study, which should follow the two preceding ones, would try to determine precisely what should be the proper role of railroad transport within an integrated national network. For this study detailed cost information is essential: both present costs, sector by sector and service by service, and the change in these costs which would result from different alternative investments. Only after the completion of these studies, as a minimum, would the country have been in a position to make a decision as momentous as the one described.

Appendix: Hypothetical Cost of Transporting by Highway all Railway Traffic of the Southern System of the Chilean State Railways in 1961.

Carload Freight

In order to estimate the theoretical cost of transporting by truck the railroad carload freight, it is necessary to make assumptions regarding the probable utilization of truck capacity. The basis for these assumptions was an analysis of the railway traffic flows in each of the sixty-nine separate sectors in which the entire Southern Network was divided. The difference between the north-south and south-north traffic in each sector represents the theoretical minimum of empty haul, which can be expressed as a percentage of the freight actually transported. The sixty-nine sectors were then aggregated into six zones in which it would be expected that the conditions of truck transport would vary from zone to zone but not within the zones.

As these theoretical estimates of minimum empty haul are exceeded even by the railroads, among other reasons because of the use of specialized equipment and because the transport on which the estimates are based is not carried out at a point of time but rather over a year, it is clearly necessary to increase them substantially before applying them to truck transport. The degree of increase is arbitrary, and for this reason three separate estimates were made, thus providing the basis for three alternative estimates of the cost of transporting by truck the railroad carload traffic. For the low estimate of this cost, the theoretical minimum empty haul was increased in the six zones between 12 and 23 percent; for the "realistic" estimate, between 39 and 45 percent; and for the high estimate, by 100 percent.

By adding the estimated empty haul to the observed ton-kilometers of freight transported by railroad, the amount of capacity which the trucks theoretically would have to provide was obtained. The ratio between the ton-kilometers of freight to be transported and the ton-kilometers of capacity provided corresponds to the traditional concept of utilization of the trucks' capacity. This percentage varied from zone to zone and among the three estimates of the costs between 44 and 77 percent.

In order to determine the number of trucks necessary to transport all railway freight, the point of departure was the relationship between the railway traffic in the peak month of March and the total for the year. For the three-year period 1958–60 the March traffic was 10.59 percent of the annual railway traffic. By applying this percentage to the total ton-capacity-kilometers which would have to have been created by the trucks in 1961, it was possible to determine the maximum ton-capacity-kilometers to be created in the peak month in each sector.

It was then arbitrarily assumed that all the truck transport would be carried out by 8-ton and 18-ton trucks. The distribution of the total ton-capacity-kilometers in each sector between the two truck types was also arbitrary; for the principal sector Santiago-Puerto Montt it was assumed that the 8-ton trucks would account for 20 percent of the peak month's ton-capacity-kilometers and the 18-ton trucks the remaining 80 percent. For the principal transversal lines, such as Santiago-Valparaíso, it was assumed that the distribution would be 40 percent for the 8-ton trucks and 60 percent for the 18-ton trucks. For the remaining transversal lines the distribution was 70 percent for the 8-ton trucks and 30 percent for the 18-ton trucks.

An estimate was then made of the number of kilometers which the two truck-types could accumulate in the peak month. This estimate varied from sector to sector and both a high and low estimate were made. For the sector Santiago-Puerto Montt the estimates for the 8-ton trucks were 11,200 and 9,450 kilometers, and for the 18-ton trucks 10,800 and 9,300 kilometers. By multiplying these kilometers by the capacity of the two truck types, the different estimates of the ton-capacity-kilometers per truck in the peak month were estimated. By dividing the total ton-capacity-kilometers to be provided in the peak month in each sector by the ton-capacity-kilometers produced by each truck, it was possible to make high, "realistic," and low estimates of the number of trucks required in each sector. The total number of 8-ton trucks varied from 600 to 871 and the 18-ton trucks from 713 to 1,017.

By comparing the number of trucks needed for the peak month with the total annual ton-capacity-kilometers calculated above, the average kilometers per year per truck were estimated. In the sector Santiago-Puerto Montt this varied from 89,250 to 105,750 kilometers for the 8-ton trucks and from 87,778 to 102,000 kilometers for the 18-ton trucks. In the other sectors the results were smaller.

In order to estimate the costs it was assumed that the typical trucking company has a capacity of around 60 tons (for example, five 8-ton trucks and one 18-ton truck). It was also assumed that the trucks use only paved roads. No insurance on the freight was included nor the costs of loading and unloading. On the basis of these assumptions and a recent study of truck costs made by the Institute of Economic Research of the University of Chile, the cost per ton-kilometer of freight transported and the cost per ton-capacity-kilometer were calculated. It was noted earlier that the exchange rate in 1961 overvalued the escudo in relation to the dollar. For this reason those parts of the truck costs which represent imported inputs were increased by 50 percent.

For the sector Santiago-Puerto Montt the results were as follows (in escudos of 1961):

	Estimated Cost per Ton-Capacity-Km. Provided			Estimated Cost per Ton-Km. of Freight Transported		
Trucks of	High	Realistic	Low	High	Realistic	Low
8-Tons	0.02754	0.02783	0.02738	0.05301	0.04730	0.04242
18-Tons	0.01993	0.02015	0.01968	0.03830	0.03427	0.03051

Multiplying the cost per ton-capacity-kilometer by the total ton-capacity-kilometers which highway trucking would have to provide in order to absorb the railroad carload freight, the total cost to the truckers was estimated.

Less-than-Carload Freight

In order to estimate the cost of transporting by truck all the less-than-carload (LCL) freight and baggage transported by the State Railways in the Southern System in 1961, it was assumed that 8-ton trucks would be used. It was also assumed that these trucks would utilize only 50 percent of their capacity and that they would operate only 73,750 kilometers annually. On the basis of these assumptions, the average cost per ton-kilometer of LCL freight and baggage transported would be 0.0551 escudos, a most prudent estimate when it is considered that during 1961 truckers transported these types of products at rates around 0.030 escudos per ton-kilometer.

Passengers

Both a high and a low estimate were made of the cost of transporting by bus the passengers carried by railway in 1961. The low estimate was made by taking the passenger fare per kilometer in Pullman buses in 1961 (which was considered to be remunerative) and adding 23 percent for the effect of an increase in the exchange rate of 50 percent. The high estimate was formed by arbitrarily adding an additional 20 percent to the low estimate. Both estimates are high, as the Pullman fare is already 30 percent higher than the first-class bus fare and 70 percent higher than the second-class fare. If all railroad passengers were transferred to buses, obviously many of them would travel first or second class rather than Pullman.

Highway Construction and Maintenance

The estimate of the part of the cost of the construction and maintenance of highways which could be allocated to the trucks and buses which would absorb the railroad traffic is considerably more arbitrary than the preceding estimates.[23] An earlier study of the Institute of Economic Research showed that the total expenditure on interurban highway construction and maintenance in 1961 was 50 million escudos. This figure was arbitrarily increased by 15 percent to take into account the undervaluation of the dollar, so that the total cost was increased to 57.5 million escudos. It was then estimated that the total gross ton-kilometers in interurban transport by all vehicles in 1961 amounted to perhaps 14.88 billion. Using gross ton-kilometers as the basis for distribution, it was estimated that the share of trucks and buses within the total cost of 57.5 million escudos was 47.77 million.

Trucks and buses in 1961, however, paid an estimated 11.95 million escudos in special "user taxes," corresponding nearly exclusively to differential taxes on gasoline and diesel oil. Had the cost of these fuels been 50 percent higher in 1961 as a consequence of a realistic exchange rate, as was assumed in the cost estimates, the user taxes would have amounted to 17.81 million escudos. Subtracting these taxes from the share of construction and maintenance costs of interurban highways corresponding to these same vehicles, the net "subsidy" which they received was 29.96 million escudos. Dividing this "subsidy" by the total gross ton-kilometers of trucks and buses in 1961, the "subsidy" per gross ton-kilometer was 0.002424 escudos.

An estimate was then made of the gross ton-kilometers of highway transport were the railway transport to be transferred to the highways according to the analysis above. The results were as follows:

	Gross Ton-Kilometers (thousands)
Carload freight	2,246,524
Less-than-carload freight	185,883
Baggage	41,108
Passengers	540,748
Total	3,014,263

By multiplying the net "subsidy" per gross ton-kilometer as calculated above by the total gross ton-kilometers resulting from the transfer of the railroad traffic, a total "subsidy" of 7.3 million escudos was obtained.

[23] Some of the most important assumptions used in the estimate follow: (1) Total construction and maintenance costs were used with no analysis of the relation between this figure and the part which can justifiably be charged to highway users in any given year. In this regard it should be noted that both construction and maintenance expenditures have been considerably higher in recent years than in the past. (2) Total costs were distributed among highway users on the basis of gross ton-kilometers, with no analysis either of marginal social costs or of the distribution of benefits. (3) The same net "subsidy" per gross ton-kilometer was assigned to the hypothetical traffic transferred from the highways, with no regard to marginal costs.

Selected Bibliography

Selected Bibliography: Transportation and Economic Development

KATHERINE D. WARDEN*

THIS SELECTED BIBLIOGRAPHY was prepared to aid those interested specifically in problems of transportation and economic development in the context of the less developed nations. Primary emphasis in the review of the literature, too, has been given to materials bearing on transport investment decisions. Thus, texts on transportation economics within the historical or normative framework of public utility regulation in developed countries have been excluded.

Unfortunately, owing to limitations of time and resources, this bibliography is both extensively and intensively limited. For the most part, references on certain subjects indirectly related to the general topic, such as treatises on economic growth and development, development planning or programing, transport engineering and design, transport administration, etc., have not been included. Furthermore, coverage in some areas (for example, cost and benefit estimation for transport projects) could greatly be expanded. Also the number of publications in foreign languages listed is particularly limited. However, the aim has been to provide an initial springboard for the researcher, and not a comprehensive survey of the field. Any additions that others might suggest are most welcome.

I. General Transportation

Arth, Maurice P., "Federal Transport Regulatory Policy," *American Economic Review*, May 1962.

Ashton, Herbert, "The Time Element in Transportation," *American Economic Review*, May 1947.

Balakrishna, R., "Transport Rates and Industrial Distribution," *Indian Journal of Economics*, January 1946.

---

* The National Bureau of Economic Research.

Barger, Harold, *The Transportation Industries, 1889-1946*. New York: National Bureau of Economic Research, 1946.

Barriger, J. W., "Transportation Problems: Discussion," *American Economic Review*, May 1957.

Beckmann, Martin, C. B. McGuire, and C. B. Winsten, *Studies in the Economics of Transportation*. New Haven: Yale University Press, 1956.

Bharadwrj, Krishna, "Notes on Some Aspects of Transportation Planning," *Indian Economic Journal*, October 1962.

Bigham, Truman Cicero, "Regulation of Minimum Rates in Transportation," *Quarterly Journal of Economics*, February 1947.

Bleile, George W. and Leon Moses, "Transportation and the Spatial Distribution of Economic Activity," Bulletin No. 311, *Highway Research Board*, National Academy of Sciences, 1962.

Boiteau, M., "Peak-Load Pricing," *Journal of Business*, April 1960.

Bonavia, Michael Robert, *The Economics of Transport*. London: Nisbet, 1936.

Bourrières, Paul and J. Bertrand, *L'Économie des Transports dans les Programmes de Développement*. Paris: Les Presses Universitaires de France, 1961.

Bourrières, Paul and L. Odier, "Transports en Économie de Développement." Paris: Études et Réalisations, 1960.

Branham, Arthur K., *Transportation Factors and National Transportation Policy: A Partial Analysis*. Lafayette, Indiana: Purdue University Press, 1951.

Buckatsch, E. J., "Reorganization of Inland Transport," *Bulletin*, Oxford University, Institute of Statistics, November 21, 1942.

Carroll, J. D. and H. W. Bevis, "Predicting Local Travel in Urban Regions," *Proceedings*, Regional Science Association, 1957.

Chiu, C. L., *The Principles of Transportation*. Shanghai: Commercial Press, 1929.

Cover, V. D., "Transportation in Capitalist and Socialized Economies: Discussion," *American Economic Review*, May 1950.

Cunningham, W. J., "The Transportation Problem," *Harvard Business Review*, Autumn 1946.

Daggett, S., "Transportation and National Policy," *Harvard Business Review*, Winter 1944.

Davies, H. Barrs, *The Rights and Duties of Transport Undertakings*. London: Pitman, 1926.

Dearing, C. L. and Wilfred Owen, "The Reorganization of Transport Regulation," *American Economic Review*, May 1950.

——. "Our National Transportation Problem," *Harvard Business Review*, March 1950.

Dewey, R. L., chairman, "Round Table of Transportation and Public Utility Problems," *American Economic Review*, May 1949.

——. "Criteria for the Establishment of an Optimum Transportation System," *American Economic Review*, May 1952.

Drury, William, *The Significance of Transport in the Production of Wealth.* London: F. Hodgson, 1921.

Duncan, C. S., and others, "The Transportation Problem: Discussion," *American Economic Review*, March 1940.

Eastman, J. B., "The Adjustment of Rates Between Competing Forms of Transportation," *American Economic Review*, March 1940.

Edwards, F. K., "Application of Market Pricing Factors in the Division of Traffic According to Principles of Economy and Fitness," *American Economic Review*, May 1955.

Fair, M. L., and others, "Transportation and Public Utilities Problems: Discussion," *American Economic Review*, May 1947.

Farris, M. T., "A Comment on J. A. McDonald's 'Some Notes on the Economics of Transportation,'" *Canadian Journal of Economics and Political Science*, May 1956.

Frederick, John H., *Improving National Transportation Policy.* Washington: American Enterprise Association, 1957.

Fromont, Philippe, *Les Transports dans les Économies Sous-Développées, Problème des Investissements Générale de Droit du Jurisprudence.* Paris: Librairie Générale de Droit et de Jurisprudence, 1957.

Germane, Gayton E., and others, *A New Concept of Transportation Movement: A System for Cargo Movement in the Communications Zone.* Prepared by the Graduate School of Business, Stanford University, Stanford, California and published for U.S. Army Transportation Research and Engineering Command, Fort Eustis, Virginia, March 1959.

Gilmore, Harlan, *Transportation and the Growth of Cities.* Glencoe, Illinois: Free Press, 1953.

Goodman, A. and L. Landon, "Automation and Transport," *British Transport Review* (House Journal of the British Transport Commission), April 1961.

Hall, H. H., *Sizes and Types of Standard Freight Containers for Universal Carrier Interchange.* Bulk Solids Handling Symposium. Washington: American Society of Mechanical Engineers, Oct. 17-18, 1961.

Harbeson, R. W., "The Transportation Act of 1958," *Land Economics*, May 1959.

Hay, William Walter, *An Introduction to Transportation Engineering.* New York: Wiley, 1961.

Healy, K. T., chairman, "Prospective Developments in Federal Regulation and Coordination of Transportation," report of round table conference, *American Economic Review*, May 1953.

——. "The Merger Movement in Transportation," *American Economic Review*, May 1962.

——. "Transportation as a Factor in Economic Growth," *Journal of Economic History Supplement*, 1947.

Heller, Frank A., "Management Skills and the Transport Industry," *British Transport Review* (House Journal of the British Transport Commission), August 1961.

Hirschman, Albert O., *The Strategy of Economic Development*. New Haven: Yale University Press, 1958.

Hunter, Holland, "Optimum Tautness in Development Planning," *Economic Development and Cultural Change*, July 1961.

——. "Resource Transportation and Economic Development," in Joseph Spengler, ed., *Conference on Natural Resources and Economic Growth*. Washington: Resources for the Future, 1961.

Industrial College of the Armed Forces, "Transportation: The Nation's Lifelines," in *The Economics of National Security*, Washington, 1961.

Innis, H. A., ed., *Essays in Transportation in Honour of W. T. Jackson*. Toronto: University of Toronto Press, 1941.

International Labour Organisation, Inland Transport Committee, *Co-ordination of Transport: Labour Problems*. Second Item on the Agenda of Fourth Session of International Labour Office. Geneva, 1951.

Isard, Walter, "Transport Development and Business Cycles," *Quarterly Journal of Economics*, November 1942.

Kaufmann, John H., "Planning for Transport Investment in the Development of Iran," *American Economic Review*, May 1962.

Koopmans, T. C., "Optimum Utilization of the Transportation System," *Econometrica*, July 1949. (Errata, April 1951.)

Kuhn, Tillo E., *Public Enterprise Economics and Transport Problems*. Berkeley, California: University of California Press, 1962.

Laight, J. C., "Transportation in the American Economy," *South African Journal of Economics*, March 1952.

Lancaster, R. K. and R. G. Lipsey, "The General Theory of Second Best," *Review of Economic Studies*, Vol. 24 (1) No. 63, 1956-57; Comment and Reply, Vol. 26 (3) No. 71, 1959.

Lefeber, Louis, *Allocation in Space, Production, Transport and Industrial Location*. Amsterdam: North Holland Publishing Company, 1958.

Lewis, William Arthur. *Overhead Costs: Some Essays in Economic Analysis*. New York: Rinehart, 1949.

Locklin, David Philip. "Economic Implications of Current Transportation Policy Recommendations (with discussion by W. H. Thompson)," *Journal of Farm Economics*, December 1956.

Long, William Rodney, *Transport Control Abroad, Recent Outstanding Measures, Trends and Developments*. Washington: Government Printing Office, 1939.

McCunniff, J. A., *Study of Economic Considerations in the Establishment of Minimum Transportation Rates and Related Problems*. San Francisco: California Public Utilities Commission, 1949.

McDonald, J. A., "Some Notes on the Economics of Transportation," *Canadian Journal of Economics and Political Science*, November 1951.

Mason, Edward S., *Economic Planning in Underdeveloped Areas*. New York: Fordham University Press, 1958.

Mater, D. H., "Wage Rates and 'Relative Economy of Fitness' in the Transportation Industry," *Journal of Business*, October 1945.

Melton, L. J., Jr., "An Integrated Approach to the Transportation Problem," *Southern Economic Journal*, April 1957.

Meyer, John R., "Economist Appraises Transport Message," *Railway Age*, June 11, 1962.

Meyer, John R., J. Kain, and M. Wohl, *Technology in Urban Transportation*. Santa Monica: RAND Corporation, 1964.

Meyer, John R., M. J. Peck, J. Stenason, and C. Zwick, *The Economics of Competition in the Transportation Industries*. Cambridge: Harvard University Press, 1959.

Milne, Alaster M., *The Economics of Inland Transport*. London: Pitman, 1960.

Mnookin, Robert, "Transportation Pricing in Underdeveloped Countries: A Welfare Analysis," Harvard Transportation and Economic Development Seminar, Discussion Paper 4 (mimeographed), May 1964.

Morgan, C. S., "Aspects of the Problem of Public Aids to Transportation," *American Economic Review*, March 1940.

National Academy of Sciences, *U. S. Transportation Resources: Performance and National Policy*. Publication 748. Washington, 1959.

———. *Transportation Design Considerations*. Publication 841. Washington, 1961.

National Resources Planning Board, *Transportation and Public Policy*, 1960 Conference on Transportation Research, Woods Hole. Washington: Government Printing Office, 1942.

Nelson, J. C., "Patterns of Competition and Monopoly in Present-Day Transport and Implications for Public Policy," *Land Economics*, August 1950.

———. "Revision of National Transportation Regulatory Policy," *American Economic Review*, December 1955.

Nightingale, E. A., "Public Utilities, Transportation, and Spatial Organization: Discussion," *American Economic Review*, May 1952.

Oi, Walter Y. and Paul W. Shuldiner, *An Analysis of Urban Travel Demands*. Evanston, Illinois: Northwestern University Press, 1962.

Organization for European Economic Cooperation, *Federal Regulation of Transport in the United States: How Transport Problems are Solved in a System of Federated States*. Paris, March 1953.

Osofsky, Sam, "A Multiple Regression Approach to Forecasting Urban Area Traffic Volumes," *Proceedings*, American Association of State Highway Officials, Washington, 1958.

Owen, Wilfred, *Cities in the Motor Age*. New York: Viking Press, 1959.

———. *The Metropolitan Transportation Problem*. Washington: Brookings Institution, 1956.

———. *Strategy for Mobility*. Washington: Brookings Institution, 1964.

———. *Transportation and Economic Development*. Washington: Brookings

Institution, Reprint No. 33, August 1959. Originally in *American Economic Review,* May 1959.

——. "Transportation and Technology," Washington: The Brookings Institution, Reprint No. 59, July 1962. Originally in *American Economic Review,* May 1962.

Pegrum, Dudley F., "Investment in the Railroad and Other Transportation Industries under Regulation," *American Economic Review,* May 1957.

——. *Transportation: Economics and Public Policy.* Homewood, Illinois: Irwin, 1962.

Plowman, E. G., "A Shipper Looks at National Transportation Policy," *Harvard Business Review,* March-April 1956.

Plummer, A. V., L. G. Wilkie, and R. F. Gran, eds., *The Transportation Usage Study.* Chicago: Cook County Highway Department, 1957.

Rahbany, K. Philip, "Cost Considerations in Transportation," *Traffic World,* Part 2, August 25, 1962.

——. "Cost Considerations in Transportation, Origin and Management of Empty Returns: A Case in Joint Costs," *Traffic World,* Part 3, October 6, 1962.

Ransmeier, J. S., "Public Utilities, Transportation, and Spatial Organization: Discussion," *American Economic Review,* May 1952.

Roberts, Merrill J., "The Motor Transportation Revolution," *Business History Review,* March 1956.

——. "Transport Dynamics and Distribution Management," *Business Horizons,* Fall 1961.

Rockwell, E., "Urban Traffic Problems and Their Effect on Public Transport," *British Transport Review* (House Journal of the British Transport Commission), August 1962.

Ruggles, N., "The Welfare Basis of the Marginal Cost Pricing Principle," *Review of Economic Studies,* XVII (1) No. 42 and XVII (2) No. 43, 1949-50.

Ruppenthal, Karl M., ed., *Transportation Frontiers.* Stanford, California: Stanford University, 1962.

Sangarapillai, P., "The Motor Traffic Act No. 14 of 1951 and Coordination of Transport," *Ceylon Economist,* June 1951.

Savage, Christopher, *An Economic History of Transport.* London: Hutchinson, 1959.

Schmidt, Robert E., and M. Earl Campbell, *Highway Traffic Estimation,* Saugatuck, Connecticut: Eno Foundation, 1953.

Science, Technology and Development. U.S. Papers Prepared for the United Nations Conference on the Application of Science and Technology for the Benefit of the Less Developed Areas. 12 vols. Washington: Government Printing Office, 1962-63.

Sharfman, I. L., chairman, "National Transportation Policy," *American Economic Review,* May 1954.

Smith, R. T., "Technical Aspects of Transportation Flow Data," *Journal of the American Statistical Association,* June 1954.

Soberman, R. M., *Some Theoretical Notes on the Supply of Transportation.* Joint Center—Guayana Project. Caracas: Corporación Venezolana de Guayana, División de Estudios, Planificación e Investigación, March 31, 1963.

Steiner, Peter O., "Peak Loads and Efficient Pricing," *Quarterly Journal of Economics,* November 1957.

Sveistrup, P. P., "Some Problems in Laying Out a New Traffic Line," *Nordisk Tidsskrift for Teknisk Økonomi,* 1948.

Thompson, W. H., and others, "Changes in National Transportation Policy: Discussion," *American Economic Review,* May 1951.

Tinbergen, Jan, *The Design of Development.* Baltimore: Johns Hopkins Press, 1958.

"Transportation Renaissance," *Annals,* American Academy of Political and Social Science, January 1963.

Transportation, Science, Technology, and Development. U.S. Papers prepared for the United Nations Conference on the Application of Science and Technology for the Benefit of the Less Developed Areas, Vol. V. Washington: Government Printing Office, 1963.

Ullman, Edward L., "The Role of Transportation and the Bases for Interaction," in W. L. Thomas, ed., *Man's Role in Changing the Face of the Earth.* Chicago: University of Chicago Press, 1956.

Ulmer, Melville J., *Capital in Transportation, Communications, and Public Utilities: Its Formation and Financing.* National Bureau of Economic Research, Studies in Capital Formation and Financing, 4. Princeton: Princeton University Press, 1960.

U.S. Congress. House of Representatives. Alaska International Rail and Highway Commission. *Transportation Requirements for the Growth of Northwest North America.* 87 Cong. 1 sess. Washington: Government Printing Office, 1961.

U.S. Department of Commerce, *Federal Transportation Policy and Program.* Washington: Government Printing Office, March 1960.

Walker, G., "Transport Policy Before and After 1953," *Oxford Economic Papers,* March 1953.

Warner, Stanley Leon, *Stochastic Choice of Mode in Urban Travel: A Study in Binary Choice.* Evanston, Illinois: Northwestern University Press, 1962.

Williams, E. W., "Discussions: Analysis of Transportation," *Proceedings,* Regional Science Association, 1957.

Williams, E. W., and David W. Bluestone, *Rationale of Federal Transportation Policy: Appendix to Federal Transportation Policy and Program,* Washington: U.S. Department of Commerce, April 1960.

Wilson, George, *Essays on Some Unsettled Questions in the Economics of Transportation.* Bloomington: Indiana University Press, 1962.

——. "On the Output Unit in Transportation," *Land Economics,* August 1959.

Zwick, Charles, *The Demand for Transportation Services in a Growing Economy.* Santa Monica: RAND Corporation (Rand P-2682), 1962.

II. General Transportation—Africa

Brown Engineers, *Report on Liberia Transportation Survey*. New York, July 1963.

Eklund, S. O. C., "Verburgh on Transportation Policy," *African Roads and Transportation*, March-April 1962.

Girard, Rene, "The Transport System of French Equatorial Africa," *Road International*, Summer 1957.

Gould, Peter R., *The Development of the Transportation Pattern in Ghana*. Evanston, Illinois: Northwestern University Press, 1960.

Hawkins, Edward K., *Roads and Road Transport in an Underdeveloped Country: A Case Study of Uganda*. London: H. M. Stationery Office, 1962.

Huston, C. T., "Transportation Costs" [in East Africa], *East African Economics Review*, January 1955.

International Bank for Reconstruction and Development. *The Economic Development of Kenya*. Report of a mission organized at the request of the Governments of Kenya and the United Kingdom. Baltimore: Johns Hopkins Press, 1963.

——. *The Economic Development of Libya*. Report of a mission organized at the request of the Government of Libya. Baltimore: Johns Hopkins Press, 1960.

——. *The Economic Development of Nigeria*. Report of a mission organized at the request of the Governments of Nigeria and the United Kingdom. Baltimore: Johns Hopkins Press, 1955.

——. *The Economic Development of Tanganyika*. Baltimore: Johns Hopkins Press, 1961.

——. *The Economic Development of Uganda*. Report of a mission organized at the request of the Government of Uganda. Baltimore: Johns Hopkins Press, 1962.

Lemon, R. M. L.: "East Africa Royal Commission 1953-1955: The Transportation Problem," *East African Economics Review*, January 1957.

Louis Berger, Incorporated, *Calabar-Ikom Highway Project: Federation of Nigeria, Eastern Region*. Harrisburg, Pennsylvania, October 1962.

Northwestern University, *Economic Survey of Liberia*. Evanston, Illinois, 1962.

Robinson, Hanlin, Stanton R. Smith, and Kenneth G. Clare, *The Economic Coordination of Transport Development in Nigeria*. SRI Report No. I-3280, prepared for Joint Planning Committee, National Economic Council, Federation of Nigeria. Menlo Park, California: Stanford Research Institute, 1961.

South Africa, Republic of, Department of Transport, *A Century of Transport: A Record of Achievement of the Ministry of Transport of the Union of South Africa*. Johannesburg: Da Gamma Publications, 1960.

Stanford Research Institute, *The Economic Coordination of Transport Development in Nigeria.* Menlo Park, California, 1961.

Thomas, Benjamin Earl, *Transportation and Physical Geography in West Africa.* Los Angeles: University of California, Department of Geography, 1960.

Transportation Consultants, Incorporated, *Transportation Survey of Sierra Leone.* Washington, March 1963.

"Transportation in Nigeria," *Research for Industry,* Vol. 14, No. 6, 1962.

United Nations Economic Commission for Africa, *East African Transport Problems in Relation to the Promotion of Economic Development.* Progress Report, E/CN.14/148, New York, 1962.

——. *Transport Problems in Relation to Economic Development in West Africa.* E/CN.14/63, New York, 1962.

Van Dongen, Irene S., *The British East African Transport Complex.* Chicago: University of Chicago Press, 1954.

Verburgh, G., *South African Transportation Policy.* Stellenbosch: Bureau for Economic Research, University of Stellenbosch, 1961.

Western Electric Company, *Republic of Nigeria Telecommunications Study.* New York, November 30, 1963.

III. General Transportation—India and Pakistan

Bhatnagar, K. P., S. Bahadur, D. N. Agrawal, and S. C. Gupta, *Transport in Modern India.* Kishore: Parade, Kanpur, India, 1953.

Bisnoi, S. L., "Problems of Transport in Coal Industry," *Economic Papers,* November 1957.

Brari, B., "Co-ordination in Transport," *Pakistan Economic Journal,* January 1950.

International Bank for Reconstruction and Development, *Development Programming and Economic Conditions in Pakistan.* Annex III-Transport, Report of Technical Information, AS-85a. Washington, May 12, 1961.

——. *Economic Development in Pakistan.* Report of Technical Information, AS-81a. Washington, August 17, 1960.

McCloskey, Donald N., "Road and Rail in India: An Institutional and Econometric Study." Harvard Transportation and Economic Development Seminar, Discussion Paper 3 (mimeographed). Cambridge: Harvard University, May 1964.

Owen, Wilfred, *Transport Survey of West Pakistan.* Karachi: Government of Pakistan Press, 1960.

Ramanadham, V. V., "Transport in Transition," *Indian Journal of Economics,* January 1945.

Srivastava, Krishma, *Transport Development in India.* Ghazeabad: Deepak Publishing House, 1956.

——. *Transport Development in India* [for Advanced Students of Economics and Commerce Offering Transport]. Ghazeabad: Deepak Publishing House, 1953.

Thadani, J. N., "Transport and Location of Industry in India," *Indian Economic Review*, August 1952.

U.S. Department of the Army, Corps of Engineers, *Transportation Survey of West Pakistan 1962*. Washington, October 1962.

——. *Transportation Survey of East Pakistan 1961*. Washington, April 1962.

Weld, William Ernest, *India's Demand for Transportation*. New York: Columbia University Press, 1920.

IV. General Transportation—Russia

Blackman, James, "Transportation [Russia]." Santa Monica, California: RAND Corporation (Rand P-288, mimeographed), 1952.

——. "Transportation Appendices." Mimeographed appendices to Chapter IV in Abram Bergson, ed., *Soviet Economic Growth: Conditions and Perspectives*. Evanston, Illinois: Row, Peterson, 1953.

Hunter, Holland, *Soviet Transportation Policy*. Cambridge: Harvard University Press, 1957.

——. "Measuring Production in the USSR: Discussion (of Soviet Transportation Development)," *American Economic Review*, May 1958.

Lebedev, I., "Development of Transportation and Communications in the USSR," *Problems of Economics*, August 1958.

Petrov, V., "Effectiveness of Capital Investment in the Transportation Industry of the USSR," *Problems of Economics*, July 1958.

Tverskoi, Konstantin N., *The Unified Transport System of the USSR*. London: V. Gollancz, 1935.

Vasilevsky, L., "An American Economist on Soviet Transport," *Problems of Economics*, January 1959.

Williams, Ernest W., "Soviet Transportation Development: A Comparison with the United States," *American Economic Review*, May 1958.

V. General Transportation—Miscellaneous Countries

Argentina, Republic of, Ministry of Public Works and Services, Transportation Planning Group, *A Long Range Transportation Plan for Argentina*. Buenos Aires, 1962.

Australia, Commonwealth of, Federal Transport Committee, *The Coordination of Transport in Australia*. Canberra, 1930.

Canadian Industrial Traffic League, Inc. *Five Traffic and Transportation Conferences, 1957-1961*. Toronto, 1961.

Currie, Archibald William, *Economics of Canadian Transportation*. Toronto: University of Toronto Press, 2nd edition, 1959.

Davies, Ernest, *Britain's Transport Crisis: A Socialist's View*. London: A. Barker, 1960.

DeFellner, Frederick Vincent, *Communications in the Far East*. London: P. S. King and Son, 1934.

DeLeuw, Cather and Company, *Land Transportation Survey for Indonesia*. Chicago, December 21, 1961.

Drewes, Wolfram U., "The Economic Development of the Western Montaña of Central Peru as Related to Transportation: A Comparison of Four Areas of Settlement," in annual Anthology from *Peruvian Times*. Lima, Peru, 1958.

Heweston, H. W., "The Report of the Royal Commission on Transportation," *Canadian Journal of Economics and Political Science*, November 1951.

——. "Transportation in the Canadian North," Arctic Survey V, *Canadian Journal of Economics and Political Science*, August 1945.

Hosono, H., "A Review of the Studies of Transportation and Communication Economics in Japan," *Japan Science Review*, Economic Series, 1953.

Hytten, T., "Some Problems of Australian Transport Development," *Economic Record*, June 1947.

Instituto de Economía, Universidad de Chile, *Una Política de Transportes para Chile*. Santiago: Publicaciones del Instituto de Economía, No. 59. 1963.

International Bank for Reconstruction and Development. *The Economic Development of Mexico*. Report of the Combined Mexican Working Party. Baltimore: Johns Hopkins Press, 1960.

——. *The Economic Development of Spain*. Baltimore: Johns Hopkins Press, 1963.

——. *The Economic Development of Venezuela*. Report of the Government of Venezuela. Baltimore: Johns Hopkins Press, 1961.

——. *A Public Development Program for Thailand*. Baltimore: Johns Hopkins Press, 1959.

Iran, Imperial Government of, Plan Organization, Transport and Communication Section, *Third Plan Frame, Transport and Communication*. Tehran, January 1961.

Koldomasov, Y., "The Influence of Transportation on the Geographic Distribution of Industry," *Problems of Economics*, July 1958.

Kolsen, H., "Economic Principles of Transportation Regulation," *Economic Record*, August 1958.

Kuhn, Tillo E., *Economic Development and Transport Investment Planning: A Case Study of Honduras*, OEA/Ser. K/1.9.1. Eng. Doc. 128, Washington: Organization of American States, 1963.

Mandel, W., *The Soviet Far East and Central Asia*. New York: Dial Press, 1944.

Maunder, W. F., "Kingston Public Passenger Transport," *Social and Economic Studies*, March 1954.

——. "Notes on the Development of Internal Transport in Jamaica," *Social and Economic Studies*, September 1954.

——. "The Significance of Transport in the Jamaican Economy: An Estimate of Gross Expenditure on Internal Transport," *Social and Economic Studies,* June 1954.

Medernach, J. A., "Transportation in Latin America," *Journal of Marketing,* April 1942.

Munby, D. L., "Transport Costs in the North of Scotland," *Scottish Journal of Political Economy,* November 1950.

Osrogin, A., "Capital Investments in Transportation Must Be Increased," *Problems of Economics,* May 1959.

Owen, Wilfred, *The Transportation Revolution in Europe.* Washington: Brookings Institution, Reprint No. 53, 1961.

Pan American Union, *A Guide to Institutions in the Washington, D.C.– New York Area Containing Bibliographical References on Transportation in Latin America.* Washington, 1961.

Parsons, Brinckerhoff, Quade, and Douglas (Engineering Consultants), *Plan for Improvements in National Transportation: Republic of Colombia and Summary Reports on Airports, Highways, Inland Waterways, Ocean Ports and Railroads.* 7 vols. Washington: International Bank for Reconstruction and Development, 1961.

Public International Development Financing in Thailand. Report No. 4, Public International Development Financing, A Research Project of the Columbia University School of Law. New York, February 1963.

Reid, E., *New Look at Transportation Policy Significance to Agriculture.* Royal Commission Report. Ottawa, 1951.

Rudzki, Adam, *Organization of Transportation of Captive Europe.* New York: Mid-European Studies Center, 1954.

Salazar Montoya, Jaime, *El Transporte en Colombia.* Bogota: Government of Colombia, National Planning Committee, 1958.

Sleeman, J. F., "Passenger Transport in Scotland," *Scottish Journal of Political Economy,* June 1956.

Soberman, R. M. *The Demand for Freight Transportation in the Guayana Region.* Joint Center–Guayana Project. Caracas: Corporación Venezolana de Guayana. División de Estudios, Planificación e Investigación, February 1963.

——. *A Transport Program for the Guayana Region.* Joint Center—Guayana Project. Caracas: Corporación Venezolana de Guayana, División de Estudios, Planificación e Investigacion, May 22, 1963.

Stanford Research Institute. *Economic Analysis of Philippine Domestic Transport.* Prepared for the National Economic Council of the Philippines. Menlo Park, California, 1957. 7 vols.

——. *The Economic Coordination of Transport Development in Nigeria.* Menlo Park, California, February, 1961.

Transportation Consultants, Incorporated, *A Comprehensive Evaluation of Thailand's Transportation System Requirements.* Washington, July 1, 1959.

United Kingdom, Ministry of Transport, *The Transport Needs of Great*

Britain in the Next Twenty Years. London: H. M. Stationery Office, 1963.

United Nations, *Programming Techniques for Economic Development with Special Reference to Asia and the Far East*. Development Programming Technique Series No. 1. Bangkok, 1960.

United Nations Economic Commission for Asia and the Far East, *Economic Development and Planning in Asia and the Far East: VI. Transport Development*, Vol. XI, No. 3. New York: December 1960.

——. "A Note on the Utilization of Transport Facilities in the ECAFE Region," *Economic Bulletin, ECAFE,* November 1950.

Walker, G., "Competition in Transport as an Instrument of Policy," *Economic Journal*, September 1956.

——. "Transport in Ireland," *Journal of Political Economy*, December 1946.

Weisskoff, Richard, "Transportation in Colombia: A Case Study in the Economics and Politics of Resource Allocation," Harvard Transportation and Economic Development Seminar, Discussion Paper 5 (mimeographed). Cambridge: Harvard University Press, June 1964.

VI. Air Transportation—General

Beckmann, Martin, "The Pricing of Fixed Services Subject to a Random Demand," *Economía Internazionale*, May 1956.

Berge, S., "Subsidies and Competition as Factors in Air Transport Policy," *American Economic Review*, May 1951.

Bluestone, David W., "The Problem of Competition Among Domestic Trunk Airlines." Unpublished doctoral thesis, American University, 1954.

Bunke, Harvey C., "Evaluation of Air Transport Policy." Unpublished doctoral thesis, University of Illinois, 1951.

Caves, Richard E., *Air Transport and its Regulators*. Cambridge: Harvard University Press, 1962.

Dale, E., and R. L. Raimon, "Management Unionism and Public Policy on the Railroads and the Airlines," *Industrial and Labor Relations Review,* July 1958.

Eichner, Herbert, "The Economics of Aircraft Utilization," *Aeroplane and Commercial Aviation News*, May 3, 1962.

Heymann, Hans, Jr., "Air Transport and Economic Development: Some Comments on Foreign Aid Programs," *American Economic Review*, May 1962.

Koontz, H. D., "Domestic Airlines Self-Sufficiency," *American Economic Review*, March 1952.

Lansing, John B. and Dwight M. Blood, "A Cross-Sectional Analysis of Non-Business Air Travel," *Journal of the American Statistical Association*, December 1958.

——, J. Liu, and D. M. Suits, "An Analysis of Interurban Air Travel," *Quarterly Journal of Economics*, February 1961.

Lester, A. M., "The Sources and Nature of Statistical Information in Special

Fields of Satistics; International Air Transport Statistics," *Journal of the Royal Statistical Society*, Series A (General), 1953.

VII. Air Transportation—Miscellaneous Countries

Airways Engineering Corporation, *Ilopango International Airport San Salvador-El Salvador: Economic and Engineering Feasibility Report*. Washington, October 1960.

Betz, Gabriel, "The Role of Commercial Aviation in Africa South of the Sahara." Unpublished doctoral thesis, Syracuse University, 1952.

Brewer, Stanley H., *The North American-Asia Market for Air Freight with Projections for 1965, 1970, 1975*. Summary edition for the Boeing Company. Seattle, Washington: College of Business Administration, University of Washington, 1963.

Cartaino, T. F., *Technological Aspects of Contemporary and Future Civil Aircraft for the World's Less Developed Areas*. Santa Monica, California: RAND Corporation, July 1962.

Cunningham, William G., "The Aircraft Industry of the United States; A Study in Industrial Location." Unpublished doctoral thesis, University of Pennsylvania, 1950.

Dhekn, Malhar Ramchandra, *Air Transport in India, Growth and Problems*. Bombay: Vora, 1953.

"Domestic Airline for the Somali Republic?" *Aeroplane and Commercial Aviation News*, September 20, 1962.

"Ethiopia Dreams of an Air Empire," *Business Week*, January 12, 1963.

Hager, Alice R., *Frontier by Air (Brazil Takes the Sky Road)*. New York: Macmillan, 1942.

Institut du Transport Aérien, *Economic Aspects of Air Transport: Air Transport in Europe and the United States Compared, Taking Account of Geographical, Demographical, Economic and Political Background*. Paris, 1951.

——. *Economic Aspects of Air Transport*. Paris, 1950.

Le Chatelier, Jean, *The Role of Air Transport in the Economic Development of the Sahara*. Paris, 1962.

Naqvi, S. K. Irtiza, *Air Transport in India*. Allahabad: Kitab Mahal, 1948.

Philips, Robin, "By Uniting We Stand," *Aeroplane and Commercial Aviation News*, June 14, 1962.

Stanford Research Institute, *Air Transport Development and Coordination in Latin America: A Study of Economic Factors*. Menlo Park, California, 1961.

Sutton, John Lawrence, *European Commercial Air Cargo, an Analysis of its Present Development*. Geneva: Imprimeries Populaires, 1949.

Tomasino, Salvatore, "Europe's Air Transport Problems—and the Common Market," *Aeroplane and Commercial Aviation News*, May 24, 1962.

Wheatcroft, S., *The Economics of European Air Transport*. Manchester: Manchester University Press, 1956.

VIII. Railroad Transportation—General

Allen, J. E., "Railways or Roads?" *Economic Journal*, March 1959.

Ashton, Herbert, "Railroad Costs in Relation to the Volume of Traffic," *American Economic Review*, June 1940.

Baker, G. P., "The Possibilities of Economies by Railroad Consolidation and Coordination," *American Economic Review*, May 1948.

Baumol, William J., and others, "The Role of Cost in the Minimum Pricing of Railroad Services," *Journal of Business*, October 1962.

Borts, G. H., "Increasing Returns in the Railway Industry," *Journal of Political Economy*, August 1954.

———. "Production Relations in the Railway Industry," *Econometrica*, January 1952.

———. "The Estimation of Rail Cost Functions," *Econometrica*, January 1960.

Boston College, Seminar Research Bureau, *Problems of the Railroads.* Boston, 1959.

Bureau of Railway Economics, *Railway Economics, a Collective Catalogue of Books in Fourteen American Libraries.* Chicago: University of Chicago Press, 1912.

"Development of Freight and Passenger Rail Transport in Member Countries." Report of the European Conference of Ministers of Transport. *Railway Gazette*, May 11, 1962.

Dewey, R. L., and H. M. Gray, "Transportation and Public Utilities: Discussion," *American Economic Review*, May 1948.

Edwards, F. K., "Cost Analysis in Transportation," *American Economic Review*, May 1947.

Feyeux, M., and M. Farrouch, "Productivity in European Railways," *European Productivity*, February 1960.

Fogel, Robert William, *Railroads and American Economic Growth: Essays in Econometric History.* Baltimore: Johns Hopkins Press, 1964.

———. *The Union Pacific Railroad, A Case in Premature Enterprise.* Baltimore: Johns Hopkins Press, 1960.

Gadgil, D. R., "Rail-Road Coordination with Special Reference to Rates Policy," *Indian Journal of Economics*, January 1946.

Gopal, M. H., "A New Basis for Railway Rates—The Social Benefit of Service Principle," *Indian Journal of Economics*, January 1946.

Healy, Kent T., "Discriminatory and Cost Based Railroad Pricing," *American Economic Review*, May 1957.

———. *The Effects of Scale in the Railroad Industry.* Committee on Transportation. New Haven: Yale University Press, 1961.

Holmstrong, John Edwin, *Railways and Roads in Pioneer Development Overseas: A Study of Their Comparative Economies.* London: P. S. King & Son, 1934.

Homberger, L. M., "Coordination of Road and Rail Transport and the Or-

292 SELECTED BIBLIOGRAPHY

ganization of the Trucking Industry: a Survey," *Land Economics*, May 1947.

Hotelling, Howard, "The General Welfare in Relation to Problems of Taxation and of Railway and Utility Rates," *Econometrica*, July 1938.

International Labour Organisation, *Social Consequences of Changing Methods and Techniques in Railways and Road Transport*, 7th Session, Inland Transport Commission, Third Item on the Agenda. Geneva, 1961.

International Union of Railways, *International Railway Statistics, Year 1961*. Paris: General Secretariat, International Union of Railways [U.I.C.], 1962.

Jenks, L. H., "Capital Movements and Transportation: Britain and American Rail Development," *Journal of Economic History*, 1951.

———. "Railroads as an Economic Force in American Development," *Journal of Economic History*, May 1944.

Kelso, H., "Waterways versus Railways," *American Economic Review*, September 1941.

Long, William Rodney, *Railway and Highway Transportation Abroad; A Study of Existing Relationship, Recent Competitive Measures and Coordination Policies*. Washington: Government Printing Office, 1935.

Mayer, H. M., "Localization of Railway Facilities in Metropolitan Centers as Typified by Chicago," *Land Economics*, November 1944.

Menzler, F. A. A., "Rail and Road Statistics," *Royal Statistical Society*, Series A, 1950.

Meyer, J. R., "Some Methodological Aspects of Statistical Costing as Illustrated by the Determination of Rail Passenger Costs," *American Economic Review*, May 1957.

Moulton, H. G., *Waterways vs. Railways*. Boston: Houghton Mifflin, 1912.

Munby, D. L., "Investment in Road and Rail Transport," *Institute of Transport Journal*, March 1962.

Nelson, James C., *Railroad Transportation and Public Policy*. Washington: Brookings Institution, 1959.

Nelson, Robert S. and Edward M. Johnson, eds., *Technological Change and the Future of the Railways*. Selected papers from a three-day conference conducted by the Transportation Center at Northwestern University. Evanston, Illinois, 1961.

"New Container Concept: Unloading from a Moving Train," *Railway Age*, July 22, 1963.

Pegrum, D. F., "Investment in the Railroad and Other Transportation Industries Under Regulation," *American Economic Review*, May 1957.

Phillips, E. J., "Diversion of Freight Traffic from the Railroads," *Land Economics*, November 1940.

Sampson, Henry, ed., *World Railways 1961-62*. Buckinghamshire, England: Low (Sampson) Marston, 7th edition, 1962.

Stevens, W. H. S., "Postwar Railroad Problems: Discussion," *American Economic Review*, May 1946.

Taussig, F. W., "A Contribution to the Theory of Railway Rates," *Quarterly Journal of Economics*, July 1891.

Taylor, M. Everard, "The Principles of Road-Rail Transport of Freight: A Survey of the Various Principles of Rail Transport, and Their Merits and Faults," *Railway Gazette*, May 4, 1962.

"Trailers—Container Showcase," *Railway Age*, August 26, 1963.

Walker, Gilbert James, *Road and Rail: An Enquiry into the Economics of Competition and State Control*. London: Allen and Unwin, 1942.

——. "Road and Rail: Transatlantic Comparison," *Journal of Political Economy*, December 1946.

Weisbrod, B. A., "The Per Diem Freight-Car Rate and Railroad Efficiency: The Short-Run Problem," *Journal of Business*, October 1959.

Wellington, Arthur Mellon, *The Economic Theory of the Location of Railways*, sixth ed. New York: John Wiley and Sons, 1904.

Williams, E. W., Jr., "Railroad Rate Levels and Earning Power in an Era of Competitive Transport," *Land Economics*, November 1959.

Wohl, Paul, *Road and Rail in Forty Countries*. London: Oxford University Press, 1935.

IX. Railroad Transportation—India

Balakrishnan, R., "Transport Rates and Industrial Distribution," *Indian Journal of Economics*, January 1946.

Gadgil, D. R., "Railroad Coordination with Special Reference to Rates Policy," *Indian Journal of Economics*, January 1946.

"Indian Railways Today: Reorganization under Five Year Plan," *Modern Transport*, June 16, 1962.

International Bank for Reconstruction and Development, *Appraisal of the Sixth Indian Railway Project*. Report on Technical Information No. TO-299b. Washington, November 2, 1961.

——. *Appraisal of the Indian Railway Project*. Report on Technical Information No. TO-353b. Washington, March 13, 1963.

——. *India's Third Five Year Plan* (mimeographed, restricted). Report on Technical Information AS-80a. Washington, August 1960.

Lefeber, Louis, with M. Datta Chaudhuri, "Transportation Policy in India," in P. N. Rosenstein-Rodan, ed., *Pricing and Fiscal Policy*. Cambridge: Massachusetts Institute of Technology, 1964.

Macpherson, W. J., "Investment in Indian Railways, 1845-1875," *Economic History Review*, December 1955.

Mitchell, Kenneth Grant, *Report on the Present State of Road and Railway Competition and the Possibilities of their Future Coordination and Development*. Calcutta: Government of India Central Publication Branch, 1933.

Patel, S. J., "Investment and Efficiency in Indian Railways During the Second Five Year Plan," *Indian Economic Review*, February 1958.

Prasad, Amba, *Indian Railways* [A Study in Public Utility Administration]. Bombay: Asia Publishing House, 1960.

——. "Operating Efficiency of Indian Railways, 1934-51," *Indian Economic Review*, February 1955.

Ramanadham, V. V., "Railways and Industrial Location, Part I," *Indian Journal of Economics*, October 1946.

——. "Railways and Industrial Location, Part II," *Indian Journal of Economics*, October 1947.

——. "Railway Convention and Surpluses," *Indian Journal of Economics*, July 1944.

——. "Road-Rail Relations," *Indian Journal of Economics*, July 1946.

Sanyal, Nalinaksha, *Development of Indian Railways*. Calcutta: University of Calcutta, 1930.

Saxena, Krishna Kumar, *Indian Railways—Problems and Prospects: A Study in the Management and Working of Indian Railways*. Bombay: Vora, 1962.

Surveys and Research Corporation, *Indian Coal Transport Study*, Vols. I and II. Washington, September 23, 1963.

Thadani, J. N., "Transport and Location of Industries in India," *Indian Economic Review*, August 1952.

Thorner, D., "Capital Movements and Transportation: Great Britain and the Development of India's Railways," *Journal of Economic History*, Fall 1951.

——. "Great Britain and the Development of India's Railways," *Journal of Economic History*. The Tasks of Economic History, Fall 1951.

Tiwari, R. D., *Railways in Modern India*. Bombay: New Book Company, 1941.

X. Railroad Transportation—Russia

Archangelsky, A. and A. K(h)reinin, "Questions of Price Formulation and the System of Railroad Freight Tariffs," *Problems of Economics*, May 1958.

Association of American Railroads, *Railroads of the USSR*. Report on the visit of the United States railroad exchange delegation to the Soviet Union during June 1960. Washington, 1961.

K(h)reinin, A., "Problems of Price Formation in Transport," *Problems of Economics*, December 1959.

Mikheyev, A., V. Dmitriyev and Y. Shukstal, "Technical Re-equipment of Railway Transportation and Problems of Economic Efficiency," *Problems of Economics*, June 1959.

Taaffe, Robert N., *Rail Transportation and the Economic Development of Soviet Central Asia*. Chicago: University of Chicago Press, 1960.

Westwood, J. N., "Soviet Railway Development," *Soviet Studies*, July 1959.

Williams, Ernest W., Jr., *Freight Transportation in the Soviet Union*. National Bureau of Economic Research. Princeton: Princeton University Press, 1962.

XI. Railroad Transportation—Miscellaneous Countries

"Australian Railways Enter a New Era of Expansion," *South African Railways and Harbours* (Government Publication), August 1962.

Australian Transport Advisory Council, *Economic Research Relative to Railways and Railroads Transport*. Report of Commission of Transport. Maribyrnong, 1958.

Carter, J. P., "Personal Discrimination in Transportation: A European Technique," *American Economic Review*, June 1957.

——. "The German Railways: An Analysis of Economic Adaptation," *Land Economics*, November 1952.

Cheng, Lin, *The Chinese Railways: A Historical Survey*. Shanghai: China United Press, 1935.

Dawson, W. B., "Interim Report on the Rhodesia Railways, 1943," *South African Journal of Economics*, December 1943.

Day, John Robert, *Railways of Southern Africa*. London: A. Barker., 1963.

Della, Porta G., "The Railway Problem in Italy," *Banca Nazionale del Lavoro Review*, July-September 1950.

DeNovo, J. A., "A Railroad for Turkey: The Chester Project, 1908-1913," *Business History Review*, 1959.

Frankel, S. H., *The Railway Policy of South Africa*. Johannesburg: Hortors, 1928.

Goodrich, Carter, *Government Promotion of American Canals and Railroads 1800-1890*. New York: Columbia University Press, 1960.

Instituto de Economía, Universidad de Chile, *Sistemas de Costos y Sus Posibles Modificaciones*. Santiago: Empresa de los Ferrocarriles del Estado, 1953.

International Bank for Reconstruction and Development, *Appraisal of a Project for the Improvement of South African Railways*. Report of Technical Information No. TO-297b. Washington, November 21, 1961.

——. *Appraisal of the Atlantic Railroad Equipment Project: Colombia*. Report of Technical Information No. TO-252a. Washington, August 31, 1960.

——. *Appraisal of the Burma Railway Development Program*. Report of Technical Information No. TO-263a. Washington, January 1, 1961.

——. *Appraisal of the Pakistan Railway Project*. Report of Technical Information No. TO-339a. Washington, August 31, 1962.

International Bank for Reconstruction and Development, Peruvian Corporation Limited, *Railway Rehabilitation Project*. Report of Technical information No. TO-313d. Washington, March 14, 1963.

Laight, J. C., "Railway Expenditure and the Volume of Traffic," *South African Journal of Economics*, September 1950.

Lochow, H. J. von, *China's National Railways: Historical Survey and Postwar Planning*. Peiping, China (published by author), 1948.

Richards, C. S. and J. C. Laight, "The South African Railways and the Newton Report," *South African Journal of Economics,* December 1950.

Roads, D. J., "The Chinese Eastern Railway," *Contemporary China,* 1955.

Robert R. Nathan Associates, *Economic Review of the Turkey-Iran Railway Link.* Washington, July 1963.

Samaratunga, S., "Road-Rail Coordination in Ceylon: Some Economic Aspects," *Ceylon Economist,* November 1950.

Saunders, W. B. and Company, *A General Appraisal.* Vol. I of *The Problems of the Canadian Railways.* Washington, 1960.

Sergeant, W., "The Place of Railways in Mass Transit," *Canadian Transportation,* May 1962.

Sharp, C. H., "The Allocation of Goods Traffic Between Road and Rail," *Journal of Industrial Economics,* July 1959.

Soemobaskoro, S., "The Alleged Unfair Competition Between Rail and Road Transportation (with Special Reference to Indonesia)," *Ekonomi dan Keuangan Indonesia,* December 1958.

South African Railways. Report by Railway Commission on the Merits of Improving the Existing Natal Main Line as Against Constructing an Alternative Main Line. Cape Town: Cape Times, 1914.

The South African Railways: History, Scope and Organization. Annual Report published by Authority of the General Manager, South African Railways. Pretoria: Government Printers, 1947.

Stewart, M., "The New Railway Agreement," *Bulletin,* Oxford University Institute of Statistics. September 20, 1941.

Sudan, Government of, *Report* [on Sudan Railways], Atbara, Sudan, 1958-59.

Varian, H., *Some African Milestones.* Wheatley: Oxford University Press, 1953.

Williams, E. W., "An Evaluation of Public Policy Towards the Railway Industry," *American Economic Review,* May 1951.

XII. Road Transportation—General

Allen, J. E., "Railways or Roads?" *Economic Journal,* March 1959.

American Association of State Highway Officials, Committee on Planning and Design Policies, *Road User Benefit Analyses for Highway Improvements.* Washington, 1952-1959.

de Beer, Alan R., "The Economic Justification of Roads in Developing Countries," *Road International,* April 1963. Also in *Traffic Engineering and Control,* January 1963; and in *Roads and Road Construction,* December 1962.

Bos, H. C. and L. M. Koyck, "The Appraisal of Road Construction Projects; a Practical Example," *Review of Economics and Statistics,* February 1961.

Brownlee, O. H. and W. W. Heller, "Highway Development and Financing," *American Economic Review,* May 1956.

Brunner, Christopher, "Assistance for Roads in Under-Developed Countries," *Traffic Engineering and Control*, April 1961.

——. *The Economic Justification of Roads*. London: International Road Federation, 1962.

——. *The Problem of Motor Transport; an Economic Analysis*. London: Ernest Benn, 1928.

Buchanan, J. M., "The Pricing of Highway Services," *National Tax Journal*, June 1952.

Charlesworth, G., D. J. Reynolds, and J. G. Wardrop, *Road Improvements: Choosing Priorities by a New Formula*. London: Road Research Laboratory, 1959.

—— and J. L. Paisley, *The Economic Assessments of Returns from Road Works*. London: Institution of Civil Engineers, 1959.

Chatburn, George R., *Highways and Highway Transportation*. New York: Thomas Y. Crowell, 1923.

Claffey, P. J., *Time and Fuel Consumption for Highway User Benefit Studies*. Washington: Highway Research Board of the National Academy of Sciences, 1960.

Colquhoun, R. S., "Low-Cost Roads—In Undeveloped Countries," *Road International*, Autumn 1950.

Dearing, Charles L., "Toll Road Rates and Highway Pricing," *American Economic Review*, May 1957.

"Developing Countries: Roads' Economic Justification," *Bulletin*, British Road Federation, December 1962.

"The Economics of Roads," *Bulletin*, Oxford University Institute of Statistics, November 1960.

Fellmann, J. D., "Emergent Urban Problems of Intercity Motor Transportation, *Land Economics*, May 1951.

Ferguson, A. R., "A Marginal Cost Function for Highway Construction and Operation," *American Economic Review*, May 1958.

Garrison, William L., and others, *Studies of Highway Development and Geographic Change*. Seattle, Washington: University of Washington Press, 1959.

Grotewold, A. and L. Grotewold, "Commercial Development of Highways in Urbanized Regions: A Case Study (of Highway 41 between Chicago and Milwaukee)," *Land Economics*, August 1958.

Groves, H. M., and others, "Highway Development and Financing," *American Economic Review*, May 1956.

Hawkins, E. K., "Investment in Roads in Under-Developed Countries," *Bulletin*, Oxford University Institute of Statistics, 4th quarter, 1960.

Homberger, L. M., "Coordination of Road and Rail Transportation and the Organization of the Trucking Industry: A Survey," *Land Economics*, May 1947.

International Road Federation, "World Highway Statistics," *IRF Staff Reports*. Washington, 1957-61.

Johnston, J., "Scale, Costs and Profitability in Road Passenger Transport," *Journal of Industrial Economics,* June 1956.

Knapp, J. Burke, "The Place of Highways in Economic Development," *Road International,* April 1963.

Krishnamurthy, V. A., "Under-Developed Areas and Road Transport," *Transport* (Bombay), March 1963.

Kuhn, Tillo E., *Economic Concepts of Highway Planning.* A paper prepared for presentation at the 40th Annual Meeting of the Highway Research Board. Washington: National Academy of Sciences, January 1961.

——. *Economic Analyses for Highway Improvements in Developing Countries,* OEA/Ser.K/1.9.Eng.Doc.130. Washington: Organization for American States, 1963.

——. "The Economics of Road Transportation." Unpublished doctoral thesis, McGill University, 1957.

——. *Use of Economic Criteria for Highway Investment Planning.* Washington: Highway Research Board, National Academy of Sciences, 1959.

Lang, A. S. and Martin Wohl, *Evaluation of Highway Impact.* 39th Annual Meeting, Highway Research Board. Washington: National Academy of Sciences, January 1960.

Lawton, L., "Evaluating Highway Improvements on Mileage and Time Cost Basis," *Traffic Quarterly,* January 1950.

McCarty, John F., *State Regulation and Taxation of Highway Carriers.* Berkeley, California: University of California, 1953.

Meazler, F. A. A., "Rail and Road Statistics," *Royal Statistical Society,* Ser. A., 1950.

Meibury, Charles O., "An Economic Analysis of Highway Services," *Quarterly Journal of Economics,* November 1963.

Melton, Lee J., "The Transportation Company: An Economic Inevitability," *Highway Research Board Proceedings,* Vol. 39. Washington: National Academy of Sciences, 1960.

Millard, R. S., *Roads, Road Transport, and Traffic in Developing Countries.* London: The Institution of Civil Engineers, June 1962.

Mitchell, Kenneth, "The Logical Stage Development of Roads in Under-Developed Countries," *Road International,* Winter 1951.

Mohring, H., "Land Values and the Measurement of Highway Benefits," *Journal of Political Economy,* June 1961.

—— and Mitchell Harwitz, *Highway Benefits, An Analytical Framework.* Evanston, Illinois: Northwestern University Press, 1962.

Munby, I. L., "Investment in Road and Rail Transport," *Institute of Transport Journal,* March 1962.

Nelson, J. C., "Highway Development, the Railroads and National Transport Policy," *American Economic Review,* May 1951.

——. "The Pricing of Highway, Waterway and Airway Facilities," *American Economic Review,* May 1962.

Odier, Lionel, *The Economic Benefits of Road Construction and Improve-*

ments (translated from the French document by Noel Lindsay). Paris: Publications ESTOUP, 1963.

Oglesby, C. H. and E. L. Grant, "The Fundamental Approach to Decisions in Highway Programming and Design." Economic analysis in *Proceedings, Highway Research Board.* Washington: National Academy of Sciences, 1958.

Owen, Wilfred, *Automotive Transportation: Trends and Problems.* Washington: Brookings Institution, 1949.

——, and Charles L. Dearing, *Toll Roads and the Problem of Highway Modernization.* Washington: Brookings Institution, 1951.

Pegrum, D. F., "The Economic Basis of Public Policy for Motor Transport," *Land Economics,* August 1952.

Ponsonby, G. J., "The Problem of the Peak, with Special Reference to Road Passenger Transport," *Economic Journal,* March 1958.

——. "The Problem of the Roads," *Lloyd's Bank Review,* January 1955.

Prentiss, Louis W., "Highway Construction as an Anti-Recession Activity," *Traffic Quarterly,* July 1962.

Reynolds, D. J., "The Economics of Rural Motorways," *Journal of Industrial Economics,* November 1961.

Roberts, Merrill J., "Some Aspects of Motor Carrier Costs: Firm Size, Efficiency and Financial Health," *Land Economics,* August 1956.

Ross, W. D., *Financial Highway Improvements in Louisiana.* Baton Rouge: Louisiana State University, 1955.

Roth, G. J., *The Economic Benefits to be Obtained by Road Improvements with Special Reference to Vehicle Operating Costs.* London: Road Research Laboratory, 1959.

St. Clair, G. P. and N. Lieder, "Evaluation of Unit Cost of Time and Strain-and- Discomfort Costs of Non-Uniform Driving," *Special Report 56,* Highway Research Board. Washington: National Academy of Sciences, September 1959.

Smykay, E. W., "An Appraisal of the Economics of Scale in the Motor Carrier Industry," *Land Economics,* May 1958.

Sussna, E., "Costs, Productivity and Welfare Problems of the Local Transit Industry," *Land Economics,* August 1959.

Tanner, J. C., "The Sampling of Road Traffic," *Applied Statistics,* November 1957.

Taylor, M. Everard, "The Principles of Road-Rail Transport of Freight: A Survey of the Various Principles of Rail Transport, and Their Merits and Faults," *Railway Gazette,* May 4, 1962.

Tinbergen, Jan, "The Appraisal of Road Construction: Two Calculation Schemes," *Review of Economics and Statistics,* August 1957.

Tucker, W. H., "The Gray Area of Transportation," *Atlantic Economic Review,* January 1963.

U.S. Congress. House of Representatives. Studies of "Economic and Social Effects of Highway Improvement," Part VI of *Final Report of the Highway*

Cost Allocation Study. H. Doc. 54, 87th Cong. 1st Sess. Washington: Government Printing Office, 1961.

——. *Final Report of the Highway Cost Allocation Study,* Parts I-V. H. Doc. 54, 87th Cong. 1st Sess. Washington: Government Printing Office, 1961.

U.S. Interstate Commerce Commission, "Cost of Transporting Freight by Class I and Class II, Motor Common Carriers of General Commodities." Washington: Government Printing Office, May 1960.

Walker, G., "Road and Rail: A Transatlantic Comparison," *Journal of Political Economy,* December 1946.

——. *Road and Rail: an Enquiry into the Economics of Competition and State Control.* London: Allen and Unwin, 1942.

Winfrey, R., "Concepts and Applications of Engineering Economy in the Highway Field." *Special Report 56,* Highway Research Board. Washington: National Academy of Sciences, September 1959.

Wohl, Paul, *Road and Rail in Forty Countries.* London: Oxford University Press, 1935.

Woods, Kenneth Brady, ed., *Highway Engineering Handbook.* New York: McGraw-Hill, 1960.

Zettel, R. M., *Highway Benefits and the Cost Allocation Problem.* Washington: American Association of State Highway Officials, 1957.

——. "The Incidence of Highways Benefits." *Special Report.* Highway Research Board. Washington: National Academy of Sciences, 1956.

XIII. Road Transportation—India

Indian Roads and Transport Development Association, *Investigation by the Indian Road Congress into Transport Costs.* Mexico City: International Road Federation, 1958.

International Bank for Reconstruction and Development, *Appraisal of a Road Project for India.* Report of Technical Information No. TO(IDA) 1b. Washington, June 7, 1961.

Nadirshah, E. A., "A Review of Roads and Road Transport in India," *Road International,* Autumn 1956.

Rao, R. V., "Nationalized Road Transport Services in Hyderabad," *Indian Journal of Economics,* July 1955.

Ramanadham, V. V., "Road-Rail Relations," *Indian Journal of Economics,* July 1946.

Ramanadham, V. V. and N. K. Nagen, "Economic Aspects of Road Transport in Punjab," *Asian Economic Review,* February 1960.

Saggar, R. K., "The Organization of Road Transport Undertakings in Punjab [India]," *Asian Economic Review,* November 1961.

Singh, D. B., "Problems of the Motor Transport Industry in India," *Indian Journal of Economics,* July 1954.

Vagh, B. V., "The Bottleneck in Indian Transport: Increased Road Transport Facilities Urgently Needed," *Road International,* Autumn 1954.

XIV. Road Transportation—Miscellaneous Countries

Amman & Whitney International Limited, *Economic and Engineering Feasibility Report, Dacca-Chittagong cum Narayanganj Road.* New York, September 1, 1963.

——. *Iran Roads Program Phase I Reconnaissance Report Burujird-Qum Route.* Tehran, December 15, 1960.

Booney, R. S. P., *The Relationship Between Road Transport and Rural Development in North Borneo.* Harmondsworth: Great Britain Road Research Laboratory, 1963.

"Brazilian Roads and the Alliance for Progress," *World Highways,* July 1962.

Burch, Phillip H., *Highway Revenue and Expenditure Policy in the United States.* New Brunswick, New Jersey: Rutgers University Press, 1962.

Campbell, J. R., *Development of Roads in the Sudan.* Report No. TAA/SUD/2. New York: United Nations Technical Assistance Program, 1957.

Coverdale and Colpitts (Consulting Engineers), *Report on Peruvian Highway Study.* New York, October 31, 1961.

Daniel, Mann, Johnson and Mendenhall (Consulting Engineers), *Khartoum-Port Sudan Highway.* Los Angeles, May 11, 1962.

"The Development of Highways in Central America," *World Highways,* 1960.

Diker, Vecdi, "Highway Development in Turkey," *Road International,* Winter 1951.

Farmer, R. N., "Motor Vehicle Transport Pricing in Lebanon," *Journal of Industrial Economics,* July 1959.

Fraenkel, Benjamin B., "Highways in Brazil's Future," *Road International,* Autumn 1955.

Hart, P. E., "The Efficiency of the Road Haulage Industry under Nationalization," *Journal of Industrial Economics,* November 1953.

Hasnat, A., "Road Transport in East Bengal," *Pakistan Economic Journal,* August 1954.

Hawkins, Edward Kenneth, *Roads and Road Transport in an Underdeveloped Country, A Case Study of Uganda.* London: H. M. Stationery Office, 1962.

——. *Road Transportation in Nigeria: A Study of African Enterprise.* London: Oxford University Press, 1958.

Hensman, P. S., "The Economics of Goods Transport by Road," *Institute of Transport Journal,* March 1962.

Hirst, R. R., "Interstate Road Transport (Australia-New Zealand)," *Economic Record,* November 1956.

Hogg, Vincent W., "Nigeria," *Road International,* Winter 1959-60.

——, and C. M. Roelandts, *Nigerian Motor Vehicle Traffic, An Economic Forecast.* London: Oxford University Press, 1962.

Grassini, Piero, "Progress of the Road Plan for Southern Italy," *Road International*, Autumn 1955.

Instituto de Economía, Universidad de Chile, *Costos del Transporte Caminero en Chile*. Santiago: Publicaciones del Instituto de Economía, No. 22, 1959.

International Bank for Reconstruction and Development, *Appraisal of the Feeder Roads Project in Panama*. Report of Technical Information No. TO-235a. Washington, August 10, 1960.

——. *Appraisal of a Highway and Maintenance Project—Peru*. Technical Report No. TO-293b. Washington, November 26, 1961.

——. *Appraisal of a Highway Construction and Maintenance Program—Argentina*. Report of Technical Information No. TO-286a. Washington, June 20, 1961.

——. *Appraisal of a Highway Construction Project—Mexico*. Report of Technical Information No. TO-256a. Washington, November 6, 1960.

——. *Appraisal of a Highway Improvement and Maintenance Project—Spain*. Report of Technical Information No. TO-378. Washington, June 19, 1963.

——. *Appraisal of a Highway Project—Costa Rica*. Report of Technical Information No. TO (IDA) 14. Washington, November 4, 1961.

——. *Appraisal of a Highway Project—Swaziland*. Report of Technical Information No. TO-312. Washington, March 5, 1962.

——. *Appraisal of a Highway Project—Yugoslavia*. Report of Technical Information TO-367a. Washington, June 7, 1963.

——. *Appraisal of a Road Project for Liberia*. Report of Technical Information TO-375. Washington, June 6, 1963.

——. *Appraisal of a Second Highway Project—Haiti*. Report of Technical Information No. TO-316. Washington, April 24, 1962.

——. *Appraisal of a Second National Highway Project—Ecuador*. Report of Technical Information TO-361. Washington, April 9, 1963.

——. *Appraisal of a Third Highway Program—Ethiopia*. Report of Technical Information No. TO-352a. Washington, February 14, 1963.

——. *Appraisal of a Third Highway Project—El Salvador*. Report of Technical Information TO-340a. Washington, November 11, 1962.

Kuhn, Tillo E., "Roads to Resources in the Canadian North," *Road International*, Spring 1960.

Lada, Julius, "Roads into the Near and Middle East," *Road International*, Spring 1956.

Laight, J. C., "Road Transport of Goods in South Africa," *South African Journal of Economics*, June 1959.

Leite, Deltro Barbosa, "Roads to Resources in Brazil," *Road International*, Autumn 1961.

Louis Berger Incorporated. *Calabar-Ikom Highway Project: Federation of Nigeria, Eastern Region*. Harrisburg, Pennsylvania, October 1962.

——. *Economic and Engineering Feasibility Report to the Government of*

East Pakistan on Dacca Sylhet cum Comilla Road. Orange, New Jersey, August 30, 1963.

——. *Economic and Engineering Feasibility Report to Government of East Pakistan on Faridpur-Jhenida Jessore-Khulna Roads.* Orange, New Jersey, August 30, 1963.

——. *Economic and Engineering Feasibility Report to Government of East Pakistan on Jaijdi-Begamganu Raipura-Chandpur Road.* Orange, New Jersey, August 30, 1963.

——. *Economic and Engineering Feasibility Report to Government of East Pakistan on Jhenida-Kushtia Ishurdi Road.* Orange, New Jersey, August 30, 1963.

——. *Economic and Engineering Feasibility Report to Government of East Pakistan on Mymensingh-Jamalpur Bahadurabad Ghat Road.* Orange, New Jersey, August 30, 1963.

——. *Engineering Report—Phase IA: Rangoon-Mandalay Highway Project, Union of Burma.* Harrisburg, Pennsylvania, December 1962.

MacDonald, A., "Road Development in Nigeria: A Review of Progress in a Varied Terrain," *Road International,* Autumn 1953.

March, Jose J., "Mexico's Highway Programme," *Road International,* Autumn 1953.

Millard, R. S., *Road Development in the Overseas Territories.* London: Royal Society of Arts, 1959.

Netzer, D., "Financing Policy for Highways: Impact of the 1956 Federal Legislation," *National Tax Journal,* June 1957.

Noble, Dudley, "Australia—A Country Ripe for the Development of Road Transport," *Road International,* Summer 1956.

Onalp, Tahsin, *Highway Activities in Turkey.* Paper presented at the 4th Conference, International Road Federation. Washington, 1962.

"Road Construction in Australia," *International Road Safety and Traffic Review,* Summer 1962.

"Road Transport in South Africa," *Road International,* Spring 1955.

Samaratunga, S., "Road-Rail Coordination in Ceylon: Some Economic Aspects," *Ceylon Economist,* November 1950.

Sargent, J. R., "Road Planning; Some Lessons Learned in British North Borneo," *Bulletin,* Oxford University Institute of Statistics, 4th Quarter, 1960.

Soberman, Richard M., *The Cost of Road Transportation in Venezuela.* Joint Center—Guayana Project. Caracas: Corporación Venezolana de Guayana, División de Estudios, Planificación e Investigación. April 17, 1963.

Soemobaskoro, S., "The Alleged Unfair Competition between Rail and Road Transportation [with special reference to Indonesia]," *Ekonomi dan Keuangan Indonesia,* December 1958.

Stanford Research Institute, *A Ten-Year Highway Program for Honduras.* Menlo Park, California, and Tegucigalpa, Honduras, December 1962.

Tippetts, Abbett, McCarthy, and Stratton (Consulting Engineers), *Proposed Highway Yapacani to Puerto Grether and Yapacani River Bridge.* Cochabamba, Bolivia, April 30, 1963.

——. *Proposed Improvement of Three Highways: Guabira-Yapacani, Guabira-Chane, and Guabira-Puerto Banegas.* Cochabamba, Boliva, May 17, 1963.

United Nations, *Aspects Economiques de la Construction des Routes.* E/CN 11 Trans Sub. 2/18, ECAFE, Geneva, December 1960.

Vezzani, Ferruccio, "Road Building in Italy." *Road International,* Spring 1952.

Walker, G., "Highway Finance," *Journal of Industrial Economics,* June 1956.

Yared, Emile, "Improving the Road System of Lebanon—A Country Where the Development and Improvement of the Road System Are Vital to Its Economic Existence," *Road International,* Summer 1955.

XVI. Water Transportation

Carter, J. P., "The New Maritime Nations (Liberia and Panama)," *Journal of Business,* July 1956.

Goodrich, Carter, *Government Promotion of American Canals and Railroads 1800-1890.* New York: Columbia University Press, 1960.

Instituto de Economía, Universidad de Chile, *Aprovechamiento de los Barcos de Cabotaje Chilenos.* Santiago: Publicaciones del Instituto de Economía, No. 30, 1960.

——. *Costos del Transporte Maritimo en Chile.* Santiago: Publicaciones del Instituto de Economía, No. 24, 1960.

——. *Eficiencia Portuaria en Chile.* Santiago: Publicaciones del Instituto de Economía, No. 31, 1960.

Ivanov, L., "Concrete Economic Problems in the Work of a Research Institute Specializing in a Branch of the Economy (Water Transport)," *Problems of Economics,* August 1958.

Kaliski, S. F., "The Demand for Passages Through the Kiel Canal: A Comment," *Canadian Journal of Economics and Political Science,* November, 1955.

Kartanahardja, R. A., "National Shipping in Indonesia (Development and Organization)," *Ekonomi dan Keuangan Indonesia,* May 1956.

Kelso, H., "Waterways Versus Railways," *American Economic Review,* September 1941.

Kopanitsas, D. E., "Differential Prices for the Service of Ships Belonging to the Same General Class: A Case of Oligopoly," *Royal Statistical Society,* 1958.

National Academy of Sciences, *Utilization in Maritime Transportation: An Annotated Bibliography,* 1960.

Netherlands Engineering Consultants, *A Study of the Future of the Port of Bangkok.* The Hague, Holland, August 1962.

Norbom, Jon O., "A Quantitative Determination of the Importance of the Shipping Industry in the Economy of Western Europe," *Weltwirtschaftliches Archiv*, Heft No. 1, 1955.

Parkinson, J. R., "Demand for Ships," *Scottish Journal of Political Economy*, April 1958.

Parsons, Brinckerhoff, Quade & Douglas (Consulting Engineers), *Deep-Water Harbor Development, St. Johns, Antigua, W. I.* Preliminary Engineering Report. New York, October 28, 1963.

Renshaw, E. F., "A Note on the Measurement of the Benefits from Public Investment in Navigation Projects," *American Economic Review*, September 1957.

Sawa, S., "The Organization of the Shipping Market," *Kyoto University Economic Review*, April 1958.

Sheldon, C. D., "Some Economic Reasons for the Marked Contrast in Japanese and Chinese Modernization as Seen in Examples from 'Pre-Modern' Shipping and Trading by Water," *Kyoto University Economic Review*, October 1953.

Sobotka, Rudolf, "Growth of Soviet Tanker Fleet Studied," *Maritime News*, May 1962.

Teichart, P. C. M., "The Development of Argentina's Four State Fleets," *Weltwirtschaftliches Archiv*, Heft No. 2, 1959.

Verburgh, C., "The Merchant Shipping Industry of South Africa," *South African Journal of Economics*, September 1958.

——. "The Competition of South African Harbours and Lourenco Marques for the Ocean Borne Imports of the Transvaal 'Competitive Area,' " *South African Journal of Economics*, December 1957.

Yanmamoto, H., "The Recovery Method of the Japanese Shipping Industry in Post-War Period," *Kobe Economic and Business Review*, 1954.

Index

Index*

Accident reduction, 121n, 130-31, 179, 186-87
Accounting prices, 229. *See also* Shadow prices
Activity analysis, 9-10
Adler, Hans A., 11, 16, 43n, 91, 170
Africa, 70, 72, 127-28
Agriculture: preserving products of, 70-71, 85, 86; in regional development models, 111-17; and transport, 5, 18, 67, 98, 136, 185, 190, 230; in underdeveloped areas, 2-3, 72, 128
Air transport: 34, 72, 74; economic characteristics of, 57-59, 62, 64; innovations in, 81-83; loans and credits for, 227, 234; in underdeveloped countries, 77, 79-80, 82-83; in various countries, 19-20, 75, 76, 78
Argentina, 44, 45, 54, 65, 172, 246, 249n
Arndt, Manuel Metz, 257n
Asia, 70, 72, 79, 127-28
Automobiles. *See* Road-highway transport

Baumol, William J., 210n
Behling, Burton N., 210n
Beneficiaries. *See* User payment for transport
Benefits. *See* Cost-benefit analysis
Bibliography, 1, 277-305
Bohannan, Paul, 67n
Boiteux, Marcel, 212n
Bonbright, James C., 210n
Brazil, 244
Brown, Robert T., 11n, 16-17, 235n, 242, 264n
Brozen, Yale, 210n
Burma, 79

* References to tables and charts are in italics.

Cambodia, 79
Canada, 74, 75-76
Canals. *See* Water transport
Capital: 34, 35, 240; opportunity costs of, 176, 178, 192-93, 230; in regional development models, 109-119
Capital-output ratios, 129-31
Carlson, Philip R., 83n
Caves, Richard E., 58n
Central America, 174
Chakravarty, S., 110n
Chamberlin, Edward H., 201-202n
Chile: 17; education in, 86-87; financial analysis of railroads in, 271-74; *map, 243*; railroad renovation in, 250-70; road-rail competition in, 242, 261-67, 271-74; transport in, 242-48
China, 77
Colombia, 77, 79-80, 87, 172, 226
Comfort and convenience, 179
Commodities: in regional models, 147-169
Communication, 81, 86-87
Comparative statics, 195, 196-210
Competition, 92, 109, 115, 118 ff., 174, 176, 206, 238
Constant returns to scale, 145 ff.
Consumption: 18, 67; in regional development models, 109, 112-16
Containers, 65, 84, 100, 138, 139-40
Cookenboo, Leslie, Jr., 47n, 48n, 49
Cost-benefit analysis: 11, 16, 90-93, 104, 170, 173 ff., 192-94, 232. *See also* Transport modes; Transport projects
Costs: 20, 32, 72, 215-17; measurement of, 171-80, 184, 231; and modes, 36-61; "sunk," 35, 36, 47, 204, 206-207, 240. *See also* Financial analysis; Transport projects

309

B2o